D0586969

POLITICAL THEORY AND THE MODERN STATE

Political Theory and the Modern State

Essays on State, Power and Democracy

David Held

Polity Press

Essays 1 and 4 © 1984 The Open University
Essay 2 as originally published © The President and Fellows of Harvard College
and the Editors, 1984
Essay 8 © 1988 The Open University
Essay 9 as originally published © Basil Blackwell Publisher Ltd 1984
This collection and all other essays © David Held 1989

First published 1989 by Polity Press
in association with Basil Blackwell.
Reprinted 1990

Editorial Office:
Polity Press, 65 Bridge Street,
Cambridge, CB2 1UR, UK

Marketing and production:
Basil Blackwell Ltd
108 Cowley Road, Oxford OX4 1JF, UK

British Library Cataloguing in Publication Data
A CIP catalogue record for this book is available from the British Library.

ISBN 0 – 7456 – 0619 – 9
ISBN 0 – 7456 – 0620 – 2 (pbk)

Typeset in 10 on 12pt Baskerville
by Downdell Limited, Oxford
Printed in Great Britain by
T J Press Ltd, Padstow

Contents

Preface

The essays in this volume, written in the main over the last five years, are concerned to map out the terms of discourse about the modern state and to offer an initial assessment of them. They examine, among other topics, the notion of the modern state, the efficacy of the concept of sovereignty, problems of power and legitimation, sources of political stability and crisis, and the future of democracy. In so doing, they provide an introduction to many of the central issues of modern politics and political thought.

Although the majority of the essays have been published before, they have all been edited and revised for this volume. Essays 6, 7 and 8 appear here for the first time and develop arguments which are central both to the earlier essays and to my most current concerns. Together, the articles continue and develop themes I approached in earlier books, especially *Introduction to Critical Theory* and *Models of Democracy*, and lay a basis for a set of arguments I will amplify further in a forthcoming work, *The Foundations of Democracy*.

Over the years in which I wrote these pieces, many friends and colleagues have provided invaluable encouragement and assistance. I should like to thank in particular David Beetham, John Dunn, John Keane, Joel Krieger, Adrian Leftwich, Greg McLennan and Christopher Pollitt. Joel Krieger and Adrian Leftwich co-authored essays 2 and 9, respectively; I am extremely grateful to them for allowing me to reproduce these essays and for the free hand they gave me in making amendments. Anthony Giddens, Stuart Hall, John Thompson and Michelle Stanworth not only provided indispensable intellectual guidance but also offered routine forms of support without which, even if I could have survived, it would have been radically less pleasurable to do so.

And thanks, finally, to Rosa and Joshua – whose adeptness at strategic manoeuvering reminds me daily that politics is an irreducible part of everyday life!

Introduction

The essays in this volume have three broad objectives: first, to provide an introduction to the main theoretical perspectives on the modern state, the type of state which emerged with the early development of the European state system from the sixteenth century; second, to examine competing interpretations of the shifting balance between order and crisis that confronts and shapes the modern state; and third, to assess how adequate our leading political theories are as a basis for understanding and acting upon the political stage today.

The essays are informed by a number of assumptions about the nature of politics as a practical activity, about politics as a discipline, and about political theory which it is as well to clarify from the outset. Politics – as a practical activity – is, in my view, the discourse and the struggle over the organization of human possibilities. As such, it is about power; that is to say, it is about the *capacity* of social agents, agencies and institutions to maintain or transform their environment, social or physical. It is about the resources which underpin this capacity and about the forces that shape and influence its exercise (see essay 9 of this volume, p. 247). Accordingly, politics is a phenomenon found in and between all groups, institutions and societies, cutting across public and private life. It is expressed in all the relations, institutions and structures that are implicated in the production and reproduction of the life of societies. Politics creates and conditions all aspects of our lives and it is at the core of the development of collective problems, and the modes of their resolution. While 'politics', thus understood, raises a number of complicated issues, it usefully highlights the nature of politics as a universal dimension of human life, independent of any specific 'site' or set of institutions.

The study of politics involves much more than the study of the state. It involves, at the very least, examining the way the state is enmeshed in the political structures of 'society' – of groups, classes and institutions (formal and informal) – and the way the latter in turn are shaped by the state. Therefore, while the focus of this book is squarely on 'the modern state', it is also, inescapably, on 'society'. To link two such ambiguous concepts together risks making the focus of the volume highly diffuse. But the fact that 'state' and 'society' are inextricably bound together does not mean that for analytic purposes one cannot distinguish particular issues or problems for attention. Nor does it mean, of course, that one cannot single out aspects of state politics alone for detailed consideration.[1]

While at a very abstract level we can talk about something called 'the state' and juxtapose it with other forms of social and economic order, this should not lead one to the view that the state itself is simply a unified entity: the state forms a set of highly complicated relations and processes. To begin with, any attempt to understand the state must consider its spatial and temporal dimensions – the horizontal stretch of the state across territory, the depth of state intervention in social and economic life and the changing form of all these things over time. Furthermore, it is important to consider the state as a cluster of agencies, departments, tiers and levels, each with their own rules and resources and often with varying purposes and objectives. Abstract statements about the state are always a shorthand for this 'cluster' and must be consistent with an exploration of its dynamics. In order to understand the relations and processes of the state and their place in shaping society, it is important to grasp the way the state is embedded in particular socio-economic systems, with distinctive structures and sets of institutions, together with its nature as a site of political negotiation and conflict.

If the first assumption underpinning these essays specifies the breadth of politics as a practical activity, the second emphasizes that if politics as a discipline is to be taken seriously, then it must seek to grasp the complex *relations* between aspects of social life – such as the polity, the economy and social structure – which are conventionally thought of and studied as distinct (see essay 9). The tendency of the social sciences to generate sound but discrete pieces of knowledge about different aspects of society has, unfortunately, done little to generate a larger picture of the modern political world. The division of labour in the social sciences is highly advanced and the resulting output highly fragmented. Whilst specialization need not always lead to the fragmentation of knowledge, this seems to have happened in the case of the social sciences (Held, 1987b). And while there have certainly been advances made in the specialist study of parts of the contemporary world and its problems, they have not been matched by comparable advances in attempts to integrate these into wider frameworks of understanding about societies and their politics. Within the social sciences it is clear that, broadly speaking, 'the political system', 'the economy' and 'the social system' (though not always called that) have been thought of and studied as if they were more or less autonomous spheres of activity in human societies. And the study of, for example, governmental decision-making, pressure group politics, inequality, conflict in the Third World, unemployment and inflation, have been confined to particular disciplinary corners with consistently disappointing results. Such is the almost inevitable outcome, I believe, of a failure to try to think through the relation between political processes and events, social structures and events and economic life. It is the interaction of all these phenomena which should be regarded as politics: what is referred to in essay 9 as 'the "lived interdisciplinarity" of all collective social life' (pp. 246–7). Hence, if politics as a discipline is to be developed systematically, it must, paradoxically, be interdisciplinary, so that it can generate frameworks of understanding and explanation which are able to illuminate successfully the interlocking structures and processes of modern politics.

A related and third underpinning assumption of the volume concerns the nature of political theory. Political theory, I believe, must concern itself both with theoretical and practical issues, with philosophical as well as organizational and institutional questions. The fundamental reason for this is that the project of political theory can be based neither purely on political *philosophy* nor purely on political *science*. All political philosophy, implicitly if not explicitly, makes complex claims about the operation of the political world, past, present and future, which require examination within modes of inquiry which go beyond those available to philosophy *per se*. The rise of the social sciences (in particular, the disciplines of 'government' and sociology) in the late nineteenth and twentieth centuries added momentum to the view that the study of politics must be based on the pursuit of science. There has been a marked shift in the weight granted to 'scientific method' in the explication of the meaning of politics. But 'science' has by no means triumphed everywhere over 'philosophy'; and a purely empirical approach to political theory has been extensively criticized (see, for example MacIntyre, 1971; Habermas, 1973). Political science inevitably raises normative questions which a dedication to the 'descriptive–explanatory' does not eradicate. The meaning, for example, of sovereignty, democracy or the state, cannot be fully explicated by science alone. Neither philosophy nor science can replace each other in the project of political theory. Successful political theory requires the philosophical analysis of principles and the empirical understanding of political processes and structures.

If political theory is concerned with the nature and structure of political practices, processes and institutions and, thereby, with 'what is going on' in the political world, then I take it to be an inextricably *hermeneutic* and *critical* enterprise (cf. MacIntyre, 1983; Taylor, 1983). It is hermeneutic because the problems of 'interpretation' are fundamental to the social sciences in general, and to politics in particular. All theoretical endeavour, whether it be that of lay people or professional political theorists, involves interpretation – interpretation which embodies a particular framework of concepts, beliefs and standards. Such a framework is not a barrier to understanding; on the contrary, it is integral to it (Gadamer, 1975). For the interpretative framework we employ determines what we apprehend, what we notice and register as significant. Furthermore, such a framework shapes our attempts to understand and assess political actions, events and processes; for it carries with it general views about human capacities, needs and motives and about the mutability or otherwise of human institutions, which are charged with normative implications (see Taylor, 1967). Accordingly, particular theories cannot be treated as *the* correct or final understanding of a phenomenon; the meaning of a phenomenon is always open to future interpretations from new perspectives, each with its own particular practical stance or interest in political life.

Having said this, it is important to stress that political theory is also a critical endeavour; that is to say, it seeks an account of politics which transcends those of lay agents. The routine monitoring of political life by ordinary men and women provides interpretations of politics which are indisputably knowledgeable and frequently illuminating. These 'interpretive schemes' are, implicitly or explicitly, political theories in germ (MacIntyre, 1983, p. 23). But they often contain elements which, for a number of diverse reasons, fall short of a satisfactory account of the conditions and possibilities of politics (see essays 3-5). Political theory aims to offer a systematic analysis of politics and of the ways in which it is always 'bounded' by, among other things, unacknowledged conditions of action (cf. Giddens, 1979, pp. 49-95 and 1984, pp. 348ff.). It can, thereby, fracture existing forms of understanding and re-form the practically generated accounts of the political in everyday life. It has an irreducible critical dimension.

The process of analysing aspects of the political world contributes to our self-understanding and self-formation. It is a means of enlightenment and, more fundamentally, a means available to be reflexively applied to the transformation of the conditions of our own lives. Political theory has had this type of critical impact since its inception in the early modern era (cf. Skinner, 1978). The discourse of and over politics can readily become a part of the concepts and theories which are utilized and applied in settings beyond those in which they were originally generated.

A fourth, additional, assumption I make in this book is that political theory can be developed as the critique of political ideology. While it is possible to interpret the work of most, if not all, modern political theorists as hermeneutic and critical in the senses set out immediately above, it cannot be said that their work in general embraces the tasks of the critique of ideology. By ideology I mean systems of signification or meaning which are mobilized to sustain asymmetrical power relations in the interests of dominant or hegemonic groups (Thompson, 1984, pp. 126-32). And by the critique of ideology I mean a programme of examining the way such systems of signification are produced and reproduced, and how they shape and mis-shape the politico-social world.

The aim of political theory as the critique of ideology is to enlighten those to whom it is addressed about the political system in which they live and, in so doing, to open up and elaborate alternative possible political worlds (Habermas , 1974, p. 32; Held, 1980, parts 2 and 3; essay 3 of this volume). The critique of political ideology is concerned both with how and why the political world is as it is and with how it might be otherwise. For what distinguishes it as a theoretical enterprise is the attempt to elaborate and project a conception of politics based on a 'thought experiment' – an experiment into how people would interpret their needs and abilities, and which rules, laws and institutions they would consider justified, if they had access to a fuller account of their position in the political system (see essay 4). This 'thought experiment' is guided by an interest in examining the ways in which politics – above all, democratic politics – might be transformed to enable citizens more effectively to understand, shape and organize their own lives (see essays 3–6).[2]

There are those who have denied the legitimacy of the project of the critique of ideology on the grounds that there is no 'Archimedean point' – no, for instance, other-worldly doctrine, natural law, proletarian interest or ideal speech situation – from which to evaluate confidently political relations and institutions. While this rejection of an Archimedean point is, in my judgement, quite correct in general terms (Held, 1980, part 3), it by no means invalidates the project of political theory as the critique of ideology. For differences of evaluative or moral appraisal are never merely a clash of discrepant 'ultimate values' which one must either simply accept or reject. The meaning of evaluative standpoints always depends, as noted previously, on a framework or web of concepts and theories in which the factual and normative inform one another, and which are open to appraisal in philosophical and empirical terms (Hesse, 1974 and 1978; Giddens, 1977, pp. 89–95). As I have argued elsewhere in relation to democratic theory, a consideration of, for instance, political principles, without an examination of the conditions of their realization, may preserve a sense of virtue, but it will leave the actual meaning of such principles barely articulated. By contrast, a consideration of social institutions and political arrangements, without reflecting upon the proper principles of their ordering, might lead to an understanding of their functioning, but it will barely help us to a judgement as to their adequacy, appropriateness and desirability (Held, 1987a, part 3).

Political theories are complex 'networks' of concepts and generalizations about political life involving ideas, assumptions and statements about the nature, purposes and key features of government, state and society and about the political capabilities of human beings. And in assessing them one must attend to the nature and coherence of their theoretical claims, to the adequacy of empirical statements, to the desirability of prescriptions, and to the practicality of political goals.

This is a very tall order! And one which makes successful political theory extremely difficult to achieve (cf. Miller, 1983; 1987). Recognizing this, it is all the more important to emphasize that the essays in this volume are only a set of tentative contributions, which aim to introduce a number of key political ideas, clarify certain central political processes and raise some questions about possible political worlds.

The essays cluster around one major preoccupation: the relationship between state and society, or, rather, that segment of society I shall generally refer to as 'civil society'. Civil society connotes those areas of social life – the domestic world, the economic sphere, cultural activities and political interaction – which are organized by private or voluntary arrangements between individuals and groups outside the *direct* control of the state (cf. Bobbio, 1985; Pelczynski, 1985; Keane, 1988). The essays in the volume seek to explore how classical and contemporary political theorists have understood the relationship between state and civil society, and they seek to assess the adequacy of the various views available to us. In addition, they seek to propose an alternative way of thinking about this relationship while at the same time being attentive to theoretical and practical problems entailed by this alternative view. The following questions are central: What is the state? How should we define it? What is its relationship to civil society? How do the structures, processes and institutions of state and civil society interrelate? Under what conditions, if any, do modern political orders face crisis or breakdown? What should be the proper form and limits of state action? What should be the proper form and limits of civil society? What does and should democracy mean today – within the state apparatus, and within civil society? Is the idea of democracy progressively compromised by the growth and progressive intersection of national and international forces and processes – the erosion of sovereignty in the global system? What new political challenges, if any, do these forces and processes create?

Each of the essays in this volume explores aspects of these and related questions. The first essay sets out four central perspectives on the relationship between state and society – those of liberalism, liberal democracy, Marxism and, for want of a better label, 'political sociology'. From Hobbes to Weber, Marx to Dahl, this essay lays out the background and the intellectual landscape to many of the crucial arguments and debates about the modern state today. The second essay focuses on contemporary theories of the state, examining, in particular, the contributions of pluralists, corporatists and Marxists to the analysis of the interrelation between class structure, power and the state. The essay offers, in conclusion, a set of propositions about the relations between state and society in Western capitalist countries, propositions explored at greater length later in the volume.

The distinctive contribution of Jürgen Habermas to political and social theory is then assessed in the third essay. The essay examines Habermas's claim that there are good grounds to suppose that contemporary capitalist societies are facing imminent crises of legitimation; and it argues that while this view is illuminating in a number of respects, it fails to take account of, among other things, the fragmentation of modern culture and the atomization of people's experiences of the social world, which often means that societies can cohere without a high degree of positive endorsement or legitimation. Further, it is argued, despite deeply felt misgivings and antagonisms to existing institutions among certain middle-class and working-class groups, the absence of a clear conception of a plausible alternative to current political arrangements is a crucial factor inhibiting the development of protest and opposition movements.

'Power and Legitimacy', the fourth essay, provides an extended analysis of problems of order and conflict in the modern state and pursues in detail the question of how political societies are reproduced over time. Taking a broad post-war canvas, the adequacy of a variety of theoretical notions – from 'civic culture' to 'overload crisis' – is critically assessed. Drawing empirical material from the British political system, it is contended that, while this system enjoys a degree of popular support, dissensus is more striking than consensus, and administrative and coercive means are ever more important to ensure political stability.

'Liberalism, Marxism and the Future Direction of Public Policy', essay 5, explores some of the theoretical implications of the above argument in the context of a consideration of the recent successes of governments of the 'New Right'. Assessing current theoretical and political disputes about the proper form and role of the state, it argues that there are fundamental flaws in both the perspectives of the New Right and of its main, New Left, critics. For the New Right's brand of liberalism ignores the fact that markets comprise power relations while Marxism neglects the threat to individual autonomy arising from the power of the state. An argument is presented that enhanced autonomy for individuals and groups can only be properly achieved – or, the 'autonomy principle', as I call it, realized – if it is linked to a twin project of enhancing the independence of the multitude of groups that compose 'civil society' and democratizing the state in a wide-ranging manner.

Essay 6 takes these arguments further by examining in greater detail the political philosophies of the New Right and New Left. Focusing on democracy, it argues that neither the perspective of the New Right nor that of the New Left can provide an adequate account of democracy as it is and as it ought to be. The case is made for a third way – for a model of 'democratic autonomy' or 'liberal socialism' – which might help create and restore the opportunities for people to establish themselves 'in their capacity of being citizens'.

Citizenship is the subject of the seventh essay, which places at its centre an appraisal of contributions of T. H. Marshall and Anthony Giddens to the study of the nature and practices of contemporary democracies. Both these writers have helped illuminate the history and development of citizenship rights and their relation to wider social and economic structures. The essay discusses at length Giddens's recent contributions to the study of class, citizenship and the modern state, and appraises the strengths and weaknesses of his approach. The essay concludes by stressing how the idea of citizenship and the theory of democracy has to be rethought in relation to substantial changes in political, social and economic life which derive from, among other things, the dynamics of the world economy, the rapid growth of transnational links and major changes to the nature of international law – a project scarcely begun today.

'Sovereignty, National Politics and the Global System', essay 8, underlines the urgency of this project through an examination of the concept of sovereignty. Sovereignty is important because it highlights both a critical 'internal' element of the modern state and the necessity to understand the 'external' framework within which the state exists, if the state's claim to supreme power is to be properly understood. The essay explores the meaning of sovereignty – as set out in the writings of figures such as Bodin, Hobbes, Locke and Rousseau – and the way the notion of national sovereignty faces a number of challenges from the nature and structure of the global system. It establishes the necessity of thinking systematically beyond the terms of reference of the nation-state if a satisfactory account of state, power and politics is to be achieved.

The last article in the volume, essay 9, focuses on the failure of politics as a discipline to examine and address central political problems – those deep-rooted problems that actually face us daily as citizens, for example, issues of war and peace, unemployment and technical change, inequality and conflict. It sets out a view of what the discipline of politics should be like in theory and in practice. In so doing, it creates a challenge to the teaching and practice of politics as a discipline and as an everyday practical activity.

In sum, essays 1 and 2 explore how the relationship between 'state' and 'civil society' has been understood; essays 3 and 4 examine how this relationship has operated in advanced capitalist countries; essays 5–7 set out how one might rethink the form and limits of the modern state and civil society; essay 8 focuses on some of the profound difficulties that face the ideas of a national politics and a democratic polity; and essay 9 explores how one might begin to think further about these pressing problems.

Notes

1 By 'state politics' I mean what has generally been regarded by contemporary political theorists and political scientists as 'the political': the form, organization and operations of a state and its relations with other states. While I will use the concept of politics throughout the volume in the broad sense I have set out (pp. 1–2), this does not mean that one cannot use it in a more restricted sense to refer to particular domains of political activity, e.g. state politics, community politics, sexual politics. The context in which various conceptions of politics are used will, I hope, leave no ambiguity as to their meaning.

2 Some political theorists have understood their activities in a comparable manner; that is to say, they have explicitly embraced an interest in political change or transformation as the guiding thread to their work, for instance, Marx and Habermas (see essays 1 and 3). Others have, by the very nature of the way they have understood the methodological status of their work, denied that a practical stance shapes their endeavours, even when these endeavours have often been explicitly directed to reshaping the political understanding and institutions of the modern world, for instance, Hobbes (see essays 1 and 8). Still others have rejected all links between theory and practice in the study of politics and resisted any claims that the latter can legitimately guide practical change even though implicitly their work has been 'rich' in normative implications, for instance, empirical democratic theorists (see essays 1 and 2 of this volume; Held, 1987a, ch. 6).

References

Bobbio, N. 1985: *Stato, Governo, Societa: Per Una Teoria Generale della Politica*. Turin: Einaudi.

Gadamer, H.-G. 1975: *Truth and Method*. London: Sheed & Ward.

Giddens, A. 1977: *Studies in Social and Political Theory*. London: Hutchinson.

Giddens, A. 1979: *Central Problems in Social Theory*. London: Macmillan.

Giddens, A. 1984: *The Constitution of Society*. Cambridge: Polity Press.

Habermas, J. 1974: The classical doctrine of politics in relation to social philosophy. In J. Habermas, *Theory and Practice*, Boston: Beacon Press.

Held, D. 1980: *Introduction to Critical Theory*. London: Hutchinson.

Held, D. 1987a: *Models of Democracy*. Cambridge: Polity Press.

Held, D. 1987b: The future prospects of sociology. *Network*, 39.

Hesse, M. 1974: *The Structure of Scientific Inference*. London: Macmillan.

Hesse, M. 1978: Theory and value in the social sciences. In C. Hookway and P. Pettit (eds), *Action and Interpretation: Studies in the Philosophy of Social Sciences*, Cambridge: Cambridge University Press.

Keane, J. 1988: *Democracy and Civil Society*. London: Verso.

MacIntyre, A. 1971: Is a science of comparative politics possible? In A. MacIntyre, *Against the Self-Images of the Age*, London: Duckworth.

MacIntyre, A. 1983: The indispensability of political theory. In D. Miller and L. Siedentop (eds), *The Nature of Political Theory*, Oxford: Clarendon Press.

Miller, D. 1983: Linguistic philosophy and political theory. In D. Miller and L. Siedentop (eds), *The Nature of Political Theory*, Oxford: Clarendon Press.

Miller, D. 1987: Political theory. In D. Miller, J. Coleman, W. Connolly and A. Ryan (eds), *The Blackwell Encyclopaedia of Political Thought*, Oxford: Basil Blackwell.

Pelczynski, Z. A. (ed.) 1985: *The State and Civil Society*. Cambridge: Cambridge University Press.

Skinner, Q. 1978: *The Foundations of Modern Political Thought*, 2 vols. Cambridge: Cambridge University Press.

Taylor, C. 1967: Neutrality in political science. In P. Laslett and W. G. Runciman (eds), *Philosophy, Politics and Society*, 3rd ser., Oxford: Basil Blackwell.

Taylor, C. 1983: Political theory and practice. In C. Lloyd (ed.), *Social Theory and Political Practice*, Oxford: Clarendon Press.

Thompson, J. B. 1984: *Studies in the Theory of Ideology*. Cambridge: Polity Press.

1

Central Perspectives on the Modern State

The state – or apparatus of 'government' – appears to be everywhere, regulating the conditions of our lives from birth registration to death certification.* Yet the nature of the state is hard to grasp. This may seem peculiar for something so pervasive in public and private life, but it is precisely this pervasiveness which makes it difficult to understand. There is nothing more central to political and social theory than the nature of the state, and nothing more contested. It is the objective of this essay to set out some of the key elements of the conflict of interpretation.

In modern Western political thought, the idea of the state is often linked to the notion of an impersonal and privileged legal or constitutional order with the capability of administering and controlling a given territory (see Skinner, 1978; cf. Neumann, 1964). This notion found its earliest expression in the ancient world (especially in Rome) but it did not become a major object of concern until the early development of the European state system from the sixteenth century onwards. It was not an element of medieval political thinking. The idea of an impersonal and sovereign political order, that is, a legally circumscribed structure of power with supreme jurisdiction over a territory, could not predominate while political rights, obligations and duties were closely tied to property rights and religious tradition. Similarly, the idea that human beings as 'individuals' or as 'a people' could be active citizens of this order – citizens of their state – and not merely dutiful subjects of a monarch or emperor could not develop under such conditions.

The historical changes that contributed to the transformation of medieval notions of political life were immensely complicated. Struggles between

* This essay first appeared in David Held et al. (eds), *States and Societies* (Oxford: Martin Robertson, 1983), pp. 1–55. © The Open University, 1984, D209: *State and Society*.

monarchs and barons over the domain of rightful authority; peasant rebellions against the weight of excess taxation and social obligation; the spread of trade, commerce and market relations; the flourishing of Renaissance culture with its renewed interest in classical political ideas (including the Greek city-state and Roman law); the consolidation of national monarchies in central parts of Europe (England, France and Spain); religious strife and the challenge to the universal claims of Catholicism; the struggle between church and state – all played a part.[1] As the grip of feudal traditions and customs was loosened, the nature and limits of political authority, law, rights and obedience emerged as a preoccupation of European political thought. Not until the end of the sixteenth century did the concept of the state become a central object of political analysis.

While the works of Niccolo Machiavelli (1469–1527) and Jean Bodin (1530–96) are of great importance in these developments, Thomas Hobbes (1588–1679) directly expressed the new concerns when he stated in *De Cive* (1642) that it was his aim 'to make a more curious search into the rights of states and duties of subjects' (quoted in Skinner, 1978, vol. 2, p. 349). Until challenged by, among others, Karl Marx in the nineteenth century, the idea of the modern state came to be associated with a 'form of public power separate from both the ruler and ruled, and constituting the supreme political authority within a certain defined boundary' (Skinner, 1978, vol. 2, p. 353). But the nature of that public power and its relationship to ruler and ruled were the subject of controversy and uncertainty. The following questions arose: What is the state? What should it be? What are its origins and foundations? What is the relationship between state and society? What is the most desirable form this relationship might take? What does and should the state do? Whose interest does and should the state represent? How might one characterize the relations among states?

This essay focuses on four strands or traditions of political analysis which sought to grapple with such questions: (1) *liberalism*, which became absorbed with the question of sovereignty and citizenship; (2) *liberal democracy*, which developed liberalism's concerns while focusing on the problem of establishing political accountability; (3) *Marxism*, which rejected the terms of reference of both liberalism and liberal democracy and concentrated upon class structure and the forces of political coercion; and (4), for want of a more satisfactory term, *political sociology*, which has, from Max Weber to Anglo-American pluralism and 'geopolitical' conceptions of the state, elaborated concerns with both the institutional mechanisms of the state and the system of nation-states more generally. None of these traditions of analysis, it should be stressed, forms a unity; that is to say, each is a heterogeneous body of thought encompassing interesting points of divergence. There is also some common ground, more noticeable in the work of contemporary figures, across these separate traditions. I shall attempt to indicate this briefly throughout the essay and in my concluding remarks. It is important to appreciate that, in a field in which there is as vast a range of literature as this, any selection has an arbitrary element to it. But I hope to introduce, and assess in a preliminary way, some of the central perspectives on the modern state.

A distinction is often made between normative political theory or political philosophy on the one hand, and the descriptive–explanatory theories of the social sciences on the other. The former refers to theories about the proper form of political organization and includes accounts of such notions as liberty and equality. The latter refers to attempts to characterize actual phenomena and events and is marked by a strong empirical element. The distinction, thus, is between theories which focus on what is desirable, what should or ought to be the case, and those that focus on what is the case. The political writings of people like Hobbes, Locke and Mill are generally placed in the first camp, while those of, for instance, Weber are put in the second; Marx occupying sometimes one domain, sometimes the other, depending on the writings one examines. But it will become clear that, while this distinction should be borne in mind, it is hard to use it as a classificatory device for theories of the state. For many political philosophers see what they think the state ought to be like in the state as it is. Social scientists, on the other hand, cannot escape the problem that facts do not simply 'speak for themselves': they are, and they have to be, interpreted; and the framework we bring to the process of interpretation determines what we 'see', what we notice and register as important.

The essay begins with the thought of Hobbes, which marks a point of transition between a commitment to the absolutist state and the struggle of liberalism against tyranny. It is important to be clear about the meaning of 'liberalism' (see Habermas, 1962; Pateman, 1979). While it is a highly controversial concept, and its meaning has shifted historically, I will use it here to signify the attempt to define a private sphere independent of the state and thus to redefine the state itself, that is, the freeing of civil society – personal, family and business life – from political interference and the simultaneous delimitation of the state's authority. With the growing division between the state and civil society, a division which followed the expansion of market economies, the struggle for a range of freedoms and rights which were in principle to be universal became more acute. Gradually, liberalism became associated with the doctrine that freedom of choice should be applied to matters as diverse as marriage, religion, economic and political affairs – in fact, to everything that affected daily life (see Macpherson, 1966, ch. 1; cf. Giddens, 1981, chs 8 and 9). Liberalism upheld the values of reason and toleration in the face of tradition and absolutism (see Dunn, 1979, ch. 2). In this view, the world consists of 'free and equal' individuals with natural rights. Politics should be about the defence of the rights of these individuals – a defence which must leave them in a position to realize their own capacities. The mechanisms for regulating individuals' pursuit of their interests were to be the constitutional state, private property, the competitive market economy – and the distinctively patriarchal family. While liberalism celebrated the rights of individuals to 'life, liberty and property', it should be noted from the outset that it was generally the male property-owning individual who was the focus of so much attention; and the new freedoms were first and foremost for the men of the new middle classes or the bourgeoisie. The Western world was liberal first, and only later, after extensive conflicts, liberal democratic or democratic; that is, only later was a universal franchise won which allowed all mature adults the chance to express their judgement about the performance of those who govern them (Macpherson, 1966, p. 6). But even now, the very meanings of the terms 'liberalism' and 'democracy' remain unsettled.

Sovereignty, citizenship and the development of liberalism

Hobbes was among the first to try to grasp the nature of public power as a special kind of institution – as he put it, an 'Artificiall Man', defined by permanence and sovereignty, the authorized representative 'giving life and motion' to society and the body politic (*Leviathan*, p. 81). He was preoccupied, above all, with the problem of order, which resolved itself into two questions: Why is 'a great Leviathan or state' necessary? and What form should the state take? Through a theory of human nature, sovereign authority and political obligation, he sought to prove that the state must be regarded as ultimately both absolute and legitimate, in order that the worst of evils – civil war – might be permanently averted (see Plamenatz, 1963, pp. 116–54).

In so arguing, Hobbes produced a political philosophy which is a fascinating point of departure for reflection on the modern theory of the state; for it is at once a profoundly liberal and illiberal view (see Dunn, 1979, pp. 23, 42–3, 50; cf. Skinner, 1966). It is liberal because Hobbes derives or explains the existence of society and the state by reference to 'free and equal' individuals, the component elements, according to him, of social life – 'men as if but even now sprung out of the earth and suddenly, like mushrooms, come to full maturity, without all kind of engagement to each other' (*De Cive*, p. 109). It is liberal because Hobbes is concerned to uncover the best circumstances for human nature – understood as naturally selfish, egoistical and self-interested – to find expression. And it is liberal because it emphasizes the importance of consent in the making of a contract or bargain, not only to regulate human affairs and secure a measure of independence and choice in society, but also to legitimate, that is, justify, such regulation. Yet Hobbes's position is also, as I shall attempt to show, profoundly illiberal: his political conclusions emphasize the necessity of a practically all-powerful state to create the laws and secure the conditions of social and political life. Hobbes remains of abiding interest today precisely because of this tension between the claims of individuality on the one hand, and the power requisite for the state to ensure 'peaceful and commodious living', on the other (cf. Macpherson, 1968, p. 81; or for a fuller account Macpherson, 1962).

In *Leviathan* (1651), Hobbes set out his argument in a highly systematic manner. Influenced by Galileo, he was concerned to build his 'civil science' upon clear principles and closely reasoned deductions. He started from a set of postulates and observations about human nature. Human beings, Hobbes contended, are moved by desires and aversions which generate a state of perpetual restlessness. Seeking always 'more intense delight', they are profoundly self-interested; a deep-rooted psychological egoism limits the possibilities for human cooperation. In order to fulfil their desires, human beings (though in different ways and degrees) seek power. And because the power gained by one 'resisteth and hindreth the power of another', conflicts of interest are inevitable: they are a fact of nature. The struggle for power, for no other reason than self-preservation and self-interest (however disguised by rationalization) defines the human condition. Hobbes thus emphasizes 'a generall inclination of all mankind, a perpetuall and restlesse desire of Power after power, that ceaseth only in Death' (*Leviathan*, p. 161). The idea that human beings might come to respect and trust one another, treat each other as if they could keep promises and honour contracts, seems remote indeed.

Hobbes desired to show, however, that a consistent concern with self-interest does not simply lead to an endless struggle for power (see Peters, 1956, ch. 9; 1967, pp. 41–3). In order to prove this he introduced a 'thought experiment' employing four interrelated concepts: state of nature, right of nature, law of nature and social contract. He imagined a situation in which individuals are in a state of nature – that is, a situation without a 'Common Power' or state to enforce rules and restrain behaviour – enjoying 'natural rights' to use all means to protect their lives and to do whatever they wish, against whoever they like and to 'possess, use, and enjoy all that he would, or could get' (see *Leviathan*, part 1, chs 13–15). The result is a constant struggle for survival: Hobbes's famous 'Warre of every one against every one'. In this state of nature individuals discover that life is 'solitary, poore, nasty, brutish and short' and, accordingly, that to avoid harm and the risk of an early death, let alone to ensure the conditions of greater comfort, the observation of certain natural laws or rules is required (*Leviathan*, ch. 13). The latter are things the individual ought to adhere to in dealings with others if there is sufficient ground for believing that others will do likewise (see Plamenatz, 1963, pp. 122–32, for a clear discussion of these ideas). Hobbes says of these laws that 'they have been contracted into one easy sum, intelligible even to the meanest capacity; and that is, *Do not that to another which thou wouldest not have done to thyself*' (see *Leviathan*, chs 14 and 15). There is much in what he says about laws of nature that is ambiguous (above all, their relation to the 'will of God'), but these difficulties need not concern us here. For the key problem, in Hobbes's view, is: under what conditions will individuals trust each other enough to 'lay down their right to all things' so that their long-term interest in security and peace can be upheld? How can individuals make a bargain with one another when it may be, in certain circumstances, in some people's interest to break it? An agreement between people to ensure the regulation of their lives is necessary, but it seems an impossible goal.

His argument, in short, is as follows: if individuals surrender their rights by transferring them to a powerful authority which can force them to keep their promises and covenants, then an effective and legitimate private and public sphere, society and state, can be formed. Thus the social contract consists in individuals handing over their rights of self-government to a single authority – thereafter authorized to act on their behalf – on the condition that every individual does the same. A unique relation of authority results: the relation of sovereign to subject. A unique political power is created: the exercise of sovereign power or sovereignty – the authorized (hence rightful) use of power by the person or assembly established as sovereign.[2] The sovereign's subjects have an obligation and duty to obey the sovereign; for the position 'sovereign' is the product of their social contract, and 'sovereignty' is above all a quality of the position rather than of the person who occupies it. The contract is a once-and-for-all affair, creating an authority able to determine the very nature and limits of the law. There can be no conditions placed on such authority because to do so would undermine its very *raison d'être*.

The sovereign has to have sufficient power to make agreements stick, to enforce contracts and to ensure that the laws governing political and economic life are upheld. Power must be effective. Since, in Hobbes's view, 'men's ambitions, avarice, anger and other passions' are strong, the 'bonds of words are too weak to bridle them . . . without some fear of coercive power' (see *Leviathan*, ch. 14). In short: 'covenants, without the sword, are but words, and of no strength to secure a man at all' (*Leviathan*, p. 223). Beyond the sovereign state's sphere of influence there will always be the chaos of constant warfare; but within the territory controlled by the state, with 'fear of some coercive power', social order can be sustained.

It is important to stress that, in Hobbes's opinion, while sovereignty must be self-perpetuating, undivided and ultimately absolute, it is established by the authority conferred by the people (*Leviathan*, pp. 227–8). The sovereign's right of command and the subjects' duty of obedience is the result of consent – the circumstances individuals would have agreed to if there had actually been a social contract. Although there is little about Hobbes's conception of the state which today we would call representative, he argues in fact that the people rule through the sovereign. The sovereign is their representative: 'A

Multitude of men, are made *One* Person, when they are by one man, or one Person, Represented' (*Leviathan*, p. 220). Through the sovereign a plurality of voices and interests can become 'one will', and to speak of a sovereign state assumes, Hobbes held, such a unity. Hence, his position is at one with all those who argue for the importance of government by consent and reject the claims of the 'divine right of Kings' and, more generally, the authority of tradition. Yet, his conclusions run wholly counter to those who often take such an argument to imply the necessity of some kind of popular sovereignty or democratic representative government (cf. Peters, 1956, ch. 9). Hobbes was trying to acknowledge, and persuade his contemporaries to acknowledge, a full obligation to a sovereign state. As one commentator usefully put it:

> Hobbes was not asking his contemporaries to make a contract, but only to acknowledge the same obligation they would have had if they had made such a contract. He was speaking not to men in a state of nature, but to men in an imperfect political society, that is to say, in a society which did not guarantee security of life and commodious living (as witness its tendency to lapse into civil war). He was telling them what they must do to establish a more nearly perfect political society, one that would be permanently free from internal disturbance. (Macpherson, 1968, p. 45; cf. *Leviathan*, p. 728)

A strong secular state was offered as the most effective, appropriate and legitimate political form. The right of citizens to change their ruler(s) was, accordingly, regarded as superfluous.

The fundamental purpose of sovereignty is to ensure 'the *safety of the people*'. By 'safety' is meant not merely minimum physical preservation. The sovereign must ensure the protection of all things held in property: 'Those that are dearest to a man are his own life, and limbs; and in the next degree, (in most men) those that concern conjugall affection; and after them riches and means of living' (*Leviathan*, pp. 376, 382-3). Moreover, the sovereign must educate the people to respect all these kinds of property so that men can pursue their trades and callings, and industry and the polity can flourish. At this point Hobbes suggests certain limits to the range of the sovereign's actions: the sovereign should neither injure individuals nor the basis of their material wellbeing, and should recognize that authority can be sustained only so long as protection can be afforded to all subjects (see *Leviathan*, ch. 21).

There are a number of particularly noteworthy things about Hobbes's conception of the state. First, the state is regarded as pre-eminent in political and social life. While individuals exist prior to the formation of civilized society and to the state itself, it is the latter that provides the conditions of existence of the former. The state alters a miserable situation for human beings by changing the conditions under which they pursue their interests. The state constitutes society through the powers of command of the sovereign (set down in the legal system) and through the capacity of the sovereign to enforce the law (established by the fear of coercive power). The state does not simply record or reflect socio-economic reality, it enters into its very construction by establishing its form and codifying its forces. Second, it is the self-seeking nature of individuals' behaviour and patterns of interaction that makes the indivisible power of the state necessary. The sovereign state must be able to act decisively to counter the threat of anarchy. Hence it must be powerful and capable of acting as a single force. Third, the state, and practically all it does, can and must be considered legitimate. For the 'thought experiment', drawing on the notions of a state of nature and social contract, shows how individuals with their own divergent interests come to commit themselves to the idea that only a great Leviathan or state or 'Mortall God' can articulate and defend the 'general' or 'public' interest. The sovereign state represents 'the public' – the sum of individual interests – and thus can create the conditions for individuals to live their lives and to go about their competitive and acquisitive business peacefully. Hobbes's argument recognizes the importance of public consent (although he was not always consistent about its significance), and concludes that it is conferred by the social contract and its covenants.

Hobbes's arguments are extraordinarily impressive. The image of an all-powerful Leviathan is a remarkably contemporary one; after all, most states in the twentieth century have been run by 'Mortall Gods', people with seemingly unlimited authority backed by the armed forces. (Consider the number of dictatorships that now exist.) Moreover, the idea that individuals are merely self-interested is also a depressingly modern one. Such a conception of human beings is presupposed in the economic and political doctrines of many writers today (see, for example, Friedman, 1962). But the impressiveness of some of Hobbes's views should not, of course, be confused with their acceptability. Hobbes's accounts, for example, of sovereignty, obligation and the duties of citizens are all contestable, as are his general doctrines about human nature. The constitutive role of the state (the degree to which the state forms society), coercive power (the degree to which such power is or must be central to political order), representation (the degree to which a sovereign authority can claim to articulate the public interest without forms of democratic accountability), and legitimacy (the degree to which states are considered just or worthy by their citizens) – all have been and still are subject to debate.

John Locke (1632–1704) raised a fundamental objection to the Hobbesian argument that individuals could only find a 'peaceful and commodious' life with one another if they were governed by the dictates of an indivisible sovereign. He said of this type of argument: 'This is to think that Men are so foolish that they take care to avoid what Mischiefs may be done them by *Pole-Cats*, or *Foxes*, but are content, nay think it Safety, to be devoured by

Lions' (*Two Treatises*, p. 372; see also note 36 on the same page). In other words, it is hardly credible that people who do not fully trust each other would place their trust in an all-powerful ruler to look after their interests. What obstacles are there to the potential 'violence and oppression', as Locke put it, 'of this Absolute Ruler'? (*Two Treatises*, p. 371). What would make such a system of rule compelling and trustworthy?

Locke approved of the revolution and settlement of 1688, which imposed certain constitutional limits on the authority of the Crown in England. He rejected the notion of a great Leviathan, pre-eminent in all social spheres, an uncontested unity establishing and enforcing law according to the sovereign's will. For Locke, the state (he spoke more often of 'government') can and should be conceived as an 'instrument' for the defence of the 'life, liberty and estate' of its citizens; that is, the state's *raison d'être* is the protection of individuals' rights as laid down by God's will and as enshrined in law (see Dunn, 1969, part 3). Society, conceived of as the sum of individuals, exists prior to the state, and the state is established to guide society. He placed a strong emphasis on the importance of government by consent – consent which could be revoked if the government and its deputies fail to sustain the 'good of the governed'. Legitimate government requires the consent of its citizens, and government can be dissolved if the trust of the people is violated. What Locke meant by 'consent' is controversial (cf. Plamenatz, 1963, ch. 6; Dunn, 1980a, pp. 29–52), but whatever position one takes on this question the contrast between the views of Locke and Hobbes remains remarkable. Moreover, while Locke did not develop a systematic doctrine about the desirability of a mixed form of government or a division of powers within the state, he has been associated for many generations with such a view (see Laslett, 1963, pp. 130–5). He accepted that the state should have supreme jurisdiction over its territory, but was critical of the notion of the indivisibility of state power and suggested an important alternative conception.

It is interesting that the idea of social contract and the state of nature can yield a variety of political positions. Locke, like Hobbes, saw the establishment of the political world as preceded by the existence of individuals endowed with natural rights. Locke, like Hobbes, was concerned to derive and explain the very possibility of government. Locke, like Hobbes, was concerned about what form legitimate government should take and about the conditions for security, peace and freedom. But the way in which he conceived these things was considerably different. In the important second of the *Two Treatises of Government* (which was published for the first time in 1690), Locke starts with the proposition that individuals are originally in a state of nature, a '*State of perfect Freedom* to order their Actions, and dispose of their Possessions, and Persons as they think fit, within the bounds of the Law of Nature, without asking leave, or depending upon the will of any other Man' (p. 309). The state of nature is a state of liberty but not 'a state of license'. Individuals are bound by duty to God and governed only by the law of nature. The law of nature (the precise meaning of which is difficult to pin down in the *Two Treatises*) specifies basic principles of morality – individuals should not take their own lives, they should try to preserve each other and should not infringe upon one another's liberty. The law can be grasped by human reason but it is the creation of God, the 'infinitely wise Maker' (p. 311).

Humans – in fact, Locke spoke here only of men – are free and equal because reason makes them capable of rationality, of following the law of nature. They enjoy natural rights. The right of governing one's affairs and enforcing the law of nature against transgressors is presupposed, as is the obligation to respect the rights of others. Individuals have the right to dispose of their own labour and to possess property. The right to property is a right to 'life, liberty and estate' (p. 395, para. 123). (Locke also uses 'property' in a narrower sense to mean just the exclusive use of objects (pp. 327–44).)[3]

Adherence to the law of nature, according to Locke, ensures that the state of nature is not a state of war. However, the natural rights of individuals are not always safeguarded in the state of nature, for certain 'inconveniences' exist: not all individuals fully respect the rights of others; when it is left to each individual to enforce the law of nature there are too many judges and hence conflicts of interpretation about the meaning of the law; and when people are loosely organized they are vulnerable to aggression from abroad (see, for example, *Two Treatises*, pp. 316–17, para. 13). The central 'inconvenience' suffered can be summarized as the inadequate regulation of property in its broad sense, the right to 'life, liberty and estate' (*Two Treatises*, p. 308, para. 3, and pp. 395–6, para. 124). Property is prior to both society and the state; and the difficulty of its regulation is the critical reason which compels 'equally free men' to the establishment of both. Thus the remedy for the inconveniences of the state of nature is an agreement or contract to create, first, an independent society and, second, a political society or government (*Two Treatises*, pp. 372–6, paras 94–7; see Laslett, 1963, pp. 127–8). The distinction between these two agreements is important, for it makes clear that authority is bestowed by individuals in society on government for the purpose of pursuing the ends of the governed; and should these ends fail to be adequately represented, the final judges are the people – the citizens of the state – who can dispense both with their deputies and, if need be, with the existing form of government itself.

In Locke's opinion, it should be stressed, the formation of the state does not signal the transfer of all subjects' rights to the state (see, for example, pp. 402–3, para. 135, and pp. 412–13, para. 149). The rights of law making and enforcement (legislative and executive rights) are transferred, but the whole process is conditional upon the state adhering to its essential purpose: the preservation of 'life, liberty and estate'. Sovereign power, that is, sovereignty, remains ultimately with the people. The legislative body enacts rules as the people's agent in accordance with the law of nature, and the executive power (to which Locke also tied the judiciary) enforces the legal system. This separation of powers was important because:

> It may be too great a temptation to humane frailty apt to grasp at Power, for the same Persons who have the Power of making Laws, to have also in their hands the power to execute them, whereby they may exempt themselves from Obedience to the Laws they make, and suit the Law, both in its making and execution, to their own private advantage, and thereby come to have a distinct interest from the rest of the community, contrary to the end of Society and Government. (p. 410)

Thus, an absolutist state and the arbitrary use of authority are inconsistent with the integrity and ultimate ends of society. Locke believed in the desirability of a constitutional monarchy holding executive power and a parliamentary assembly holding the rights of legislation, although he did not think this was the only form government might take and his views are compatible with a variety of other conceptions of political institutions. Moreover, it is not always clear who was qualified to vote for the assembly: it sometimes appears simply as if 'the people' (minus women and slaves of both sexes!) are entitled, but it is almost certain that Locke would not have dissented from a franchise based strictly on property-holding (cf. Dunn, 1969, ch. 10; Franklin, 1978).

The government rules, and its legitimacy is sustained, by the 'consent' of individuals. 'Consent' is a crucial and difficult notion in Locke's writings. It could be interpreted to suggest that only the continually active personal agreement of individuals would be sufficient to ensure a duty of obedience, that is, to ensure a government's authority and legitimacy (see Plamenatz, 1963, p. 228). However, as one critic aptly put it, 'Locke took much of the sting (and interest) out of this view by his doctrine of "tacit consent", according to which individuals may be said to have consented to a government in any society subsequent to the supposed contract simply by owning property, or by "lodging only for a week", by "travelling freely on the highway" and indeed even by being "within the territories of that government"' (Lukes, 1973, pp. 80-1). Locke seems to have thought of the active consent of individuals as having been crucial only to the initial inauguration of a legitimate state. Thereafter consent follows from majority decisions of 'the people's' representatives and from the fact of adherence or acquiescence to the legal system; for what property now is, and what protection and security people can enjoy, is specified by law (see Dunn, 1980a, pp. 36-7). The government, by virtue of the original contract and its covenants, is bound by the law of nature and, thus, bound to guarantee 'life, liberty and estate'. The price of this is a duty to obey the law, an obligation to the state, unless the law of nature is consistently violated by a series of tyrannical political actions. Should such a situation occur, rebellion to form a new government, Locke contended, might not only be unavoidable but just.

One commentator has summarized Locke's views well:

> God, the Creator, determined the ends of man, his creature . . . God gave men reason to understand their situation on earth and, above all, their duty within this situation. He gave them senses as channels through which they could apprehend this situation. Government and social order were contrivances devised for them through their own reason and sense experience to improve this situation. It was a *subordinate practical convenience*, not a focus of value in itself. (Dunn, 1979, p. 39; my emphasis)

The duties of the state are the maintenance of law and order at home and protection against aggression from abroad. In Locke's famous words: 'Wherever Law ends Tyranny begins.' Free from tyranny, people would enjoy the maximum scope to pursue their own privately initiated interests. The state should be the regulator and protector of society: individuals are best able by their own efforts to satisfy their needs and develop their capacities in a process of free exchange with others.

Political activity for Locke is instrumental; it secures the framework or conditions for freedom so that the private ends of individuals might be met in civil society. The creation of a political community or government is the burden individuals have to bear to secure their ends. Thus, membership of a political community, that is, citizenship, bestows upon the individual both responsibilities and rights, duties and powers, constraints and liberties (cf. Laslett, 1963, pp. 134–5). In relation to Hobbes's ideas this was a most significant and radical view. For it helped inaugurate one of the most central tenets of European liberalism; that is, that the state exists to safeguard the rights and liberties of citizens who are ultimately the best judges of their own interests; and that accordingly the state must be restricted in scope and constrained in practice in order to ensure the maximum possible freedom of every citizen. In most respects it was Locke's rather than Hobbes's views which helped to lay the foundation for the development of liberalism and prepared the way for the tradition of popular representative government. Compared to Hobbes, Locke's influence on the world of practical politics has been considerable.

Locke's writings seem to point in a number of directions at once. They suggest the importance of securing the rights of individuals, popular sovereignty, majority rule, a division of powers within the state, constitutional monarchy and a representative system of parliamentary government – a direct anticipation of key aspects of British government as it developed in the nineteenth and early twentieth centuries, and of central tenets of the modern representative state. But, at best, most of these ideas are only in rudimentary form and it is certain that Locke did not foresee many of the vital components of democratic representative government, for instance, competitive parties, party rule, and the maintenance of political liberties irrespective of class, sex, colour and creed (Laslett, 1963, p. 123). It is not a condition of legitimate government or government by consent, on Locke's account, that there be regular periodic elections of a legislative assembly, let alone universal suffrage (cf. Plamenatz, 1963, pp. 231, 251–2; Dunn, 1969, ch. 10). Moreover, he did not develop a detailed account of what the limits might be to state interference in people's lives and under what conditions civil disobedience is justified. He thought that political power was held 'on trust' by and for the people, but failed to specify adequately who were to count as 'the people' and under what conditions 'trust' should be bestowed. He certainly never imagined that such power might be exercised directly by the citizens themselves, that is, in some form of direct or self-government. While Locke was unquestionably one of the first great champions of liberalism he cannot, in the end, be considered a democrat (even if we restrict the meaning of this term to support for a universal franchise), although his works clearly stimulated the development of both liberal and democratic government, what we may call liberal democracy.[4]

Power, accountability and liberal democracy

If Hobbes and Locke saw the state as a regulator and protector, it was above all because of fears about the problems and dangers individuals faced if left to their own devices. People could not live adequately without a guiding force, although Locke added that the guiding force – the trustee of the people – could not be fully trusted either: there must be limits upon legally sanctioned political power. This latter argument was taken significantly further by two of the very first advocates of liberal democracy: Jeremy Bentham (1748–1832) and James Mill (1773–1836) who, for my purposes here, can be treated together. For these two thinkers, liberal democracy was associated with a political apparatus that would ensure the accountability of the governors to the governed. Only through democratic government would there be a satisfactory means for choosing, authorizing and controlling political decisions commensurate with the public interest, that is, the interests of the mass of individuals. As Bentham wrote: 'A democracy . . . has for its characteristic object and effect . . . securing its members against oppression and depredation at the hands of those functionaries which it employs for its defence' (*Constitutional Code*, book 1, p. 47). Democratic government is required to protect citizens from despotic use of political power whether it be by a monarch, the aristocracy or other groups. Bentham's and Mill's argument has been usefully referred to as the 'protective case for democracy' (see Macpherson, 1977, ch. 2). Only through the vote, secret ballot, competition between potential political leaders (representatives), elections, separation of powers and the liberty of the press, speech and public association could 'the interest of the community in general' be sustained (cf. Bentham, *Fragment on Government* and Mill, *An Essay on Government*).

Bentham and Mill were impressed by the progress and methods of the natural sciences and were decidedly secular in their orientations. They thought of the concepts of social contract, natural rights and natural law as misleading philosophical fictions which failed to explain the real basis of the citizen's commitment and duty to the state. This basis could be uncovered by grasping the primitive and irreducible elements of actual human behaviour. The key to their understanding of people, and of the system of governance most suited to human beings, lies in the thesis that humans act to satisfy desire and avoid pain. In brief their argument is as follows: the overriding motivation of human beings is to fulfil their desires, maximize their satisfactions or utilities, and minimize their suffering; society consists of individuals seeking as much utility as they can get from whatever it is they want; individuals' interests conflict with one another for 'a grand governing law of human nature', as Hobbes thought, is to subordinate 'the persons and properties of human beings to our pleasures' (see Bentham, *Fragment on Government*). Since those who govern will naturally act in the same way as the governed, government must, to avoid abuse, be directly accountable to an electorate called upon frequently to decide if their objectives have been met.

What, then, should be the government's objectives? Government must act according to the principle of utility: it must aim to ensure, by means of careful calculation, the achievement of the greatest happiness for the greatest number – the only scientifically defensible criterion, Bentham and Mill contended, of the public good. It has four subsidiary goals: 'to provide subsistence; to produce abundance; to favour equality; to maintain security' (see Bentham, *Principles of the Civil Code*). Of these four the last is by far the most critical; for without security of life and property there would be no incentive for individuals to work and generate wealth: labour would be insufficiently productive and commerce could not prosper. If the state pursues this goal (along with the others to the extent that they are compatible), it will therefore be in the citizen's self-interest to obey it.

Bentham, Mill and the Utilitarians generally provided one of the clearest justifications for the liberal democratic state that ensures the conditions necessary for individuals to pursue their interests without risk of arbitrary political interference, to participate freely in economic transactions, to exchange labour and goods on the market and to appropriate resources privately. These ideas became the basis of classical nineteenth-century 'English liberalism': the state was to have the role of the umpire or referee while individuals pursued, according to the rules of economic competition and free exchange, their own interests. Periodic elections, the abolition of the powers of the monarchy, the division of powers within the state plus the free market would lead to the maximum benefit for all citizens. The free vote and the free market were *sine qua non*. For a key presupposition was that the collective good could be properly realized in many domains of life only if individuals interacted in competitive exchanges, pursuing their utility with minimal state interference. Significantly, however, this argument had another side. Tied to the advocacy of a 'minimal' state whose scope and power was to be strictly limited, there was a strong commitment in fact to certain types of state intervention, for instance, the curtailment of the behaviour of the disobedient, whether they be individuals, groups or classes (see Mill, 'Prisons and prison discipline'). Those who challenge the security of property or the market society undermine the realization of the public good. In the name of the public good, the Utilitarians advocated a new system of administrative power for 'person management' (cf. Foucault, 1977, part 3; Ignatieff, 1978, ch. 6). Prisons were a mark of this new age. Moreover, whenever *laissez-faire* was inadequate to ensure the best possible outcomes, state intervention was justified to reorder social relations and institutions. The enactment and enforcement of law, backed by the coercive powers of the state, and the creation of new state institutions was legitimate to the extent that it upheld the general principle of utility.

Bentham and Mill were reluctant democrats. In considering the extent of the franchise they found grounds at one time for excluding, among others, the whole of the labouring classes and female population, despite the fact that many of their arguments seemed to point squarely in the direction of universal suffrage. (Bentham became more radical on the question of the suffrage than Mill and, in later works, abandoned his earlier reservations about universal manhood suffrage, though he retained some reservations about the proper extent of women's political involvement.) Their ideas have been aptly referred to as 'the founding model of democracy for a modern industrial society' (Macpherson, 1977, pp. 42–3). Their account of democracy establishes it as nothing but a logical requirement for the governance of a society, freed from absolute power and tradition, in which individuals have endless desires, form a body of mass consumers and are dedicated to the maximization of private gain. Democracy, accordingly, becomes a means for the enhancement of these ends – not an end in itself, for perhaps the cultivation and development of all citizens. As such it is at best a partial form of democratic theory (cf. Pateman, 1970, ch. 1).

The 'highest and harmonious' development of individual capacities was, however, a central concern of James Mill's son, John Stuart Mill (1806–73) (see J. S. Mill, *Considerations on Representative Government*, and in particular the extracts from this work in Held et al., 1983, part 1). If Bentham and James Mill were reluctant democrats but prepared to develop arguments to justify democratic institutions, John Stuart Mill was a clear advocate of democracy, preoccupied with the extent of individual liberty in all spheres of human endeavour. Liberal democratic or representative government was important for him, not just because it established boundaries for the pursuit of individual satisfaction, but because it was an important aspect of the free development of individuality: participation in political life (voting, involvement in local administration and jury service) was vital to create a direct interest in government and, consequently, a basis for an involved, informed and developing citizenry. Mill conceived of democratic politics as a prime mechanism of moral self-development (cf. Macpherson, 1977, ch. 3; Dunn, 1979, pp. 51–3). He likened periodic voting to the passing of a 'verdict by a juryman' – ideally the considered outcome of a process of active deliberation about the facts of public affairs, not a mere expression of personal interest.

John Stuart Mill's absorption with the question of the autonomy of individuals and minorities is brought out most clearly in his famous and influential study, *On Liberty* (1859). The aim of this work is to elaborate and defend a principle which will establish 'the nature and limits of the power which can be legitimately exercised by society over the individual'. Mill recognized that some regulation and interference in individuals' lives is necessary but sought an obstacle to arbitrary and self-interested intervention. He put the crucial point thus:

> The object . . . is to assert one very simple principle, as entitled to govern absolutely the dealings of society with the individual in the way of compulsion and control, whether the means used be physical force in the form of legal penalties or the moral coercion of public opinion. That principle is that the sole end for which mankind are warranted, individually or collectively, in interfering with the liberty of action of any of their number is self-protection. That the only purpose for which power can be rightfully exercised over any member of a civilised community, against his will, is to prevent harm to others. (*On Liberty*, p. 68)

Social or political interference with individual liberty may be justified only when an act (or a failure to act), whether it be intended or not, 'concerns others' and then only when it 'harms' others. The sole end of interference with liberty should be self-protection. In those activities which are merely 'self-regarding', that is, only of concern to the individual, 'independence is, of right, absolute'; for 'over himself, over his own body and mind, the individual is sovereign' (*On Liberty*, p. 69).

Mill's principle is, in fact, anything but 'very simple': its meaning and implications remain controversial (see Ryan, 1970). For instance, what exactly constitutes 'harm to others'? Does inadequate education cause harm?

Does the publication of pornography cause harm? But leaving aside difficulties such as these, it should be noted that in his hands the principle generated a defence of many of the key liberties associated with liberal democratic government. The 'appropriate region of human liberty' became: first, liberty of thought, feeling, discussion and publication; second, liberty of tastes and pursuits ('framing the plan of our life to suit our own character'); and third, liberty of association or combination assuming, of course, it causes no harm to others (*On Liberty*, pp. 71–2). The 'only freedom which deserves the name is that of pursuing our own good in our own way, so long as we do not attempt to deprive others of theirs or impede their efforts to obtain it' (p. 72). Mill contended, moreover, that the current practice of both rulers and citizens was generally opposed to his doctrine and unless a 'strong barrier of moral conviction' can be established against such bad habits, growing infringements on the liberty of citizens can be expected as the centralized bureaucratic state expands to cope with the problems of the modern age (*On Liberty*, ch. 5).

Liberty and democracy create, according to Mill, the possibility of 'human excellence'. Liberty of thought, discussion and action are necessary conditions for the development of independence of mind and autonomous judgement; they are vital for the formation of human reason or rationality. In turn, the cultivation of reason stimulates and sustains liberty. Representative government is essential for the protection and enhancement of both liberty and reason. Without it arbitrary laws might, for instance, be created which enhance the likelihood of tyranny. Representative democracy is the most suitable mode of government for the enactment of laws consistent with the principle of liberty, as the free exchange of goods in the market place is the most appropriate way of maximizing economic liberty and economic good.[5] A system of representative democracy makes government accountable to the citizenry and creates wiser citizens capable of pursuing the public interest. It is thus both a means to develop self-identity, individuality and social difference – a pluralistic society – and an end in itself, an essential democratic order.

Given that individuals are capable of different kinds of things and only a few have developed their full capacities, would it not be appropriate if some citizens have more sway over government than others? Regrettably for the cogency of Mill's argument he thought as much and recommended a plural system of voting; all adults should have a vote but the wiser and more talented should have more votes than the ignorant and less able. Mill took occupational status as a rough guide to the allocation of votes and adjusted his conception of democracy accordingly: those with the most knowledge and skill – who happened to have most property and privilege – could not be outvoted by those with less, that is, the working classes (see Macpherson, 1977, pp. 57–64). Mill was extremely critical of vast inequalities of income, wealth and power; he recognized that they prevented the full development of most members of the labouring classes and yet he stopped short – far short – of a commitment to political and social equality. The idea that all citizens should have equal weight in the political system remained outside his actual doctrine. Moreover, since he ultimately trusted so little in the judgement of the electorate and the elected, he defended the notion that Parliament should have only a right of veto on legislation proposed and drawn up by a non-elected commission of experts.

It was left by and large to the extensive and often violently repressed struggles of working-class and feminist activists in the nineteenth and twentieth centuries to achieve in some countries genuinely universal suffrage. This achievement was to remain fragile in countries such as Germany, Italy, Spain and was in practice denied to some groups, for instance, many Blacks in the United States before the civil rights movement in the 1950s and 1960s. Through these struggles the idea that 'citizenship rights' should apply to all adults became slowly established;[6] many of the arguments of the liberal democrats could be turned against the *status quo* to reveal the extent to which the principle and aspirations of equal political participation and equal human development remained unfulfilled. It was only with the actual achievement of full citizenship that liberal democracy took on its distinctively modern form:

> a cluster of rules . . . permitting the broadest . . . participation of the majority of citizens in political decisions, i.e. in decisions affecting the whole society. The rules are more or less the following: (a) all citizens who have reached legal age, without regard to race, religion, economic status, sex etc. must enjoy political rights, i.e. the right to express their own opinion through their vote and/or to elect those who express it for them; (b) the vote of all citizens must have equal weight; (c) all citizens enjoying political rights must be free to vote according to their own opinion, formed as freely as possible, i.e. in a free contest between organized political groups competing among themselves so as to aggregate demands and transform them into collective deliberations; (d) they must also be free in the sense that they must be in a position of having real alternatives, i.e. of choosing between different solutions; (e) whether for collective deliberations or for the election of representatives, the principle of numerical majority holds – even though different forms of majority rule can be established (relative, absolute, qualified), under certain circumstances established in advance; (f) no decision taken by a majority must limit minority rights, especially the right to become eventually, under normal conditions, a majority. (Bobbio, 1978, p. 17)

The idea of democracy remains complex and contested. The development towards the notion of the liberal democratic state in the works of Hobbes, Locke, Bentham and the two Mills comprises a most heterogeneous body of thought. Its enormous influence, especially in the Anglo-American world, has spawned seemingly endless debates and conflicts.[7] However, the whole liberal democratic tradition stands apart from an alternative perspective: the theory of what can be called 'direct' or 'participatory' democracy, which had one of its earliest exponents in Rousseau (1712–78). It is worth saying something briefly about Rousseau, not only because of the importance of his thought, but because he had, according to some writers at least, a direct influence on the development of the key counterpoint to liberal democracy – the Marxist tradition (see, for example, Colletti, 1972).

The idea that the consent of individuals legitimates government and the state system more generally was central to both seventeenth- and eighteenth-century liberals as well as to nineteenth- and twentieth-century liberal democrats. The former regarded the social contract as the original mechanism of individual consent, while the latter focused on the ballot box as the mechanism whereby the citizen periodically conferred authority on government to enact laws and regulate economic and social life. Rousseau was dissatisfied, for reasons I can only briefly allude to, with arguments of both these types. Like Hobbes and Locke, he was concerned with the question of whether there is a legitimate and secure principle of government (Rousseau, *The Social Contract*, p. 49). Like Hobbes and Locke he offered an account of a state of nature and the social contract. In his classic *Social Contract* (published in 1762), he assumed that although humans were happy in the original state of nature, they were driven from it by a variety of obstacles to their preservation (individual weaknesses, common miseries, natural disasters) (*The Social Contract*, p. 59). Human beings came to realize that the development of their nature, the realization of their capacity for reason, the fullest experience of liberty, could be achieved only by a social contract which established a system of cooperation through a law-making and enforcing body. Thus there is a contract, but it is a contract which creates the possibility of *self*-regulation or *self*-government. In Hobbes's and Locke's versions of the social contract, sovereignty is transferred from the people to the state and its ruler(s) (although for Locke the surrender of the rights of self-government was a conditional affair). By contrast Rousseau was original, as one commentator aptly put it, 'in holding that no such transfer of sovereignty need or should take place: sovereignty not only originates in the people; it ought to stay there' (Cranston, 1968, p. 30). Accordingly, not only did Rousseau find the political doctrines offered by Hobbes and Locke unacceptable, but those of the type put forward by the liberal democrats as well. In a justly famous passage he wrote:

> Sovereignty cannot be represented, for the same reason that it cannot be alienated
> . . . the people's deputies are not, and could not be, its representatives; they are
> merely its agents; and they cannot decide anything finally. Any law which the
> people has not ratified in person is void; it is not law at all. The English people
> believes itself to be free; it is gravely mistaken; it is free only during the election
> of Members of Parliament; as soon as the Members are elected, the people is
> enslaved; it is nothing. (*The Social Contract*, p. 141)

Rousseau saw individuals as ideally involved in the direct creation of the laws by which their lives are regulated. The sovereign authority is the people making the rules by which they live. Like John Stuart Mill after him, Rousseau celebrated the notion of an active, involved citizenry in a developing process of government, but he interpreted this in a more radical manner: all citizens should meet together to decide what is best for the community and enact the appropriate laws. The governed, in essence, should be the governors. In Rousseau's account, the idea of self-government is posited as an end in itself; a political order offering opportunities for participation in the arrangement of public affairs should not just be a state, but rather the formation of a type of society – a society in which the affairs of the state are integrated into the affairs of ordinary citizens.[8]

The role of the citizen is the highest to which an individual can aspire. The considered exercise of power by citizens is the only legitimate way in which liberty can be sustained. The citizen must both create and be bound by 'the supreme direction of the general will' – the publicly generated conception of the common good (*The Social Contract*, pp. 60–1). The people are sovereign only to the extent that they participate actively in articulating the 'general will'. It is important to distinguish the latter from the 'will of all': it is the difference between the sum of judgements about the common good and the mere aggregate of personal fancies and individual desires (pp. 72–3, 75). Citizens are only obligated to a system of laws and regulations on the grounds of publicly reached agreement, for they can only be genuinely obligated to a law they have prescribed for themselves with the general good in mind (p. 65; cf. p. 82). Hence, Rousseau draws a critical distinction between independence and liberty:

> Many have been the attempts to confound independence and liberty: two things so essentially different, that they reciprocally exclude each other. When every one does what he pleases, he will, of course, often do things displeasing to others; and this is not properly called a free state. Liberty consists less in acting according to one's own pleasure, than in not being subject to the will and pleasure of other people. It consists also in our not subjecting the wills of other people to our own. Whoever is the master over others is not himself free, and even to reign is to obey. (*Lettres écrites de la montagne*, p. 227, quoted in Keane, 1984)

Liberty and equality are inextricably linked. For the social contract 'establishes equality among the citizens in that they . . . must all enjoy the same rights' (*The Social Contract*, p. 76; cf. p. 46).

Rousseau argued in favour of a political system in which the legislative and executive functions are clearly demarcated. The former belong to the people and the latter to a 'government' or 'prince'. The people form the legislative assembly and constitute the authority of the state; the 'government' or 'prince' (composed of one or more administrators or magistrates) executes the people's laws (*The Social Contract*, book 3, ch. 1, pp. 11-14, 18).[9] Such a 'government' is necessary on the grounds of expediency: the people require a government to coordinate public meetings, serve as a means of communication, draft laws and enforce the legal system (*The Social Contract*, p. 102). The government is a result of an agreement among the citizenry and is legitimate only to the extent to which it fulfils 'the instructions of the general will'. Should it fail to so behave it can be revoked and changed (pp. 136-9, 148).

Rousseau's work had a significant (though ambiguous) influence on the ideas in currency during the French Revolution as well as on traditions of revolutionary thought, from Marxism to anarchism. His conception of self-government has been among the most provocative, challenging at its core some of the critical assumptions of liberal democracy, especially the notion that democracy is the name for a particular kind of state which can only be held accountable to the citizenry once in a while. But Rousseau's ideas do not represent a completely coherent system or recipe for straightforward action. He appreciated some of the problems created by large-scale, complex, densely populated societies, but did not pursue these as far as one must (see, for example, *The Social Contract*, book 3, ch. 4). He too excluded all women from 'the people', that is, the citizenry, as well as, it seems, the poor. The latter appear to be outcasts because citizenship is made conditional upon a small property qualification (land) and/or upon the absence of dependency on others (cf. Connolly, 1981, ch. 7). Rousseau's primary concern was with what might be thought of as the future of democracy in a non-industrial, agriculturally based community. As a vision of democracy it was and remains evocative and challenging, but it was not connected to an account of political life in an industrial capitalist society. It was left to Marx, Engels and Lenin, among others, to pursue these connections.

Class, coercion and the Marxist critique

Individuals; individuals in competition with one another; freedom of choice; politics as the arena for the maintenance of individual interests, the protection of 'life, liberty and estate'; the democratic state as the institutional mechanism for the articulation of the general or public interest (as opposed to simple private desires): all these are essential preoccupations of the liberal democratic tradition. While Marx (1818-83) and Engels (1820-95) did not deny that people had unique capacities, desires and an interest in free choice, they attacked relentlessly the idea that the starting-point of the analysis of the state can be the individual, and his or her relation to the state. As Marx put it, 'man is not an abstract being squatting outside the world. Man is the human world, the state, society' (*The Critique of Hegel's Philosophy of Right*, p. 131; modified translation). Individuals only exist in interaction with and in relation to others; their nature can only be grasped as a social and historical product. It is not the single, isolated individual who is active in historical and political processes, but rather human beings who live in definite relations with others and whose nature is defined through these relations. An individual, or a social activity, or an institution (in fact, any aspect of human life) can only be properly explained in terms of its historically evolving interaction with other social phenomena – a dynamic and changing process of inextricably related elements.

The key to understanding the relations between people is, according to Marx and Engels, class structure.[10] Class divisions are not, they maintain, found in all forms of society: classes are a creation of history, and in the future will disappear. The earliest types of 'tribal' society were classless. This is because, in such types of society, there was no surplus production and no private property; production was based upon communal resources and the fruits of productive activity were distributed through the community as a whole. Class divisions arise only when a surplus is generated, such that it becomes possible for a class of non-producers to live off the productive activity of others. Those who are able to gain control of the means of production form a dominant or ruling class both economically and politically. Class relations for Marx and Engels are thus necessarily exploitative and imply divisions of interest between ruling and subordinate classes. Class divisions are, furthermore, inherently conflictual and frequently give rise to active class struggle. Such struggles form the chief mechanism or 'motor' of historical development.

With the break-up of feudalism and the expansion of market economies, the class system of modern Western capitalist societies became slowly established. The class divisions of these societies are based, above all, Marx and Engels argued, upon one dominant exploitative relationship: that between those with capital and those who only have their labouring capacity to sell. 'Capitalists' own factories and technology while wage-labourers, or 'wage-workers', are propertyless. As capitalism matures, the vast majority of the population become wage-workers, who have to sell their labour-power on the market to secure a living. Societies are capitalist to the extent that they can be characterized as dominated by a mode of production which extracts surplus from wage-workers in the form of 'surplus value' – the value generated by workers in the productive process over and above their wages, and appropriated by the owners of capital (see Giddens and Held, 1982, pp. 28–35). This relationship between capital and wage-labour designates, in Marx's and Engel's account, the essential social and political structure of the modern epoch.

How then can the nature of the state be understood? What is the role of the state in the context of a class society? Central to the liberal and liberal democratic traditions is the idea that the state can claim to represent the community or public interest, in contrast to individuals' private aims and concerns. But, according to Marx and Engels, the opposition between interests that are public and general, and those that are private and particular is, to a large extent, illusory (see Maguire, 1978, ch. 1). The state defends the 'public' or the 'community' as if: classes did not exist; the relationship between classes was not exploitative; classes did not have fundamental differences of interest; these differences of interest did not define economic and political life. In treating everyone in the same way, according to principles which protect the freedom of individuals and defend their right to property, the state may act 'neutrally' while generating effects which are partial – sustaining the privileges of those with property. Moreover, the very claim that there is a clear distinction between the private and the public, the world of civil society and the political, is dubious. The key source of contemporary power – private ownership of the means of production – is ostensibly *depoliticized*; that is, treated as if it were not a proper subject of politics. The economy is regarded as non-political, in that the massive division between those who own and control the means of production, and those who must live by wage-labour, is regarded as the outcome of free private contracts, not a matter for the state. But by defending private property the state already has taken a side. The state, then, is not an independent structure or set of institutions above society, that is, a 'public power' acting for 'the public'. On the contrary, it is deeply embedded in socio-economic relations and linked to particular interests.

There are at least two strands in Marx's account of the relation between classes and the state; while they are by no means explicitly distinguished by Marx himself, it is illuminating to disentangle them.[11] The first, henceforth referred to as position 1, stresses that the state generally, and bureaucratic institutions in particular, may take a variety of forms and constitute a source of power which need not be directly linked to the interests, or be under the unambiguous control of, the dominant class in the short term. By this account, the state retains a degree of power independent of this class: its institutional forms and operational dynamics cannot be inferred directly from the configuration of class forces – they are 'relatively autonomous'. The second strand, position 2, is without doubt the dominant one in his writings: the state and its bureaucracy are class instruments which emerged to coordinate a divided society in the interests of the ruling class. Position 1 is certainly a more complex and subtle vision. Both positions are elaborated below. I shall begin with position 1, for it is expressed most clearly in Marx's early writings and highlights the degree to which the second view involves a narrowing down of the terms of reference of Marx's analysis of the state.

Marx's engagement with the theoretical problems posed by state power developed from an early confrontation with Hegel (1770–1831), a central figure in German idealist philosophy and a crucial intellectual influence on his life. In the *Philosophy of Right*, Hegel portrayed the Prussian state as divided into three substantive divisions – the legislature, the executive and the crown – which together express 'universal insight and will'.[12] For him, the most important institution of the state is the bureaucracy, an organization in which particular interests are subordinated to a system of hierarchy, specialization, expertise and coordination on the one hand, and internal and external pressures for competence and impartiality on the other. According to Marx, in the *Critique of Hegel's Philosophy of Right* (pp. 41–54), Hegel failed to challenge the self-image of the state and, in particular, of the bureaucracy.

The bureaucracy is the 'state's consciousness'. Marx describes the bureaucracy, by which he means the corps of state officials, as 'a particular closed society within the state', which extends its power or capacity through secrecy and mystery (*Critique*, p. 46). The individual bureaucrat is initiated into this closed society through 'a bureaucratic confession of faith' – the examination system – and the caprice of the politically dominant group. Subsequently the bureaucrat's career becomes everything, passive obedience to those in higher authority becomes a necessity and 'the state's interest becomes a particular private aim'. But the state's aims are not thereby achieved, nor is competence guaranteed (*Critique*, pp. 48, 51). For, as Marx wrote,

> The bureaucracy asserts itself to be the final end of the state . . . The aims of the state are transformed into aims of bureaus, or the aims of bureaus into the aims of the state. The bureaucracy is a circle from which no one can escape. Its hierarchy is a hierarchy of knowledge. The highest point entrusts the understanding of the particulars to the lower echelons, whereas these, on the other hand, credit the highest with an understanding in regard to the universal [the general interest]; and thus they deceive one another. (*Critique*, pp. 46–7)

Marx's critique of Hegel involves several points, but one in particular is crucial: in the sphere of what Hegel referred to as 'the absolutely universal interest of the state proper' there is, in Marx's view, nothing but 'bureaucratic officialdom' and 'unresolved conflict' (p. 54). Marx's emphasis on the structure and corporate nature of bureaucracies is significant because it throws into relief the 'relative autonomy' of these organizations and foreshadows the arguments elaborated in what may be his most interesting work on the state, *The Eighteenth Brumaire of Louis Bonaparte*.

The Eighteenth Brumaire is an eloquent analysis of the rise to power between 1848 and 1852 of Louis Napoleon Bonaparte and of the way power accumulated in the hands of the executive at the expense of, in the first instance, both civil society and the political representatives of the capitalist class, the bourgeoisie. The study highlights Marx's distance from any view of the state as an 'instrument of universal insight' or 'ethical community' for he emphasized that the state apparatus is simultaneously a 'parasitic body' on civil society and an autonomous source of political action. Thus, in describing Bonaparte's regime, he wrote:

> This executive power, with its enormous bureaucratic and military organization, with its ingenious state machinery, embracing wide strata, with a host of officials numbering half a million, beside an army of another half million, this appalling parasitic body . . . enmeshes the body of French society like a net and chokes all its pores. (*The Eighteenth Brumaire*, p. 121)

The state is portrayed as an immense set of institutions, with the capacity to shape civil society and even to curtail the bourgeoisie's capacity to control the state (see Maguire, 1978; Spencer, 1979). Marx granted the state a certain autonomy from society: political outcomes are the result of the interlocking of complex coalitions and constitutional arrangements.

The analysis offered in *The Eighteenth Brumaire*, like that in the *Critique*, suggests that the agents of the state do not simply coordinate political life in the interests of the dominant class of civil society. The executive, under particular circumstances – for example, when there is a relative balance of social forces – has the capacity to promote change as well as to coordinate it. But Marx's focus, even when discussing this idea, was essentially on the state as a conservative force. He emphasized the importance of its information network as a mechanism for surveillance, and the way in which the state's political autonomy is interlocked with its capacity to undermine social movements threatening to the *status quo*. Moreover, the repressive dimension of the state is complemented by its capacity to sustain belief in the inviolability of existing arrangements. Far then from being the basis for the articulation of the general interest, the state, Marx argued, transforms 'universal aims into another form of private interest'.

There were ultimate constraints on the initiatives Bonaparte could take, however, without throwing society into a major crisis, as there are on any legislative or executive branch of the state. For the state in a capitalist society, Marx concluded from his study of the Bonapartist regime, cannot escape its dependence upon that society and, above all, upon those who own and control the productive process. Its dependence is revealed whenever the economy is beset by crises; for economic organizations of all kinds create the material resources on which the state apparatus survives. The state's overall policies have to be compatible in the long run with the objectives of manufacturers and traders, otherwise civil society and the stability of the state itself are jeopardized. Hence, though Bonaparte usurped the political power of the bourgeoisie's representatives, he protected the 'material power' of the bourgeoisie itself – a vital source of loans and revenue. Accordingly, Bonaparte could not help but sustain the long-term economic interests of the bourgeoisie and lay the foundation for the regeneration of its direct political power in the future, whatever else he chose to do while in office (see *The Eighteenth Brumaire*, pp. 118ff.).

Marx attacked the claim that the distribution of property lies outside the constitution of political power. This attack is, of course, a central aspect of Marx's legacy and of what I am calling position 2. Throughout his political essays and especially in his more polemical pamphlets such as the *Communist Manifesto*, Marx (and indeed Engels) insisted on the direct dependence of the state on the economic, social and political power of the dominant class. The state is a 'superstructure' which develops on the 'foundation' of economic and social relations (see Marx and Engels, *The Communist Manifesto*; Marx, 'Preface' to *A Contribution to the Critique of Political Economy*). The state, in this formulation, serves directly the interest of the economically dominant class: the notion of the state as a site of autonomous political action is supplanted by an emphasis upon class power, an emphasis illustrated by the famous slogan of the *Communist Manifesto*: 'The executive of the modern state is but a committee for managing the common affairs of the whole bourgeoisie.' This formula does not imply that the state is dominated by the bourgeoisie as a whole: it may be independent of sections of the bourgeois class (cf. Miliband, 1965). The state, nevertheless, is characterized as essentially dependent upon society and upon those who dominate the economy: 'independence' is exercised only to the extent that conflicts must be settled between different sections of capital (industrialists and financiers, for example), and between 'domestic capitalism' and pressures generated by international capitalist markets. The state maintains the overall interests of the bourgeoisie in the name of the public or general interest.

There are, then, two (often interconnected) strands in Marx's account of the relation between classes and the state: the first conceives the state with a degree of power independent of class forces; the second upholds the view that the state is merely a 'superstructure' serving the interests of the dominant class. On the basis of position 1 it is possible to think of the state as a potential arena of struggle which can become a key force for socialist change. The social democratic tradition, as developed by people like Eduard Bernstein (1850–1932), elaborated this notion: through the ballot box the heights of state power could be scaled and used against the most privileged, while one by one institutions of the state could be progressively turned against the interests of capital (Bernstein, 1961). In contradistinction, revolutionary socialist traditions developed from position 2. Following Marx's analysis, Lenin insisted that the eradication of capitalist relations of production must be accompanied by the destruction of the capitalist state apparatus: the state, as a class instrument, had to be destroyed and direct democracy – as imagined in part by Rousseau – installed (see Lenin, *State and Revolution*).

Position 1 has been emphasized above because it is generally downplayed in the secondary literature on Marx. (Some important exceptions are: Draper, 1977; Maguire, 1978; Perez-Diaz, 1978.) Marx's work on the state remained incomplete. Position 1 left several important questions insufficiently explored. What is the basis of state power? How do state bureaucracies function? What precise interest do political officials develop? Position 2 is even more problematic: it postulates a capitalist-specific (or, as it has been called more recently, 'capital logic') organization of the state and takes for granted a simple causal relation between the facts of class domination and the vicissitudes of political life. But Marx's combined writings do indicate that he regards the state as central to the integration and control of class-divided societies. Furthermore, his work suggests important limits to state intervention within capitalist societies. If intervention undermines the process of capital accumulation, it simultaneously undermines the material basis of the state; hence, state policies must be consistent with capitalist relations of production. Accordingly, a dominant economic class can rule without directly governing, that is, it can exert determinate political influence without even having representatives in government. This idea retains a vital place in contemporary debates among Marxists, liberal democratic theorists and others.

On the whole, Lenin (1870–1924) followed the tenets of Marx's position 2. His views are stated succinctly in *State and Revolution* (1917), where he listed his first task as the 'resuscitation of the real teaching of Marx on the state' (p. 7).[13] Lenin conceived of the state as a 'machine for the oppression of one class by another'. The modern representative state was 'the instrument for the exploitation of wage-labour by capital' – 'a special repressive force' (p. 17). Thus, the distinguishing feature of the state, apart from its grouping of people on a territorial basis, is its dependence on force, exercised through specialized bodies such as the army, police and prison service. Many of the routine activities of the state, from taxation to legislation concerned with the protection of officials, exist essentially to ensure the survival of these repressive institutions.

The ruling classes maintain their grip on the state through alliances with government – alliances created both by government dependence on the stock exchange and by the corruption of ministers and officials. The vital business of the state takes place, not in representative assemblies, but in the state bureaucracies, where alliances can be established out of public view. Further, even democratic rights such as freedom of association, freedom of the press, or freedom of assembly, are a major benefit to the dominant classes. They can claim these institutions are 'open' while controlling them 'through ownership of the media, control over meeting places, money, and other resources' (pp. 72–3).

Although *State and Revolution* reiterates what I have called Marx's position 2, Lenin made more than Marx did of one central point: the crystallization of class power within the organs of state administration. For the Lenin of *State and Revolution*, 'so long as the state exists, there is no freedom. When freedom exists, there will be no state.' Strong central control would be necessary after the Revolution, but a precondition of revolutionary success is the destruction of the 'old state machine': 'The bureaucracy and the standing army, direct products of class oppression, have to be smashed. The army would be replaced by armed workers and the bureaucrats by elected officials subject to recall' (pp. 35–9). There would be 'immediate introduction of control and supervision by *all*, so that all may become "bureaucrats" for a time and that, therefore, nobody may be able to become a "bureaucrat"'. Officials and soldiers would be necessary but they would not become 'privileged persons divorced from the people and standing *above* the people'. Lenin never doubted that discipline was essential in political organizations, but he argued that this does not entail the creation of an elite of functionaries.[14] Following the lessons which Marx and Engels drew from the Paris Commune – lessons interpreted to some degree in the spirit of Rousseau's vision of direct democracy – Lenin maintained that the new socialist order must and could replace 'the government of persons' by 'the administration of things' (*State and Revolution*, p. 16).

The survival of bureaucracy in the early days of post-Revolutionary Russia was frequently explained by Lenin in terms of the lingering influence of capitalism and the old regime. He continually affirmed a causal relation between forms of state organization and classes, even in his famous 'last testament', where problems concerning central administration and the bureaucratization of the party and the state were sources of great anxiety (see Lewin, 1975). This position had dire consequences: it led, in part, to the widespread belief among Bolsheviks that, with the abolition of capitalist property relations (and the expansion of forces of production), problems of organization, control and coordination could be easily resolved.

There are many tensions in Lenin's treatment of the state and political organization. He thought that the work of the new socialist order could be conducted by workers organized in a framework of direct democracy (soviets), yet he defended the authority of the party in nearly all spheres. His argument that state bureaucracies need not entail fixed positions of power and privilege is suggestive, but it remains, especially in light of the massive problems of organization faced during and after the Revolution, a very incomplete statement. Lenin failed to examine the degree to which state organizations are influenced by diverse interests, political compromises and complex circumstances which do not merely reflect 'class antagonisms which must be reconciled from above'. To this extent his views on the state do not represent an advance on Marx's position 1.

In the last twenty years there has been a massive revival of interest in the analysis of state power among contemporary Marxist writers.[15] Marx left an ambiguous heritage, never fully reconciling his understanding of the state as an instrument of class domination with his acknowledgement that the state might also have significant political independence. Lenin's emphasis on the oppressive nature of capitalist state institutions certainly did not resolve this ambiguity; and his writings seem even less compelling after Stalin's purges and the massive growth of the Soviet state itself. Since the deaths of Marx and Engels, many Marxist writers have made contributions of decisive importance to the analysis of politics (for instance, Lukács, Korsch and Gramsci explored the many complex and subtle ways dominant classes sustain power), but not until recently has the relation between state and society been fully re-examined in Marxist circles. (The key contributions to this re-examination are assessed in essay 2, pp. 67–73.)

Contemporary Marxism is, however, in a state of flux. There are now as many differences between Marxists as between liberals or liberal democrats. Moreover, the reconsideration of the classical Marxist account of the state – in part stimulated by the state's growth in Western and Eastern Europe during recent decades – has led to a reappraisal by some Marxists of the liberal democratic tradition with its emphasis on the importance of individual liberties and rights, that is, citizenship (see essays 5–7 in this volume). The significance of 'citizenship rights' as a limit to the extension of state power has been more fully appreciated. At the same time, it is interesting to note, some liberal democrats have come to understand the limitations placed on political life by, among other things, massive concentrations of economic ownership and control (for example, Lindblom, 1977, whose work is discussed briefly in the next section). But exactly how one reconciles some of the most important insights of these fundamentally competing traditions of thought remains an open and extremely difficult question.

Bureaucracy, parliaments and the nation-state

The notion that the state, and bureaucratic organization in particular, constitute 'parasitic' entities is a position Marx and many other Marxists have espoused. Max Weber (1864–1920), a founder of sociology, a champion of European liberalism and of the German nation-state, contested this view. Although he drew extensively upon Marx's writings, he did so critically and nowhere more critically perhaps than with reference to the modern state. In contrast to Marx, Engels and Lenin, Weber resisted all suggestion that forms of state organization were 'parasitic' and a direct product of the activities of classes. He stressed the similarities between private and public organizations as well as their independent dynamics. Moreover, the idea that institutions of the modern state should be 'smashed' in a revolutionary process of transformation was, according to him, at best a foolhardy view.

Centralized administration may be inescapable. Weber's consideration of this issue makes his work especially important. He dismissed the feasibility of direct democracy,

> where the group grows beyond a certain size or where the administrative function becomes too difficult to be satisfactorily taken care of by anyone whom rotation, the lot, or election may happen to designate. The conditions of administration of mass structures are radically different from those obtaining in small associations resting upon neighborly or personal relationships . . . The growing complexity of the administrative tasks and the sheer expansion of their scope increasingly result in the technical superiority of those who have had training and experience, and will thus inevitably favor the continuity of at least some of the functionaries. Hence, there always exists the probability of the rise of a special, perennial structure for administrative purposes, which of necessity means for the exercise of rule. (*Economy and Society*, vol. 2, pp. 951–2)

The question of the class nature of the state is, Weber maintained, distinct from the question of whether a centralized bureaucratic administration is a necessary feature of political and social organization. It is simply misleading to conflate problems concerning the nature of administration in itself with problems concerning the control of the state apparatus (see Albrow, 1970, pp. 37–49). In Weber's opinion, Lenin's commitment to the 'smashing' of the state was based on his failure to see these as two distinct issues.

Weber developed one of the most significant definitions of the modern state, placing emphasis upon two distinctive elements of its history: territoriality and violence. The modern state, unlike its predecessors which were troubled by constantly warring factions, has a capability of monopolizing the legitimate use of violence within a given territory; it is a nation-state in embattled relations with other nation-states rather than with armed segments of its own population. 'Of course,' Weber emphasized,

> force is certainly not the normal or only means of the state – nobody says that – but force is a means specific to the state . . . the state is a relation of men dominating men [and generally – one should add – men dominating women], a relation supported by means of legitimate (i.e. considered to be legitimate) violence. ('Politics as a vocation', p. 78)

The state maintains compliance or order within a given territory; in individual capitalist societies this involves crucially the defence of the order of property and the enhancement of domestic economic interests overseas, although by no means all the problems of order can be reduced to these. The state's web of agencies and institutions finds its ultimate sanction in the claim to the monopoly of coercion, and a political order is only, in the last instance, vulnerable to crises when this monopoly erodes.

However, there is a third key term in Weber's definition of the state:

legitimacy. The state is based on a monopoly of physical coercion which is legitimized (that is, sustained) by a belief in the justifiability and/or legality of this monopoly. Today, Weber argued, people no longer comply with the authority claimed by the powers that be merely on the grounds, as was common once, of habit and tradition or the charisma and personal appeal of individual leaders. Rather, there is general obedience by 'virtue of "legality"', by virtue of the belief in the validity of legal statute and functional "competence" based on rationally created *rules*' ('Politics as a vocation', p. 79). The legitimacy of the modern state is founded predominantly on 'legal authority', that is, commitment to a 'code of legal regulations'.

Foremost among the state's institutions are the administrative apparatuses – a vast network of organizations run by appointed officials. Although such organizations have been essential to states at many times and places in history, 'only the Occident', on Weber's account, 'knows the state in its modern scale, with a professional administration, specialized officialdom, and law based on the concept of citizenship'. These institutions had 'beginnings in antiquity and the Orient', but there they 'were never able to develop' (Weber, *General Economic History*, p. 232).

The modern state is not, Weber contended, an effect of capitalism; it preceded and helped promote capitalist development (*Economy and Society*, vol. 2, pp. 1381ff.). Capitalism, however, provided an enormous impetus to the expansion of rational administration, that is, the type of bureaucracy founded on legal authority. Weber extended the meaning of the concept of bureaucracy: when Marx and Lenin wrote about it, they had in mind the civil service, the bureaucratic apparatus of the state, but Weber applied the concept much more broadly, as characterizing all forms of large-scale organization (the civil service, political parties, industrial enterprises, universities, etc.). In the contemporary world, he believed, private and public administration are becoming more and more bureaucratized (*Economy and Society*, vol. 2, p. 1465). That is to say, there is a growth of office hierarchy; administration is based upon written documents; specialist training is presupposed and candidates are appointed according to qualification; formal responsibilities demand the full working capacities of officials; officials are 'separated from ownership of the means of administration' (*Economy and Society*, vol. 1, pp. 220–1).

Under practically every imaginable circumstance, bureaucracy is, according to Weber, 'completely indispensable' (*Economy and Society*, vol. 1, p. 223). The choice is only 'between bureaucracy and dilettantism in the field of administration'. Weber explained the spread of bureaucracy in the following terms:

> The decisive reason for the advance of bureaucratic organization has always been its purely *technical* superiority over any other form of organization. The fully developed bureaucratic apparatus compares with the non-mechanical modes of

production. Precision, speed, unambiguity, knowledge of the files, continuity, discretion, unity, strict subordination, reduction of friction and of material and personal costs – these are raised to the optimum point in the strictly bureaucratic administration, and especially in its monocratic form. (*Economy and Society*, vol. 2, p. 973)

As economic life becomes more complex and differentiated, bureaucratic administration becomes more essential.

While rule by officials is not inevitable, considerable power accrues to bureaucrats through their expertise, information and access to secrets. This power can become, Weber says, 'overtowering'. Politicians and political actors of all kinds can find themselves dependent on the bureaucracy. A central question – if not preoccupation – for Weber was, how can 'bureaucratic power' be checked? He was convinced that, in the absence of checks, public organization would fall prey to powerful private interests (among others, organized capitalists and major landholders) who would not have the nation-state as their prime concern; moreover, in times of national emergency, there would be ineffective leadership. Bureaucrats, unlike politicians, cannot take a passionate stand. They do not have the training – and bureaucracies are not structurally designed – for the consideration of political, alongside technical or economic, criteria. However, Weber's solution to the problem of unlimited bureaucratization was not one that depended merely on the capacity of individual politicians for innovation. Writing about Germany, he advocated a strong parliament which would create a competitive training ground for strong leadership and serve as a balance to public and private bureaucracy (see Mommsen, 1974). In so arguing, Weber was taking 'national' power and prestige' as his prime concern. As one commentator aptly noted, 'Weber's enthusiasm for the representative system owed more to his conviction that national greatness depended on finding able leaders than to any concern for democratic values' (Albrow, 1970; Mommsen, 1974, ch. 5).

Weber's position on the relationship between social structure, bureaucracy and the state can be clarified further by examining his assessment of socialism. He believed that the abolition of private capitalism 'would simply mean that . . . the *top management* of the nationalized or socialized enterprises would become bureaucratic' (*Economy and Society*, vol. 2, p. 1402). Reliance upon those who control resources would be enhanced, for the abolition of the market would be the abolition of a key countervailing power to the state. The market generates change and social mobility: it is the very source of capitalist dynamism.

State bureaucracy would rule alone if private capitalism were eliminated. The private and public bureaucracies, which now work next to, and potentially against, each other and hence check one another to a degree, would be merged into a single hierarchy. This would be similar to the situation in ancient Egypt, but it would occur in a much more rational – and hence unbreakable – form. (*Economy and Society*, vol. 2, p. 143)

While Weber argued that 'progress' toward the bureaucratic state is given an enormous impetus by capitalist development, he believed that this very development itself, coupled with parliamentary government and the party system, provided the best obstacle to the usurpation of state power by officials.

Weber accepted that intense class struggles have occurred in various phases of history and that the relationship between capital and wage-labour is of considerable importance in explaining many of the features of industrial capitalism. However, he dissented strongly from the view that the analysis of power could be assimilated to the analysis of classes. For Weber, classes cannot be reduced to economic relations, and they constitute in themselves only one aspect of the distribution of and struggle for power. What Weber calls 'status groups', political parties and nation-states, are at least as significant (Giddens and Held, 1982, pp. 60–86). The fervour created by sentiments of group solidarity, or of ethnic community, or of power prestige, or of nationalism generally, is a vital part of the creation and mobilization of political power in the modern age. But of all these the most important for Weber was the struggle between nation-states – a decisive feature of the modern world which promised to keep history open to 'human will' and the 'competition of values' in an ever more rationalized, bureaucratic world (see Roth and Schluchter, 1979).

Weber's attempt to analyse the internal workings of public (and private) organizations and his observations about trends in bureaucratization constitute a major contribution to understanding the state. His work provides a counterbalance to the Marxist and particularly Leninist emphasis on the intimate connection between state activities, forms of organization and class relations (cf. Wright, 1978, ch. 4). The argument that private and public administrations are similarly structured – as opposed to causally determined by class power – is important and provocative.

But Weber's analysis also has severe limits. His assumption that the development of bureaucracy leads to an increased power for those at the highest levels of administration leads him to neglect the ways in which those in subordinate positions may increase their power (Giddens, 1979, ch. 4). In modern bureaucratic systems there appear to be considerable 'openings' for those in 'formally subordinate positions to acquire or regain control over their organizational tasks' (for example, by hindering or blocking the collection of vital information for centralized decision-making). Bureaucracies may enhance the potential for disruption from 'below' and increase the spaces for circumventing hierarchical control. Weber did not characterize adequately internal organizational processes and their significance for developments in other political spheres. In addition, one can search his writings in vain for a satisfactory explanation of the precise character of the relation between the growing bureaucratic centralization of the state and modern capitalism.[16] In his historical account of patterns of bureaucratization in diverse societies, he did not isolate the degree to which certain bureaucratic processes may be specific to, or influenced by, capitalist development *per se*. He failed to disentangle the 'impact of cultural, economic and technological forces' on the growth of bureaucracy, and to say to what extent these were independent of capitalist development. In the end, the particular connection between the state, bureaucratization and capitalism is left obscure. Further, although Weber's stress on the conflicts between nation-states captures an important aspect of the international context of states, it is also left clouded by a variety of intriguing but incomplete reflections on the nature of such states and by a dubious patriotic fervour.

Weber's writings have had an enormous influence on the development of sociology and political science in the Anglo-American world. They have stimulated a rich variety of developments, two of which deserve some attention here: 'pluralism' or empirical democratic theory (which takes as a starting-point Weberian ideas about the multi-dimensionality of power) and 'geopolitical' conceptions of politics (which focus on the state at the intersection of national and international conditions and pressures). While neither of these bodies of work has grown out of Weber's work alone, his writings have certainly had a notable impact on both.

A variety of pluralist theories have been expounded, but I shall focus initially on what may be regarded as the 'classical version' of pluralism developed in the writings of Laswell, Truman and Dahl, among others (cf. Truman, 1951; Dahl, 1956; 1971; 1975). This version had a pervasive influence in the 1950s and 1960s. Relatively few political and social theorists would accept it in unmodified form today, though many politicians, journalists and others in the mass media still appear to do so. Dahl and his colleagues deployed Weberian ideas as part of their effort to challenge fundamental Marxian axioms about class as the central structural determinant of the state and political outcomes. In the process they totally recast the connections between state, bureaucratic organizations and classes, and shifted the attention of political sociology and political science to those institutional arrangements designed to ensure a responsiveness by political leaders to citizens – in particular, the competition for electoral support and the activities of social groups or organized interests in relation to government (see Pateman, 1970, ch. 1).

The essence of the classical pluralist position stems from the view that there are many determinants of the distribution of power other than class and, therefore, many power centres. But this idea is taken much further than Weber took it himself. In the pluralist account, power is non-hierarchically and competitively arranged. It is an inextricable part of an 'endless process of bargaining' between numerous groups representing different interests, for example, business organizations, trade unions, parties, ethnic groups, students, prison officers, women's institutes, religious groups (see the extract from Dahl in part 1 of Held et al., 1983). Clearly there are many inequalities in society (of schooling, health, income, wealth, etc.) and not all groups have equal access to equal resources. However, nearly every 'interest group' has some advantage which can be utilized in the democratic process to make an impact. Hence the determination of political decisions at either a local or national level cannot reflect a 'majestic march' of 'the public' united upon matters of basic policy – as imagined, albeit in quite different ways, by Locke, Bentham and Rousseau (Dahl, 1956, p. 146). Political outcomes are, rather, the result of governments and, ultimately, the executive trying to mediate and adjudicate between competing demands. In this process the state becomes almost indistinguishable from the ebb and flow of bargaining, the competitive pressure of interests. Indeed, individual government departments are sometimes conceived as just another kind of interest group.

This situation is not regarded as a bad thing; for competition among social groups, in the context of the open contest for government – the rules of democratic procedure – ensures that the competition is fair and creates government by multiple groups or multiple minorities which, in turn, secures the democratic character of a regime. Dahl calls this 'polyarchy' or rule by the many or 'minorities government' (Dahl, 1956, p. 133). It is, in his view, both a desirable state of affairs and one to which most liberal democracies approximate.

The position can be criticized on many grounds – grounds which many 'pluralists', among them Dahl, would now accept (Dahl, 1978). The existence of many power centres hardly guarantees that government will (1) listen to them all equally; (2) do anything other than communicate with leaders of such groups; (3) be susceptible to influence by anybody other than those in powerful positions; (4) do anything about the issues under discussion, and so on. (See Lively, 1975, pp. 20–4, 54–6, 71–2, 141–5, for a discussion of these points; cf. Lukes, 1977.) Additionally, it is patently clear that not only do many groups not have the resources to compete in the national political arena with the clout of, say, multinational corporations, but many people do not even have access to the minimum resources for political mobilization. Moreover, the very capacity of governments to act in ways that interest groups may desire is constrained, as many Marxists have argued and as 'neo-pluralists' like Charles E. Lindblom now accept. The constraints on Western governments and state institutions – constraints imposed by the requirements of private accumulation – systematically limit policy options. The system of private investment, private property, etc., creates objective exigencies which must be met if economic growth and stable development are to be sustained. If these arrangements are threatened, economic chaos quickly ensues and the legitimacy of governments can be undermined. As Lindblom put it, 'depression, inflation, or other economic disasters can bring down a government. A major function of government, therefore, is to see to it that businessmen perform their tasks' (1977, pp. 122–3). The state must follow a political agenda which is at least favourable to, that is, biased towards, the development of the system of private enterprise and corporate power. Of course, 'neo-pluralists' retain some of the essential tenets of 'classical pluralism', including the account of the way liberal democracy generates a variety of interest groups and provides a crucial obstacle to the development of a monolithic unresponsive state.

One of the most severe deficiencies of existing theories of the state is their tendency to concentrate on, for example, group bargaining within *a* nation-state (pluralism), or on the citizen and his or her relation to *the* state (liberal democracy), or on the relation between classes, the economy and the state in *a* capitalist country albeit with imperialist ambitions (Marxism). It is important to relate 'the state' to the context of international conditions and pressures. For instance, the capitalist world was created in dependence on an international market – the 'European world economy' – which generated multiple interconnections between nation-states that were beyond the control of any one such state (Wallerstein, 1974a). Weber's work has had a notable impact on the development of ideas such as these, emphasizing how the very nature of the state crystallizes at the intersection of international and national conditions and pressures.

Among social scientists who have pursued this perspective today is Theda Skocpol. Her work bears the mark of Weber as well as other closely related figures, including the historian Otto Hintze (1861–1940) (see Skocpol, 1979, p. 307, n. 77; cf. Hintze, 1975, chs 4–6, 11). Hintze sought to show how two phenomena, above all, condition the real organization of the state. 'These are, first, the structure of social classes, and second, the external ordering of . . . states – their position relative to each other, and their overall position in the world' (Hintze, 1975, p. 183). Struggles among social classes at home and conflicts among nations have a dramatic impact on the organization and power of states. The 'shape' of a state – its size, external configuration, military structure, ethnic composition and relations, labour composition, among other things – is deeply rooted in the history of external events and conditions.[17] The state is, as Skocpol put it, 'Janus-faced, with an intrinsically dual anchorage in class-divided socio-economic structures and an international system of states' (1979, p. 32).

Skocpol rejects 'society-centred' approaches to the explanation of the state and governmental activities because their explanatory strategies involve conceiving of the state simply as an 'arena' for the struggle of groups, movements and/or classes contending for advantage, or as merely a 'functional entity' responding to the 'imperatives' or 'needs' of civil society or the capitalist economy. Either way the focus is on societal 'inputs' and 'outputs' to and from the state and the state itself *qua* specific kinds of organizations, resources and relations is blocked from view (pp. 25–33). There are intrinsic limits to all theories, whether pluralist or Marxist, which adopt such approaches: they cannot provide an adequate focus on states 'as distinctive structures with their own specific histories' (see Zeitlin, 1985, pp. 26–7).

If class relations as well as complex international circumstances provide the context of the state, how should the state itself be conceptualized? In Skocpol's account,

> The state properly conceived . . . is a set of administrative, policing, and military organizations headed, and more or less well coordinated by, an executive authority. Any state first and fundamentally extracts resources from society and deploys those to create and support coercive and administrative organizations . . . Of course . . . political systems . . . also may contain institutions through which social interests are represented in state policy making as well as institutions through which non-state actors are mobilised to participate in policy implementation. Nevertheless, the administrative and coercive organizations are the basis of state power. (1979, p. 29)

Such a perspective helps illuminate: the way state organizations themselves vary; how the capacities of state organizations change in relation to the organization and interest of socio-economic groups and the 'transnational' environment; how state personnel develop interests in internal security, policy formulation, and competition with other nation-states which may be at variance with the interests of other social groups or classes. It allows, Skocpol argues, the distinctiveness and histories of particular state agencies to be unpacked, thus 'bringing the state back in' to the abstract theory of the state (1982).

These reflections were developed by Skocpol in relation to the theory of revolutions, but on their own it is clear that they constitute less a theory and more a framework for analysis of the state – a useful framework, none the less, to the extent that it offsets some of the limitations of 'society-centred' theories (cf. Zeitlin, 1985, pp. 26ff.). At the same time, however, it may fail, as Wallerstein's work implies, to stress adequately the way the sovereignty of nation-states has been, and is ever more, compromised by the international interconnections of the world economy (cf. Wallerstein, 1974a, b). Further, while it is indeed important to examine the 'corporate identity' of state organizations and the interests state personnel develop, it is critical not to overstate this; for among the most valuable contributions of both Marxists and pluralists are insights into how social struggle is 'inscribed' into the organization, administration and policies of the state – the extent, for example, to which parliamentary forms themselves are the outcome of conflicts over the old powers of the monarchy, landed nobility and bourgeoisie. Moreover, the economic and electoral constraints on state activities mean that state autonomy from societal relations will almost always, at least in Western capitalist societies, be compromised, with the exception perhaps of phases of military adventure and war – although, it must be admitted, this exception begins to look ever more significant as the means of waging war become more menacing (cf. Giddens, 1981, ch. 10).

Concluding remarks

There are many conceptual problems in surveying over four hundred years of writing on 'the modern state'. Even if writers since the late sixteenth century have taken the state to mean all the institutions and relations associated with 'government', these terms of reference have been profoundly altered. Most of the writers dealt with have taken different positions on what the state could, and indeed should, do; and in the case of figures like Bentham, Marx and Weber, it is clear that their analyses actually refer to disparate political phenomena. In concluding this essay, it may be useful to highlight some of the problems and disagreements.

Among the developments in the theory of the state since the sixteenth century, two notable innovations stand out: the concept of the state as an impersonal or 'anonymous' structure of power, and the problem of reconciling authority and liberty through a fundamentally new view of the 'rights, obligations and duties' of subjects. While Hobbes marks an intermediate point between absolutism and liberalism, liberal political theory since Locke clearly affirms the state as an impersonal (legally circumscribed) structure, and connects this idea to an institutional theory of political power, such as the division between legislatures and executives. The central problem facing liberal and liberal democratic theory concerned the relationship between the state, as an independent authority with supreme right to declare and administer law over a given territory, and the individual, with a right and interest to determine the nature and limits of the state's authority. In short, the question was: how should the 'sovereign state' be related to the 'sovereign people' who were in principle the source of its powers?

Modern liberal and liberal democratic theory has constantly sought to justify the sovereign power of the state while at the same time justifying limits upon that power. The history of this attempt since Machiavelli and Hobbes is the history of arguments to balance might and right, power and law, duties and rights. On the one hand, the state must have a monopoly of coercive power in order to provide a secure basis upon which trade, commerce and family life can prosper. On the other hand, by granting the state a regulatory and coercive capability, liberal political theorists were aware that they had accepted a force which could (and frequently did) deprive citizens of political and social freedoms.

It was the liberal democrats who provided the key institutional innovation to try to overcome this dilemma – representative democracy. The liberal concern with reason, law and freedom of choice could only be upheld properly by recognizing the political equality of mature individuals. Such equality would ensure not only a secure social environment in which people would be free to pursue their private activities and interests, but also that the state's personnel would do what was best in the general or public interest, for example, pursue the greatest happiness of the greatest number. Thus, the democratic constitutional state, linked to the free market, resolved, the liberal democrats argued, the problems of ensuring both authority and liberty.

The struggle of liberalism against tyranny and the struggle by liberal democrats for political equality represented, according to Marx and Engels, a major step forward in the history of human emancipation. But for them the great universal ideals of 'liberty, equality and justice' could not be realized simply by the 'free' struggle for votes in the political system and by the 'free' struggle for profit in the market place. The advocates of the democratic state and the market economy present them as the only institutions under which liberty can be sustained and inequalities minimized. However, by virtue of its internal dynamics, the capitalist economy inevitably produces systematic inequality and hence massive restrictions on real freedom. While each step towards formal political equality is an advance, its liberating potential is severely curtailed by inequalities of class. As Marx wryly put it: 'Just as Christians are equal in heaven yet unequal on earth, so the individual members of a people are equal in the heaven of their political world yet unequal in the earthly existence of society' (*Critique*, p. 80).

In class societies, Marx and Engels maintained, the state cannot become the vehicle for the pursuit of the 'common good' or 'public interest'. Far from the state playing the role of emancipator, protective knight, umpire or judge in the face of disorder, the agencies of the state are enmeshed in the struggles of civil society. Marxists conceive of the state as an extension of civil society, reinforcing the social order for the enhancement of particular interests – in capitalist society, the long-run interests of the capitalist class. It is not the state, as Marx put it in his early writings, which underlies the social order, but the social order which underlies the state. Marx did not deny the desirability of liberty and equality – far from it. His argument is that political emancipation is only a step toward human emancipation, that is, the *complete* democratization of society as well as the state. In his view, liberal democratic society fails when judged by its own principles; and to take these principles seriously is to become a socialist. 'True democracy' can only be established with the destruction of social classes and ultimately the abolition of the state itself: the state must 'wither away' leaving a system of self-government linked to collectively shared duties and work.

The history of Marxism, and of socialism more generally since Marx, has been distinguished by deep conflicts about how to define appropriate political goals and about how to develop political strategy in historical conditions often quite different from those envisaged by Marx himself. A preoccupation with actually taking power shifted attention, at least in much of the work of Lenin and his followers, to questions about the role of the Party, Party organization and the nature of the transition to socialism. In the process, consideration of the problem of state power was regarded as of secondary importance to the practical exigencies of making revolution.

Weber believed that the Bolsheviks' political ambitions were premissed on a deficient understanding of the nature of the modern state and the complexity of political life. In his account, the history of the state and the history of political struggle could not in any way (even 'in the last instance') be reduced to class relations: the origins and tasks of the modern state suggested it was far more than a 'superstructure' on an economic 'base'. Moreover, even if class relations were transformed, institutions of direct democracy could not replace the state; for there would be a massive problem of coordination and regulation which would inevitably be 'resolved' by bureaucracy, and by bureaucracy alone unless other institutions were nourished to check its power. The problems posed in the liberal pursuit of a balance between might and right, power and law, are, Weber thought, inescapable elements of modernity.

Weber feared that political life in West and East would be ever more ensnared by a rationalized, bureaucratic system of administration – a 'steel-hard cage', as he wrote. Against this he championed the countervailing power of private capital, the competitive party system and strong political leadership to secure national power and prestige; all of which could prevent the domination of politics by state officials. In so arguing, the limitations of his political thought become apparent: some of the key insights and principles of both Marxist and liberal political theory seem to have been set aside. The significance of massive inequalities of political and class power are played down because of the priority of power, that is, interstate, politics; and this priority leaves the balance betwen might and right in the end to the judgement of 'charismatic' political leaders locked into the competition between state and economic bureaucracies – a situation which comes perilously close to accepting that even the tenets of traditional liberalism can no longer be upheld in the modern age.

The difficulties of coming to a judgement about the modern state are compounded when one examines it in relation to the system of nation-states and the international interconnections of the world economy. The more one explores this context, the more tenuous appears the abstract idea of 'the state'. Historical and geographical variation in the relations between states, as well as in the nature of the states themselves, forces us to ask whether the search for a theory of 'the state' is misplaced. Yet while we must be sensitive to the existence of 'states' and 'societies', we recognize a continuity through states in their modern guise – a peculiar mix of force and right, that constrains and shapes the lives of generations. This presence compels us to pursue seriously – and ever more urgently in the face of the global struggle for resources and the escalating capacity for mass destruction – the issues of might and right, liberty and equality, class power and domination, violence and the nation-state.

Notes

1 See, e.g., Benn and Peters (1959); Tilly (1975); Poggi (1978); Skocpol (1979); Bendix (1980); Keane (1984).
2 An interesting discussion of this idea of sovereignty in relation to other conceptions can be found in Benn (1955).
3 Interesting and contrasting accounts of Locke on property can be found in Macpherson (1962); Plamenatz (1963); and Dunn (1969).
4 One must guard against exaggerating this claim; see Dunn (1980b).
5 Mill was committed to *laissez-faire* in economic policy in his early works, but he later modified his views.
6 For a fuller account of 'citizenship rights' and some of the struggles concerning them, see essay 7 of this volume.
7 In Britain and the United States a variety of theories of the liberal democratic state have developed in recent times, including various theories of pluralism elaborated by, among others, Laswell, Truman and Dahl, and 'liberal anarchist' or 'libertarian' views expounded by, e.g., Hayek and Nozick; see Held (1987).
8 Caution is required about the use of the term 'democracy' in relation to Rousseau's writings. He refers to the political system under discussion as 'republicanism'; see Rousseau, *The Social Contract*, pp. 114 and 82, and for a general account, book 3, chs 1–5.
9 There are additional institutional positions set out by Rousseau, for instance that of 'the Lawgiver', which cannot be elaborated here; see *The Social Contract*, pp. 83–8, 95–6.
10 For an overview of Marx's and Engel's account of class see Giddens and Held (1982).
11 This discussion draws on Held and Krieger (1984). See essay 2 in this volume.
12 See Perez-Diaz (1978) for a clear and helpful discussion of Marx's relation to Hegel. The view of Hegel I have briefly presented here is very much Marx's view – a view which is challengeable in many respects; cf. Rose (1981, especially ch. 7).
13 For an account which is sensitive to the complexities of the development of Lenin's thought, see Harding (1977 and 1981).

14 Lenin was far from consistent on these matters. For a useful discussion see Kamenka and Krygier (1979).

15 For surveys of this material see Gold et al. (1975) and Jessop (1977).

16 See Krieger (1983) for an interesting discussion of Weber's concept of bureaucracy.

17 For some of the theoretical background to these ideas see Dyson (1980).

References

Albrow, M. 1970: *Bureaucracy*. London: Pall Mall.

Bendix, R. 1980: *Kings or People*. Berkeley: University of California Press.

Benn, S. I. 1955: The uses of sovereignty. *Political Studies*, 3(2).

Benn, S. I. and Peters, R. S. 1959: *Social Principles and the Democratic State*. London: Allen & Unwin.

Bentham, J.: *Constitutional Code*, book 1. In *The Works of Jeremy Bentham*, vol. IX, ed. Jeremy Bowring, Edinburgh: W. Tait, 1843.

Bentham, J.: *Principles of the Civil Code*. In *The Works of Jeremy Bentham*, vol. I, pp. 299–364, ed. Jeremy Bowring, Edinburgh: W. Tait, 1843.

Bentham, J.: *Fragment on Government*, ed. W. Harrison, Oxford: Basil Blackwell, 1960.

Bernstein, E. 1961: *Evolutionary Socialism*. New York: Schocken Books.

Bobbio, N. 1978: Are there alternatives to representative democracy? *Telos*, 35.

Colletti, L. 1972: *From Rousseau to Lenin*. London: New Left Books.

Connolly, W. 1981: *Appearance and Reality*. Cambridge: Cambridge University Press.

Cranston, M. 1968: Introduction to J.-J. Rousseau, *The Social Contract*, Harmondsworth: Penguin.

Dahl, R. A. 1956: *A Preface to Democratic Theory*. Chicago: University of Chicago Press.

Dahl, R. A. 1971: *Polyarchy: Participation and Opposition*. New Haven: Yale University Press.

Dahl, R. A. 1975: *Who Governs? Democracy and Power in an American City*. New Haven and London: Yale University Press.

Dahl, R. A. 1978: Pluralism revisited. *Comparative Politics*, 10(2).

Draper, H. 1977: *Karl Marx's Theory of Revolution*, vol. 1. New York: Monthly Review Press.

Dunn, J. 1969: *The Political Thought of John Locke*. Cambridge: Cambridge University Press.

Dunn, J. 1979: *Western Political Theory in the Face of the Future*. Cambridge: Cambridge University Press.

Dunn, J. 1980a: Consent in the political theory of John Locke. In *Political Obligation in its Historical Context*, Cambridge: Cambridge University Press.

Dunn, J. 1980b: The politics of Locke in England and America in the eighteenth century. In *Political Obligation in its Historical Context*, Cambridge: Cambridge University Press.

Dyson, K. 1980: *The State Tradition in Western Europe*. Oxford: Martin Robertson.

Foucault, M. 1977: *Discipline and Punish*. London: Allen Lane.

Franklin, J. H. 1978: *John Locke and the Theory of Sovereignty*. Cambridge: Cambridge University Press.

CENTRAL PERSPECTIVES ON THE MODERN STATE 53

Friedman, M. 1962: *Capitalism and Freedom*. Chicago: University of Chicago Press.

Giddens, A. 1979: *Central Problems in Social Theory*. London: Macmillan.

Giddens, A. 1981: *A Contemporary Critique of Historical Materialism*. London: Macmillan.

Giddens, A. and Held, D. (eds) 1982: *Classes, Power and Conflict*. London: Macmillan.

Gold, D. A. et al. 1975: Recent developments in Marxist theories of the capitalist state. *Monthly Review*, 27(5–6).

Habermas, J. 1962: *Strukturwandel der Öffentlichkeit*. Neuwied: Luchterhand.

Harding, N. 1977 and 1981: *Lenin's Political Thought*, 2 vols. London: Macmillan.

Hegel, G. W. F.: *The Philosophy of Right*, tr. T. M. Knox, Oxford: Oxford University Press, 1967.

Held, D. 1987: *Models of Democracy*. Cambridge: Polity Press.

Held, D. and Krieger, J. 1984: Theories of the state: some competing claims. In S. Bornstein, D. Held and J. Krieger (eds), *The State in Capitalist Europe*, London: Allen & Unwin.

Held, D. et al. (eds) 1983: *States and Societies*. Oxford: Martin Robertson.

Hintze, O. 1975: In *Historical Essays*, ed. Felix Gilbert. New York: Oxford University Press.

Hobbes, T.: *De Cive*. In *The English Works of Thomas Hobbes*, ed. Sir William Molesworth, vol. 2, London, 1839–44.

Hobbes, T.: *Leviathan*, ed. C. B. Macpherson, Harmondsworth: Penguin, 1968.

Ignatieff, M. 1978: *A Just Measure of Pain*. London: Macmillan.

Jessop, B. 1977: Recent theories of the capitalist state. *Cambridge Journal of Economics*, 1(4).

Kamenka, E. and Krygier, M. (eds) 1979: *Bureaucracy*. Port Melbourne: Edward Arnold.

Keane, J. 1984: *Public Life and Late Capitalism*, essay 6. Cambridge: Cambridge University Press.

Krieger, J. 1983: *Undermining Capitalism*. Princeton, NJ: Princeton University Press.

Laslett, P. 1963: Introduction to John Locke, *Two Treatises of Government*. Cambridge: Cambridge University Press.

Lenin, V. I.: *State and Revolution*. New York: International Publishers, 1971.

Lewin, M. 1975: *Lenin's Last Struggle*. London: Pluto Press.

Lindblom, C. E. 1977: *Politics and Markets*. New York: Basic Books.

Lively, J. 1975: *Democracy*. Oxford: Basil Blackwell.

Locke, J.: *Two Treatises of Government*. Cambridge: Cambridge University Press, 1963.

Lukes, S. 1973: *Individualism*. New York: Harper & Row.

Lukes, S. 1977: *Power*. London: Macmillan.

Macpherson, C. B. 1962: *The Political Theory of Possessive Individualism*. Oxford: Clarendon Press.

Macpherson, C. B. 1966: *The Real World of Democracy*. Oxford: Oxford University Press.

Macpherson, C. B. 1968: Introduction to Thomas Hobbes, *Leviathan*, ed. C. B. Macpherson, Harmondsworth: Penguin.

Macpherson, C. B. 1977: *The Life and Times of Liberal Democracy*. Oxford: Oxford University Press.

Maguire, J. 1978: *Marx's Theory of Politics*. Cambridge: Cambridge University Press.

Marx, K.: *The Eighteenth Brumaire of Louis Bonaparte*, New York: International Publishers, 1963.

Marx, K.: *The Critique of Hegel's Philosophy of Right*, Cambridge: Cambridge University Press, 1970.

Marx, K.: Preface to *A Contribution to the Critique of Political Economy*, London: Lawrence & Wishart, 1971.

Marx, K. and Engels, F.: *The Communist Manifesto*, New York: International Publishers, 1948.

Miliband, R. 1965: Marx and the state. In *Socialist Register 1965*. London: Merlin Press.

Mill, J.: Prisons and prison discipline. In *Essays on Government*, London: J. Innis, 1828.

Mill, J.: *An Essay on Government*, Cambridge: Cambridge University Press, 1937.

Mill, J. S.: *Considerations on Representative Government*. In H. B. Acton (ed.), *Utilitarianism, Liberty, and Representative Government*, London: Dent, 1951.

Mill, J. S.: *On Liberty*, Harmondsworth: Penguin, 1982.

Mommsen, W. J. 1974: *The Age of Bureaucracy*. Oxford: Basil Blackwell.

Neumann, F. 1964: *The Democratic and the Authoritarian State*. New York: Free Press.

Pateman, C. 1970: *Participation and Democratic Theory*. Cambridge: Cambridge University Press.

Pateman, C. 1979: *The Problem of Political Obligation*. Chichester: John Wiley.

Perez-Diaz, M. 1978: *State, Bureaucracy and Civil Society*. London: Macmillan.

Peters, R. S. 1956: *Hobbes*. Harmondsworth: Penguin.

Peters, R. S. 1967: Hobbes. In *The Encyclopedia of Philosophy*, vol. 4. New York: Macmillan.

Plamenatz, J. 1963: *Man and Society*, vol. 1. London: Longman.

Poggi, G. 1978: *The Development of the Modern State*. London: Hutchinson.

Rose, G. 1981: *Hegel Contra Sociology*. London: Athlone.

Roth, G. and Schluchter, W. 1979: *Max Weber's Vision of History*. Berkeley: University of California Press.

Rousseau, J.-J.: *Lettres écrites de la montagne*, 2, letter 8. In J.-J. Rousseau, *Oeuvres complètes de J.-J. Rousseau*, Paris, 1911.

Rousseau, J.-J.: *The Social Contract*, Harmondsworth: Penguin, 1968.

Ryan, A. 1970: *The Philosophy of John Stuart Mill*. London: Macmillan.

Skinner, Q. 1966: The ideological context of Hobbes's political thought. *The Historical Journal*, IX(3).

Skinner, Q. 1978: *The Foundations of Modern Political Thought*, 2 vols. Cambridge: Cambridge University Press.

Skocpol, T. 1979: *States and Social Revolutions: A Comparative Analysis of France, Russia and China*. Cambridge: Cambridge University Press.

Skocpol, T. 1982: Bringing the state back in. *Items* (SSRC), 36.

Spencer, M. E. 1979: Marx on the state. *Theory and Society*, 7(1–2).

Tilly, C. 1975: Reflections on the history of European state-making. In C. Tilly (ed.), *The Formation of National States in Western Europe*, Princeton, NJ: Princeton University Press.

Truman, D. B. 1951: *The Governmental Process*. New York: Knopf.

Wallerstein, I. 1974a: *The Modern World-System*. New York: Academic Press.

Wallerstein, I. 1974b: The rise and future demise of the world capitalist system. *Comparative Studies in Society and History*, 16(4).

Weber, M.: *General Economic History*. London: Allen & Unwin, 1923.

Weber, M.: Politics as a vocation. In H. H. Gerth and C. W. Mills (eds), *From Max Weber*, New York: Oxford University Press, 1972.

Weber, M.: *Economy and Society*, 2 vols. Berkeley: University of California Press, 1978.

Wright, E. O. 1978: *Class, Crisis and the State*. London: New Left Books.

Zeitlin, J. 1985: Shop floor bargaining and the state: a contradictory relationship. In S. Tolliday and J. Zeitlin (eds), *Shop Floor Bargaining and the State: Historical and Comparative Perspectives*. Cambridge: Cambridge University Press.

2

Class, Power and the State

In recent years there has been burgeoning interest in the state as an object of theoretical and empirical inquiry, triggered in part by practical concerns with the exercise of state power.* The discussion has been particularly lively in the writings of contemporary Marxists, but questions concerning the relationship between state and society have long been on the agenda of political and social theory. These questions, however, have often been posed in radically different terms.

Responding to the rapid and disorienting processes of nineteenth-century industrial development in Europe, Marx, Lenin and Weber provided many of the crucial points of reference for subsequent debate on state–society relations, by focusing on class, power and the nature of state organization. But the views of these figures could not simply be accepted, except by their most dedicated epigones. Marx left a thoroughly ambiguous heritage, never fully reconciling his understanding of the state as an instrument of class domination with his acknowledgement that the state might also have significant political independence. Lenin forged a conception of capitalist state institutions which stressed their oppressive and undemocratic nature, but in so doing failed to examine the degree to which state organizations are shaped and influenced by diverse interests, political compromises and complex circumstances which do not merely reflect 'class antagonisms'. In contrast to both Marx and Lenin, Weber resisted all suggestions that forms of state organization were directly caused by class relations. He stressed the internally homologous nature of private and public administration as well as their independent dynamics. However, Weber's writings do not contain a satisfactory explanation of the

---

* This essay, co-authored with Joel Krieger, was first published under the title 'Theories of the state: some competing claims' in Stephen Bornstein, David Held and Joel Krieger (eds), *The State in Capitalist Europe* (London: Allen & Unwin, 1984), pp. 1–20. I have substantially abridged and modified it for this volume.

precise character of the relation between the growing bureaucratic centralization of the state and modern capitalism. His assumption of a functional and
ultimately harmonious codevelopment of private and public institutional
forms cannot take the place of a well-worked-out theory of state–society
relations. (For an elaboration and assessment of Marx's, Lenin's and Weber's
positions see essay 1, especially pp. 31–44.)

Twentieth-century social and political science has, to a large degree, been
preoccupied with an examination of the contributions of these three classical
thinkers. A variety of diverse and competing traditions has been spawned.
A central, if not *the* central, tradition in Anglo-American political science has
elaborated a pluralist conception of society and posed a set of claims about the
state which contrast strongly with Marxist positions – rejecting all claims that
state power has a class basis. In opposition to pluralists, contemporary Marxists
have attempted to revise the interpretations of the state as a class state in the
light of the complex practices of Western post-war governments. While modifying Marx's original analysis, they have preserved some of the essential links
he drew between political power and class power and adopted some of Weber's
insights into the workings of state administration. A third school, which
emerged forcefully in the 1970s, found the claims of neither pluralist theory,
nor Marxist theory, fully satisfactory. Theorists of 'corporatism' challenged
the validity of these theories, focusing particularly on an explanation of state
policies and institutional arrangements which sought to harmonize conflicting
social interests.

This essay examines each of the three major contemporary approaches to
the understanding of state–society relations: first, the analysis of pluralists or
empirical democratic theorists which focuses on the fragmentation of power
within society; second, the writings by theorists of corporatism which
emphasize the importance of extragovernmental institutions in determining
state outcomes; third, the works of contemporary Marxists and their efforts to
reconstruct the Marxist project. Finally, a set of propositions about state–
society relations is offered which synthesizes the most salient contributions of
state theory to date, and indicates a direction for future investigations.[1]

Pluralism and the fragmentation of social interests

Applying a Weberian notion of power – 'the chance of a man or of a number
of men to realize their own will in a communal action against the resistance of
others' (Weber, 1972, p. 180) – to a basic inquiry into the distribution of
power in Western parliamentary democracies, a school of empirical democratic theory, widely referred to as 'pluralism', gained a commanding position
within American university studies of politics, beginning in the 1950s. While

its hold is not as secure now as it was then in academic circles, and its understandings of power, class and the state are ones which I will ultimately reject,
aspects of this form of democratic theory remain important. Although many
have dismissed pluralism as a wholly naive, and/or narrowly ideological,
celebration of American society, the tradition offers a clear framework for
viewing political behaviour – which is not always the case for Marxism and
Weberianism – and one which unquestionably illuminates some elements of
modern politics.

By 'power', pluralists have generally meant an ability to achieve one's aims
in the face of opposition. As Dahl, perhaps the central figure in American
pluralist theory, suggests, 'by "power" we mean to describe a . . . reasonable
relationship, such as A's capacity for acting in such a manner as to control B's
responses' (Dahl, 1956, p. 13). In other formulations Dahl refers to the power
relation as involving 'a successful attempt by A to get [B] . . . to do something
he would not otherwise do' (Dahl, 1957; see Nagel, 1975, pp. 9–15). Whether
one stresses capacity (the first definition) or actual behavioural outcomes in
the exercise of power (the second definition), Dahl's notion of power, like
Weber's, stresses the subjective elements of purpose and willing, and implies a
comparable, narrowly conflictual basis. The issue is the overcoming of B's
resistance – getting B to act against his or her preferences – and in that sense
power hinges on the exercise of control over immediate events.

Dahl's research design for an empirical investigation of the distribution of
power in American societies follows from this conceptual basis. Wanting to
discover who had power over what in New Haven politics (hence the title of his
famous study of 'pluralist democracy', *Who Governs?*) Dahl concentrates on
discovering the capacity of actors involved in particular policy decisions to
'initiate alternatives that were finally adopted' or to veto alternatives initiated
by others (Dahl, 1961). Which A could overcome the resistance of which B in
securing discrete and observable political outcomes? Focusing on the explicit
results of the governmental decision-making process in New Haven, Dahl
concludes that the city is a pluralist democracy of multiple coalitions leading to
the mayor. Power is disaggregated and non-cumulative; it is shared and
bartered by numerous groups spread throughout society and representing
diverse and competitive interests. There are inequalities of power, to be sure,
as there is an unequal distribution of wealth, status, education and so on, but
nearly everyone can be 'more equal' than another with regard to some
relevant resource. There are conflicts over the power to determine policy
outcomes, as different interests press their sectional claims on the mayor, but
the very process of interest bartering assumes a general direction of policy
which is positive for the citizenry at large.

This last notion – that the process of diverse interests competing for power is
a source of democratic equilibrium and generally favourable policy articu-

lation – remains, alongside the individualist and voluntarist notion of power, a second critical assumption of American empirical democratic theory. It is a vintage argument which dates from James Madison (1751–1836), and one which provides 'a basic rationale for the American political system' (Dahl, 1956, p. 5). Beginning from the Hobbesian assumption that people's natural inclinations include the desire for power over others, Madison wrote in *The Federalist*, no. 10, that 'the latent causes of faction are . . . sown in the nature of men' (Hamilton et al., 1945, p. 56). He argued accordingly that factions are a necessary part of political life unless snuffed out by repression, a process he likened to the elimination of air out of concern for the danger of fires. Madison's additional point, that 'the most common and durable source of factions has been the various and unequal distribution of property', has unfortunately been undervalued by empirical democratic theorists, who assert a relative equality of influence among diverse sources of interest.

Characteristically, Dahl argues that religion, race, ethnic group and regional identities are as significant as class (what Madison terms 'the unequal division of property') in the division of society into distinctive 'subcultures' or interests (Dahl, 1971, pp. 106–7). Empirical democratic theorists accept that Madison's factions – creditors, debtors, mercantile interests and so on – persevere in today's voluntary associations, interest groups, peak organizations of business and labour and, one step removed, in political parties. Mainly, Madison argued for a strong American state negatively, as a safeguard against tyranny and a means to 'break and control the violence of faction'. His contemporary adherents, however, radically alter this argument. Despite substantial disagreement among themselves, empirical democratic theorists claim that factions are more than the natural counterpart of free association – and they are not an obstacle to democratic government. Rather, Madison's factions, in their modern guise as interest groups, are viewed positively as the structural source of stability and the central expression of democracy.

This direction in democratic theory is perhaps most clear in the case of group theorists, who focus on the competing 'claims through or upon the institutions of government' by interest groups, and assert the importance of group interaction for securing equilibrium in American democracy (Truman, 1951, p. 505). According to David Truman,

> Only the highly routinized governmental activities show any stability . . . and these may as easily be subordinated to elements in the legislature as to the chief executive . . . [O]rganized interest groups . . . may play one segment of the structure against another as circumstances and strategic considerations permit. The total pattern of government over a period of time thus presents a protean complex of crisscrossing relationships that change in strength and direction with alterations in the power and standing of interests, organized and unorganized. (Truman, 1951, p. 508)

Power for group theorists like Truman is conceived along Weberian lines, while the configuration of power, expressed through factions, is strictly Madisonian. The state is not autonomous either in the Weberian sense, or in the sense of Marx's position 1 which emphasizes the state's centrality in society and its capacity to promote as well as to coordinate change (see essay 1, pp. 33–6). Rather, the state *reacts* to the purposive exercise of power which is fragmented within society, non-hierarchically and competitively configured. Moreover, Truman is explicitly Madisonian in providing mechanisms for guaranteeing that out of the diversity of competing interests relatively coherent policy (and policy within 'the democratic mold') will nevertheless emerge. Beginning from Madison's assumption that the very diversity of interests in society will protect the republic from the 'tyranny of the factious majority' (by splintering potential factions that would threaten the rights of others), Truman suggests that 'overlapping membership' is an additional safeguard. Since, in Truman's language, all 'tolerably normal' persons have multiple memberships scattered among groups with diverse – and even incompatible – interests, each interest group remains too weak and internally divided in purpose to secure a share of power incommensurate with its (assumed to be small) numbers and (assumed to be narrow) interests. Policy emerges behind the backs of state officials as the result of a series of uncoordinated impacts upon government, directed from all sides by competing forces (Truman, 1951, pp. 503–16).

Dahl, writing later than Truman, criticizes many aspects of Madison's ideas and notes the anachronistic character of his eighteenth-century views. Nevertheless, Dahl assimilates the central Madisonian concern with factional interests recast in its positive guise as the exemplary expression of – rather than a formidable threat to – democracy (Dahl, 1956). Indeed, Dahl argues that democracy may be defined as rule by multiple minority oppositions. For Dahl, a tyrannical majority is improbable, since elections, the central democratic procedure for selecting and 'controlling' leaders, express the preferences of various competitive groups, rather than the rule of a firm majority. Hence, supporters of democracy need suffer no fear of tyranny by an excessively strong interest. Rather, what Dahl calls 'polyarchy' (a situation of open contest for electoral support among a large proportion of the adult population) ensures competition among interests (minorities) – and the existence of competitive interests is the safeguard of democracy. Thus, Dahl writes:

> The real world issue has not turned out to be whether a majority, much less 'the' majority, will act in a tyrannical way through democratic procedures to impose its will on a (or the) minority. Instead, the more relevant question is the extent to which various minorities in a society will frustrate the ambitions of one another with the passive acquiescence or indifference of a majority of adults or voters.
> . . . [I]f there is anything to be said for the processes that actually distinguish

democracy (or polyarchy) from dictatorship . . . [t]he distinction comes [very close] to being one between government by a minority and government by minorities. As compared with the political processes of a dictatorship, the characteristics of polyarchy greatly extend the number, size, and diversity of the minorities whose preferences will influence the outcome of government decisions. (Dahl, 1956, p. 133)

More sophisticated than Truman in his appreciation of the nuances of power and in his comparative understanding of institutional arrangements in parliamentary democracies, Dahl nevertheless reinforces the view that competition among organized interests structures the policy outcomes and secures the democratic character of Western governments.[2] To this degree, at least, whatever their differences, nearly all empirical democratic theorists preserve their Madisonian heritage and perpetuate an interpretation of democracy as a set of institutional arrangements which allow for the rule of multiple minorities through competition for the selection and influence of elites, subject to periodic voter approval (Pateman, 1970, p. 8).

Dahl's position itself does not require that control over political decisions is equally distributed; nor does it require that all individuals and groups have equal political 'weight' (Dahl, 1956, pp. 145–6). In addition, he clearly recognizes that organizations and institutions can take on 'a life of their own', which may lead them to depart, as Weber predicted, from the wishes and interests of their members. There are 'oligarchical tendencies': bureaucratic structures can ossify and leaders can become unresponsive elites in the public or private sectors. Accordingly, public policy can be skewed towards certain interest groups which have the best organization and most resources; it can be skewed towards certain politically powerful state agencies; and it can be skewed by intense rivalries between different sectors of government itself. Policy-making as a process will always be affected and constrained by a number of factors, including intense political competition; electoral strategies; scarce resources; and limited knowledge and competence. Democratic decision-making is inevitably incremental and frequently disjointed. But the classical pluralist position does not explore these potentially highly significant issues very fully; their implications are not pursued. For the central premises of this position – the existence of multiple power centres, diverse and fragmented interests, the marked propensity of one group to offset the power of another, the state as arbitrator between factions – cannot begin to explain a world in which there may be systematic imbalances in the distribution of power, influence and resources. The full consideration of such issues is incompatible with the assumptions and terms of reference of empirical democratic theory.

In combination, a Weberian notion of power and a Madisonian view of the necessity of factions (transmuted into the positive basis of democracy), mark a dramatic turn in democratic theory and invite a series of substantial criticisms.

In the first instance, the pluralist emphasis on the 'empirical' nature of democracy creates a difficulty in democratic thought. By defining democracy in terms of what is conventionally called 'democracy' in the West – the practices and institutions of liberal democracy – and by focusing exclusively on those mechanisms through which it is said citizens can control political leaders (periodic elections and pressure-group politics), pluralists neither systematically examined nor compared the justification, features and general conditions of competing democratic models. The writings of the key pluralist authors tended to slide from a descriptive–explanatory account of democracy to a new normative theory (see Duncan and Lukes, 1963, pp. 40–7). Their 'realism' entailed conceiving of democracy in terms of the actual features of Western polities. In thinking of democracy in this way, they recast its meaning and, in so doing, surrendered the rich history of the idea of democracy to the existent. Questions about the appropriate extent of citizen participation, the proper scope of political rule and the most suitable spheres of democratic regulation – questions that have been part of democratic theory from Athens to nineteenth-century England – were put aside, or, rather, answered merely by reference to current practice. The ideals and methods of democracy become, by default, the ideals and methods of the existing democratic systems.

Suggestions about ways in which democratic public life might be enriched cannot be explored within the terms of reference of classical pluralism. This is illustrated most clearly by the use of the findings of the degree to which citizens are uninformed and/or apathetic about politics. For the most part, the classical pluralists regard such findings simply as evidence of how little political participation is necessary for the successful functioning of democracy. Limited or non-participation among large segments of the citizenry – for instance, non-whites – is not a troubling problem for them, because their theoretical framework does not allow discussion of the extent to which such phenomena might be taken to negate the definition of Western politics as democratic. Empirical findings tend to become inadequately justified theoretical virtues (cf. Krouse, 1983).

The question remains, of course, how satisfactory is pluralism as an account of political 'reality'? An intriguing place to begin in this context is with the concept of power. In an influential critique of the pluralist conception of power, Bachrach and Baratz (1962) drew attention to exercises of power which may have already determined the (observable) instances of control by A over B which constitutes power in the pluralist view (Bachrach and Baratz, 1962, pp. 947–52). They rightly pointed out – adopting Schattschneider's concept of the 'mobilization of bias' – that persons or groups may exercise power by 'creating or reinforcing barriers to the airing of policy conflicts' (cf. Schattschneider, 1960). In other words, A may be able to control B's behaviour by participating in a non-decision-making process.

Of course, power is exercised when A participates in the making of decisions that affect B. But power is also exercised when A devotes his energies to creating or reinforcing social and political values and institutional practices that limit the scope of the political process to public consideration of only those issues which are comparatively innocuous to A. To the extent that A succeeds in doing this, B is prevented, for all practical purposes, from bringing to the fore any issues that might in their resolution be seriously detrimental to A's set of preferences. (Bachrach and Baratz, 1962, p. 949)

Bachrach and Baratz's critique is of considerable significance, drawing attention as it does to the way in which power is deployed not only when things happen (decision-making) but also when they do not appear to do so (non-decision-making). However, power cannot simply be conceived in terms of what individuals do or do not do, a position which Bachrach and Baratz themselves seemed to adopt. For, as Lukes observed in a telling analysis of the concept of power, 'the bias of a system is not sustained simply by a series of individually chosen acts, but also, most importantly, by the socially structured and culturally patterned behaviour of groups, and practices of institutions' (Lukes, 1974, p. 22). If power is defined in terms of the capacity of individuals to realize their wills against resistance, collective forces and social arrangements will be neglected. It is not surprising, then, that classical pluralists failed to begin to grasp those asymmetries of power – between classes, races, men and women, politicians and ordinary citizens – which were behind, in large part, the decay of what they called 'consensus politics' in the late 1960s and 1970s.

The period 1968–9 represents something of a watershed (Hall et al., 1978). The anti-Vietnam-war movement, the student movement and a host of other political groups associated with the New Left began to alter the political pace: it was a time of marked political polarization. The new movements seemed to define themselves against almost everything that the traditional political system defended (see essay 4). While it is easy to exaggerate the coherence of these movements and the degree of support they enjoyed, it is not easy to exaggerate the extent to which they shattered the premises of classical pluralism. Within pluralist terms, the events and circumstances of the late 1960s onward were wholly unexpected, and certainly not predicted.

There is a range of other difficulties with the pluralist position, all of which stem from the inadequate grasp of the nature and distribution of power. The existence of many power centres hardly guarantees that government will attend to them all or be susceptible to influence by anybody other than those in powerful positions (Lively, 1975, pp. 20–4, 54–6, 71–2, 141–5). In addition, it is clear that, as already pointed out in essay 1, many groups do not have the resources to compete in the national political arena with the clout of, for instance, powerful corporations, national or multinational. And many do not have the minimum resources for political mobilization at all. The pluralists' analysis of the conditions of political involvement requires radical recasting.

Some of these objections would now be accepted by key 'pluralists', among them Dahl (1978; 1985). In fact, as a result of both conceptual and empirical problems with pluralist theory, classical pluralism has effectively been dissolved in recent years into a series of competing schools and tendencies (see McLennan, 1984). This is a noteworthy theoretical development which is particularly apparent in Dahl's writings (see Held, 1987, ch. 6, for a critical overview).

Corporatist theory

Beyond the debates about the concept of power, many have focused their attacks on pluralism in terms of the problems of policy formulation. These critics have viewed the policy process less as an issue about power and more as a concrete problem of institutional arrangements, both within and outside the traditional structures of the state bureaucracy. In the late 1970s none so forcefully attacked the assumptions of empirical democratic theory as the new generation of theorists of corporatism, many of whom nevertheless share some important conceptual ground with pluralist theory.[3] How far have they come from an assumption that stability is the 'invisible hand' result of diverse pressures and from an understanding of state policy as the contingent outcome of diverse societal influences?

At first glance, corporatist theory and empirical democratic theory – for simplicity here reduced to classical pluralism – seem wholly incompatible. The corporatist view of state–society relations began, as one of its most able practitioners, Leo Panitch, explains, from the 'common premise . . . that class harmony and organic unity were essential to society and could be secured if the various functional groups, and especially the organizations of capital and labour, were imbued with a conception of natural rights and obligations somewhat similar to that presumed to have unified the medieval estates' (Panitch, 1977, p. 61). This principle of organic unity is central to many versions of corporatist theory and incompatible with the tenets of pluralism. In corporatism, observed J. T. Winkler, '[s]ociety is seen as consisting of diverse elements unified into one body, forming one *corpus*, hence the word corporatism'. Whereas pluralism assumes a competition among divided interests with the struggle for factional advantage resulting in a political equilibrium which defines the policy options of a weak state, corporatism presupposes 'a shared interest in collective existence' and cooperation expressed through the strategic exercise of power by a strong central state (Winkler, 1976, p. 105).

Until recently, corporatism has referred exclusively to state corporatism –

corporatism from above – and pointed to the Fascist states of Italy and Germany in the 1930s as 'exemplary' instances of modern European corporatism. In these cases corporatism was no more than a 'decorative façade, for an organic unity won through the consistent exercise of repression' (Harris, 1972, cited in Panitch, 1977). However, a new conceptual variant of corporatism – corporatism from below or societal corporatism – has been developed as an explanation of contemporary European political realities which challenges the understandings of both Marxist and democratic theory.

In the central work of societal corporatism (or liberal corporatism) Philippe Schmitter defines corporatism as the specific political structure which typically accompanies the 'post liberal, advanced capitalist, organized democratic welfare state' (Schmitter, 1974, p. 105). As an ideal type, argues Schmitter in the definition which has become the standard reference point for subsequent debates, contemporary corporatism can be conceived as:

> a system of interest representation in which the constituent units are organized into a limited number of singular, compulsory, hierarchically ordered and functionally differentiated categories, recognized or licensed (if not created) by the state and granted a deliberate representational monopoly within their respective categories in exchange for observing certain controls on their selection of leaders and articulation of demands and supports. (Schmitter, 1974, pp. 93–4)

With Schmitter and others, the relationship between corporatism and pluralism both as empirical accounts of the existing pattern of state–society relations, and as alternative conceptions, is explicitly drawn. The 'needs of capitalism to reproduce the conditions of its existence' and particularly varying requirements generated by the changing balance of class forces since the First World War, have led to 'the decay of pluralism and its gradual displacement by societal corporatism' (Schmitter, 1974, pp. 107–8; see also Schmitter, 1979). There *was* pluralism, but there is no more; there are critical class forces which structure political relations, but the state was never the instrumental reserve of capitalist interests, and policy was never directly linked to the requirements of accumulation. The assumption of class struggle is, albeit with new institutional specifications, appropriated from Marxist theory and, at the same time, the lines are drawn sharply against pluralism as an account of contemporary politics. Any models in democratic theory, argues Schmitter, which suggest that diverse interests are pursued by 'an unspecified number of multiple, voluntary, competitive, non-hierarchically ordered and self-determined . . . categories' (Schmitter, 1974, p. 93) are no longer valid.

By the corporatist account the directive capacities of the state have increased, and 'interest intermediation' has become systematized along stricter (less plural and less voluntary) lines of power: membership is compulsory in the few peak associations (trade union or business confederations) with clout; a single organization negotiates binding settlements which are recognized as legitimate by the state; and in return for this 'representational monopoly', the representatives of the corporate interests (for example, the Trades Union Congress in Britain or Confindustria in Italy) deliver support for agreed policies and discipline their members.

Some of the appeal of corporatist theory follows from its presentation (by Schmitter, for example) as a descriptively rich 'synthesis' of central conceptual premises of Marxist and pluralist theory. From pluralism, corporatists adopt the basic understanding that policy outcomes are determined by the competitive claims of interest associations – but the associations are now oligopolistically configured. Equally significant, corporatist thinkers adopt the pluralist assumptions that competition among disparate groups tends to result in state policy equilibrium, with no shifts toward labour or capital which would force a fundamental revision of the structural arrangements of capitalism. From Marxist theory, the liberal corporatists accept that beneath the intricacies of 'interest intermediation' lie basic class conflicts, and beneath the apparent indeterminacy of policy lie activities which are designed to reproduce class relations.

Remarkably, within this theoretical amalgam, the traditional corporatist premise of organic unity is also preserved. In the liberal corporatist model an incomes policy, for example, jointly agreed between government and peak trade union associations – ideally, with tripartite negotiations securing the support of business as a full partner – becomes the modern cathedral, whose painstaking construction represents the solidity, organic unity and ostensible harmony of the society. Claims above class, the higher claims of stability and the pursuit of economic well-being, forge unity among societal factions which are manipulated by the state to disengage from class conflict and to achieve a compromise which freezes the balance of class power.

There is a conceptual ingenuity to the corporatist enterprise and a descriptive elegance which is noteworthy. More successfully than Marxist theory or modern empirical democratic theory, corporatist theory exposes what until recently has been one of the most significant patterns of post-war state management, that is, the proliferation of tripartite agreements, the tendency for the conventions of collective bargaining to be writ large in the processes of governmental decision-making, particularly in areas of macro-economic policy. Moreover, by highlighting these extraparliamentary negotiations about critical policies (wages, prices, investment and planning), corporatists seem to explain best the much-discussed weakening of formal representative structures, the undermining of the sovereignty of parliamentary bodies, the 'crisis of democracy' in the face of excessive economic pressures.

Nevertheless, serious weaknesses limit the utility of corporatist theory as a general framework for understanding the contemporary state. Descriptively, to begin with, few things besides incomes policies reflect the attributes of the tripartite model and even agreements over incomes have often been insubstantial, voluntary, ineffective and transitory. Indeed, corporatist arrangements remain fragile, because they require the consistent presence of a relatively uncommon set of conditions which secure the integration of organized labour including:

1 An attitude within the labour movement which favours 'crisis management' over structural or redistributive measures of macro-economic policy.
2 The presence of state institutions for tripartite management initiatives.
3 The institutionalization of trade union and party power within a coordinated working-class movement.
4 Sufficient centralization that decisions by confederations are binding upon individual industrial unions.
5 Adequate elite influence within unions to ensure rank-and-file compliance with agreed policies.

While broad corporatist arrangements have been generally successful in Austria and the Netherlands, these five conditions have been so difficult to realize elsewhere that even incomes policies – the minimal and most common corporatist arrangement – have failed to appear (or proved to be transitory). The failure in France has been due to the anticapitalist attitude of the largest and Communist-oriented union, the Confédération générale du travail (CGT) (absence of condition 1); in Germany, due to the low level of institutionalization for tripartite management at the federal level (absence of condition 2); and in Britain the failure is distinctly overdetermined, due (at a minimum) to the absence of factors 3, 4 and 5 (see Lehmbruch, 1979).

Temporary, one-sided agreements to limit wages, while profits and prices are left to private and market determination, hardly rival the medieval cathedral as examples of organic social architecture. Not only is instability frequently associated with efforts at the construction of durable agreements, but the central premise – that incomes policies involve freely contracting parties who represent functionally equivalent partners – seems illusory. More likely, corporatist structures temporarily obscure the asymmetries in the distribution of power (see Martin, 1975). Rather than demonstrating the end of class conflict, corporatist arrangements institutionally fix a short term balance of class power. At the same time the presence of corporatist institutions which erode the responsibility of representative organs for economic management challenges the pluralist interpretation of democracy as a set of institutional arrangements subject to the control of periodic voter approval.

Developments in contemporary Marxist theory

In the last two decades there has been a massive revival of interest in problems of state power among contemporary Marxist writers (see, for example, Jessop,

1977; Frankel, 1979). Ralph Miliband provided an important stimulus with his publication of *The State in Capitalist Society* (1969). Noting the growing centrality of the state in Western societies he sought on the one hand to assess the relationship Marx posited between class and state, and on the other to evaluate the pluralist model of state–society relations which was then the reigning orthodoxy.

Against those who held that the state is a neutral arbiter among social interests, he argued (1) that in contemporary Western societies there is a dominant or ruling class which owns and controls the means of production; (2) that it has close links with powerful institutions, among them political parties, the military, universities and the media; and (3) that it has disproportionate representation at all levels of the state, especially in the 'command positions'. The social background of civil servants ('overwhelmingly . . . from the world of business and property, or from the professional middle classes'), their own interests ('a smooth career path'), their ideological dispositions ('accepting beyond question the capitalist context in which they operate'), mean that the state apparatus 'is a crucially important and committed element in the maintenance and defense of the structure of power and privilege inherent in advanced capitalism' (Miliband, 1969, pp. 128–9).

Nevertheless, Miliband contends, there is an important distinction between governing (making day-to-day decisions) and ruling (exercising ultimate control). Members of the dominant economic class do not generally comprise the government. However, the state remains an 'instrument for the domination of society acting on behalf of ruling-class interests'. The socio-economic constraints on Western governments and state institutions – constraints imposed by the requirements of private accumulation – systematically limit their policy options. If the system of private property and investment is threatened, economic chaos quickly ensues and the legitimacy of governments can be undermined. Hence, social-democratic or labour-oriented governments are constrained: confidence in their ability to manage is easily eroded.

According to Miliband, the commitments of state administrations to private enterprise and market rationality define their class character. Miliband insists, however – defending what I earlier called Marx's position 1 (see pp. 33–6) – that in order to be politically effective, the state must be able to separate itself routinely from ruling-class factions. Government policy may even be directed against the short-run interests of the capitalist class. He is also quick to point out that under exceptional circumstances the state can achieve a high order of independence from class interests, for example, in national crises and war.

Nicos Poulantzas challenged Miliband's views in a debate which has received much attention (Poulantzas, 1972). In so doing, he sought to clarify Marx's understanding of the state's scope for 'autonomous action'. He rejects the view that the state is 'an instrument for the domination of society' and what he considers Miliband's 'subjectivist' approach – his attempt to explore the relation among classes, bureaucracy and the state through 'interpersonal relations' (for Miliband, the social background of state officials and links between them and members of powerful institutions). As Poulantzas wrote: 'The direct participation of members of the capitalist class in the state apparatus and in government, even where it exists, is not the important side of the matter' (1972, p. 245).

Although Poulantzas exaggerates the differences between his position and Miliband's, his starting-point is radically different. He does not ask: Who influences important decisions and determines policy? What is the social background of those who occupy key administrative positions? The 'class affiliation' of those in the state apparatus is not, according to Poulantzas, crucial to its 'concrete functioning' (Poulantzas, 1973, pp. 331–40). Much more important for Poulantzas are the structural components of the capitalist state which lead it to protect the long-term framework of capitalist production even if this means severe conflict with some segments of the capitalist class.

In order to grasp these structural components, it is essential, Poulantzas argues, to understand that the state is the unifying element in capitalism. More specifically, the state must function to ensure (1) the 'political organization' of the dominant classes, which because of competitive pressures and differences of immediate interest are continually broken up into 'class fractions'; (2) the 'political disorganization' of the working classes which, because of the concentration of production, among other things, can threaten the hegemony of the dominant classes; and (3) the political 'regrouping' by a complex 'ideological process' of classes from the non-dominant modes of production (for instance, peasants) who could act against the state (Poulantzas, 1973, pp. 287–8).

Since the dominant classes are vulnerable to fragmentation, their long-term interests require protection by the state. The state can sustain this function only if it is, in Poulantzas's well-known term, 'relatively autonomous' from the particular interests of diverse fractions. What is more, the state itself, Poulantzas stresses, is not a monolithic bloc; it is an arena of conflict and schism (the 'condensation of class forces') (Poulantzas, 1975). The degree of autonomy actual states acquire depends on the relations among classes and class fractions and on the intensity of social struggles.

The state's autonomy is incomplete, Poulantzas stresses, because the state bureaucracy does not in itself have political power. Bureaucratic power is 'the exercise of the state's functions', articulating political power actually belonging to classes. Insistent, at least in his early works, that power is 'the capacity to realize class interests', Poulantzas contends that state institutions are 'power centres'; but classes 'hold power'. Relative autonomy 'devolves' on the state 'in the power relations of the class struggle' (Poulantzas, 1973, pp. 335–6).

Thus, the centralized modern state is both a necessary result of 'the anarchic competition of civil society' and a force in the reproduction of such competition and division. Its hierarchical–bureaucratic apparatus along with its electoral institutions simultaneously represent unity (the 'people-nation') and atomize and fragment the body politic (Poulantzas, 1980). The state does not simply record socio-economic reality, it enters into its very construction by reinforcing its form and codifying its elements.

There are, however, inconsistencies in Poulantzas's formulation of the relationship among classes, the bureaucracy and the state. These are especially acute in his early work, *Political Power and Social Classes* (1973), where he at one and the same time grants a certain autonomy to the state and argues that all power is class power. Apart from such difficulties, he grossly underestimates the state's own capacity to influence social and political developments. Viewing the state essentially in terms of its protective role *vis-à-vis* the capitalist class, Poulantzas loses sight of an entire range of concrete undertakings – from military adventures to welfare expenditures – which cannot be explained in simple class terms. To this extent, Poulantzas's formulation collapses into Marx's 'position 2' (as reinforced by Lenin) which assumes that state organization directly expresses class power (see pp. 36–9). Among the attendant problems is a peculiar de-emphasis of the capacity of the working classes to influence the course and the organization of state administration (Frankel, 1979). By stressing that the state responds to the functional requirements of capitalism Poulantzas may, as Giddens has argued, 'overestimate the "relative autonomy" of the state in capitalist liberal democracy'. As Giddens points out, 'if the state participates in the contradictions of capitalism', it is 'not merely a defender of the status quo . . . nor a mere functional vehicle of the "needs" of the capitalist mode of production' (Giddens, 1981, pp. 217–20).

Further, Poulantzas's emphasis on the state as the 'condensation of class forces' means that his account of the state is drawn without sufficient internal definition or institutional differentiation. How institutions operate and the manner in which the relationship among elites, government officials and parliamentarians evolves are neglected. Poulantzas's disregard for non-structural considerations – the behaviour of actors which represents the central focus, for example, of pluralist theory – leads him to ignore the concrete social practices through which structural relations are reproduced.[4]

Invigorating the debate in Marxist circles about state, power and class, Claus Offe has challenged – and attempted to recast – the terms of reference of both Miliband and Poulantzas (see Keane, 1984). For Offe, the state is neither simply a 'capitalist state' as Poulantzas contends (a state determined by class power), nor 'a state in capitalist society' as Miliband argues (a state which preserves political power free from immediate class interests). Starting from a conception of contemporary capitalism which stresses its internal differentiation into four sectors (the competitive and oligopolistic private sectors, the residual labour sector and the state sector) Offe maintains that the most significant feature of the state is the way it is enmeshed in the contradictions of capitalism. Hence, the state is faced with contradictory tasks. On the one hand the state must sustain the process of accumulation and the private appropriation of resources, on the other hand it must preserve belief in itself as the impartial arbiter of class interests, thereby legitimating its power (see Offe, 1984).

The institutional separation of state and economy means that the state is dependent upon the flow of resources from the organization of profitable production, through taxation and finance from capital markets. Since in the main the resources from the accumulation process are 'beyond its power to *organize*', there is an 'institutional *self-interest* of the state' and an interest of those with state power to safeguard the vitality of the capitalist economy (see Offe and Ronge, 1975). With this argument, Offe differentiates himself from Miliband and Poulantzas. As Offe puts it, the institutional self-interest of the state 'does not result from alliance of a particular government with particular classes also interested in accumulation, nor does it result from any political power of the capitalist class which "puts pressure" on the incumbents of state power to pursue its class interest' (Offe and Ronge, 1975, p. 140). For its own sake, the state is interested in sustaining accumulation.

Political power is determined, then, in a dual way: by formal rules of democratic and representative government which fix the institutional form of access to power and by the material content of the accumulation process which sets the boundaries of successful policies. Given that governments require electoral victory and the financial wherewithal to implement policy, they are forced increasingly to intervene to manage economic crisis. The growing pressure for intervention is contradicted, however, by capitalists' concern for freedom of investment and their obstinate resistance to state efforts to control productive processes (seen, for example, in efforts by business to avoid 'excessive regulation').

The state, therefore, faces contradictory imperatives: it must maintain the accumulation process without either undermining *private* accumulation or the belief in the market as a fair distributor of scarce resources. Intervention into the economy is unavoidable and yet the exercise of political control over the economy risks challenging the traditional basis of the legitimacy of the whole social order – the belief that collective goals can be properly realized only by private individuals acting in competitive isolation and pursuing their sectoral aims with minimal state interference. The state, then, must intervene but conceal its purpose. Thus, Offe defines the capitalist state '(a) by its exclusion from accumulation, (b) by its necessary function for accumulation, (c) by its dependence upon accumulation, and (d) by its function to conceal and deny (a), (b) and (c)' (Offe, 1975, p. 144).

He argues that if these analytical propositions are valid, then 'it is hard to imagine that any state in capitalist society could succeed to perform the functions that are part of this definition simultaneously and successfully for any length of time' (Offe, 1975, p. 144). To investigate this hypothesis, he focuses on the nature of state administration and, in particular, on its capacity for rational administration. The problems of administration are especially severe, Offe suggests, since many of the policies undertaken by contemporary governments do not simply complement market activities, but actually replace them. Accordingly, Offe argues in an interesting parallel to the corporatist view, that the state selectively favours those groups whose acquiescence and support are crucial to the untroubled continuity of the existing order: oligopoly capital and organized labour. The state helps to defray the costs of production for capital (by providing cheap energy for heavy users through the pricing policies of nationalized industries, for example) and provides a range of benefits for organized labour (for instance, by tacitly supporting high wage demands and enhanced wage differentials and relativities). Offe contends, furthermore, that the representatives of these 'strategic groups' increasingly step in to resolve threats to political stability through a highly informal, extra-parliamentary negotiation process (Offe, 1979, p. 9).

Starting from a critique of Weber's basic assumption that the main reason for the expansion of bureaucratic forms of organization in modern capitalist societies is their technical superiority, Offe attempts to demonstrate that no method of state administration can be 'adequate for solving the specific problem of the capitalist state'. This he characterizes as the 'establish[ment] of a balance between its *required functions*' which result from a certain state of the accumulation process on the one side, and its '*internal structure*' on the other side (Offe, 1975, p. 140). Offe argues that the 'three "logics" of policy production' which are available to the capitalist state – based in turn on bureaucratic rules, purposive action and consensus formation – necessarily undermine its operation once the burgeoning demands from the economic sphere impel the state decisively into market-replacing activities (Offe, 1975, p. 136). For Offe, each logic of policy production encounters a particular dynamic of failure: bureaucratic policy production cannot escape its dependence upon fixed hierarchical rules and therefore cannot respond flexibly to externally determined policy objectives; policy production governed by purposive action fails for lack of clearcut, uncontroversial and operational goals transmitted from the environment; the consensus mode of policy production fails because it generates conflict by inviting 'more demands and interests to articulate themselves than can be *satisfied*' by the capitalist state, bound as it is by considerations of accumulation (Offe, 1975, p.140). Modern states are hamstrung by a bureaucracy which operates by invariant rules and

procedures and by too limited goals or with overly narrow and strict juris-
dictional areas of responsibility which limit the flexibility and, in a word, the
rationality of administrative responses to externally formulated demands.[5]

Offe's writings on the internal workings of bureaucracy within capitalist
states are important: he has offered significant insights about the limitations of
rule-bound administration in promoting aims which are beyond its juris-
dictional competence. When, for example, national railways consider the
elimination of an 'unprofitable' service, by what rules – and from what
rational stance – can they evaluate the complex consequences of the decision
for the pursuit of leisure activities, investment in local industry, employment,
settlement patterns, tourism and so on? Moreover, Offe's emphasis on the
way capitalist states are pushed into providing a range of services which
directly benefit the best-organized sectors of the working class, surmounts
some of the limitations of Poulantzas's account of the state as functionally
interlocked to the needs of capital. As Offe and Ronge argue provocatively,
the state 'does not defend the interests of one class, but the *common* interests of
all members of a *capitalist class society*' (Offe and Ronge, 1975, p. 139).

But Offe may skew his understanding of state power and administrative
capacity by underestimating the ability of political representatives and administrators to be effective agents of *political strategy* (see essays 4 and 5). Although
he does formally recognize this capacity, he does not give it sufficient weight.
His own tendency to explain the development and limitations of state policy
by reference to functional imperatives (the necessity to satisfy capital and
labour, accumulation and legitimation) encourages him to play down 'the
strategic intelligence' which government and state agencies can often display,
and which is particularly apparent in a historical and comparative appreciation
of the *diverse patterns* of state activity in parliamentary capitalist societies (see
Bornstein et al., 1984). An additional shortcoming, related to this, is his
neglect of the different forms of institutional arrangements which constitute
'states' and 'democracies' in different countries. How these arrangements are
reproduced over time, and how and why they differ from one country to
another, with what consequences, are important considerations for any
adequate assessment of the nature of the state.

Conclusions: summary and propositions

The traditions of state theory examined above focus on different aspects of
state–society relations and defend positions which seem radically at odds. For
too long, these differences have been stressed with such vehemence that possibilities for fruitful synthesis have been neglected. It has already been indicated

that what I called Marx's position 1 shares significant ground with Weber's account of bureaucracy (see essay 1), such that its elaboration and reconsideration – as attempted by Offe, for example – signals a powerful approach to questions of class, power and the state. In addition, the undeniable importance of examining the exercise of power within the context of interest-group intermediation, as emphasized in empirical democratic theory, recommends a significant area of inquiry which has been too frequently ignored by Marxists concerned with general structural arrangements. Indeed, the theorists of corporatism have attempted to assimilate an understanding of interest-group behaviour within an appreciation of the boundaries restricting state–society relations under capitalism. Moreover, if these relations are understood with the subtlety expressed in the best works of contemporary Marxists, a powerful framework is available for the historical and comparative analysis of patterns of state activity in parliamentary capitalist societies.

Difficulties with each of the traditions discussed, and points of compatibility and incompatibility, have already been noted. In summary, there follows a set of propositions about government and state administration which seeks to draw together and reformulate some of their most interesting insights.

State power   Power is not merely the voluntarist expression of the capacity of an actor to influence the conduct of others, nor is it merely structured power following from institutional bias. Rather, power is the facility of agents to act within institutions and collectivities – to apply the resources of these institutions and collectivities to their own ends, even while institutional arrangements narrow the scope of their activities. Hence, state power expresses at once the intentions and purposes of government and state personnel (they could have acted differently) and the parameters set by the institutionalized context of state–society relations.

Administrative capacity   The state's capacity to administer is constrained by dominant collectivities (for example, the willingness of corporations to invest limits the scope of intervention into the process of accumulation and appropriation of capital, while trade unions can block attempts to erode hard-won social benefits). The capacity of regimes to govern is limited not only by the power of dominant groups, but by the requirements of parliamentary and electoral acceptance. The power of regimes and the pattern of state policy are determined in three ways: by formal rules which set the mode of access to governmental power; by the institutional arrangements which determine the articulation and implementation of state policies; and by the capacity of the economy to provide sufficient resources for state policies. As Offe argues, the state is not controlled directly by the dominant class; the state defends democratic capitalist class institutions.

Policy formulation The criteria by which state agencies make decisions are distinct from the logic of market operations and the imperatives of profit maximization. The criteria for failure in the policy realm are not the same as in the economic realm, for example, bankruptcy. The state can make its policy alternatives visible to clients with conflicting interests, thereby creating a possible opportunity for compromise. State managers can consciously formulate objectives and alternatives which respond to different pressures and in accordance with a regime's strategy for electoral–parliamentary success.

The primacy of the state apparatus The state apparatus has sufficient primacy over social classes and collectivities that discrete political outcomes – constitutional forms, coalitional arrangements, particular exercises of state coercion, and the like – are not foreordained. Political developments cannot be inferred directly from the configuration of class forces (although the latter surely will condition outcomes). As Marx acknowledges, considerable power may accrue to the executive, and as Weber stresses, state managers will be influenced in practice by particular interests, although they are independent from direct control by the capitalist class (or any other sectional interest). No groups are secure from (unfavourable) administrative intrusion.

Displacement strategies The capacity of a regime to manoeuvre is enhanced by its ability to displace the effects of economic problems on to vulnerable groups, for instance, the elderly, consumers, the sick, non-unionized, non-white and so on, and on to vulnerable regions, while appeasing those able to mobilize claims most effectively. Thus, crucial fronts of social struggle can be repeatedly fragmented.

The limits of corporatist arrangements A displacement strategy can be successful only to the degree that crucial policies sustain the electoral–parliamentary viability of a regime and, at the same time, the arrangements for economic and social management. Hence, corporatist arrangements are simultaneously attractive to regimes and problematic. On the one hand tripartite arrangements may secure the support of the dominant trade union and business associations and their direct constituencies; on the other hand the favouritism toward these dominant groups expressed by corporatist arrangements – and the content of the tripartite bargains reached – may erode the electoral–parliamentary support of the more vulnerable groups, which is required for regime survival. Moreover, corporatist arrangements may also erode the mass acceptability of institutions which have traditionally channelled conflict, for example, party systems and conventions of collective bargaining (see Offe, 1979). Thus, new arrangements may backfire, encouraging the formation of opposition movements based on those excluded from key decision-making processes, for instance, shopfloor workers and shop stewards, those concerned with ecological issues and the women's movement activists.

The limits of state intervention   To the extent that all states in democratic capitalist class society defend their core institutions (notably private property and a variety of democratic norms), state policies are limited to 'crisis management'. While these policies might mitigate the worst effects of crises, thus preserving the social order, they cannot by design threaten these core institutions. Nevertheless, policies may erode the basic principles of capitalist market relations (for example, planning erodes the traditional private capitalist prerogatives in determining investment).

The ambiguity of the state   The state may introduce a variety of policies which increase the social wage, extend public goods, enhance democratic rights and alter the balance between public and private sectors. As a result, social struggle is 'inscribed' into the organization, administration and policies of the state. The multiplicity of economic and electoral constraints on state action – and regime survival – means that the state is not an unambiguous agent of capitalist reproduction.

Notes

1   The discussion of state theory which follows represents only an incomplete effort to illuminate patterns of state–society relations. For example, theoretical debates – and empirical investigations – concerning the emergence of the international system of nation-states and the continuous influence of international political and political–economic forces upon the practices of state intervention will not be discussed systematically (but see essay 8 for an account of some of these issues).

2   There is always danger in presenting a telescoped view of pluralism 'in general'. I am particularly concerned not to imply an inappropriate equivalence between Dahl's and Truman's positions. For example, Dahl preserves a crucial distinction within his argument about polyarchies. He argues (1) that if competitive electoral systems are characterized by a multiplicity of minorities who feel intensely enough about diverse issues, then rights will be protected and severe inequalities avoided with a certainty beyond that guaranteed by mere legal or constitutional arrangements; and (2) that there is empirical evidence to suggest that at least certain polities – for example the US in light of findings about New Haven – satisfies these conditions. These two claims are logically distinct in Dahl, which separates him in an important way from Truman.

3   Corporatist theory includes various schools of interpretation and normative perspectives. For Winkler, corporatism is 'an economic system in which the state directs and controls predominantly privately-owned business' (1976, p. 3), while for Schmitter, it is a 'system of interest representation' or 'interest intermediation'

(1974, p. 85; 1979, p. 9). For Panitch (1977), corporatism is an ideology and a structural tendency in advanced capitalism, viewed within a Marxist perspective. In this essay the normative issues are not raised explicitly, and the emphasis is on Schmitter's interpretation of corporatism, since it has been a most influential stance within Anglo-American university circles.

4   In his last work Poulantzas took several steps to resolve these difficulties: *State, Power, Socialism* (1980) is his most successful work. However, I do not think that it fully surmounts the problems noted.

5   In a paper written in 1979 Offe states that 'only if economic policy makers loosen their institutional ties to their parties and parliaments can they hope to remain effective in responding to rapidly changing economic imperatives' (1979, p. 18). The suggestion seems to be that the corporatist mode of organization may present the state with a fourth form of policy formation.

References

Bachrach, P. and Baratz, M. S. 1962: The two faces of power. *American Political Science Review*, 56(4).

Bornstein, S., Held, D. and Kreiger, J. (eds) 1984: *The State in Capitalist Europe*. London: Allen & Unwin.

Dahl, R. A. 1956: *A Preface to Democratic Theory*. Chicago: University of Chicago Press.

Dahl, R. A. 1957: The concept of power. *Behavioural Science*, 2(3).

Dahl, R. A. 1961: *Who Governs? Democracy and Power in an American City*. New Haven: Yale University Press.

Dahl, R. A. 1971: *Polyarchy: Participation and Opposition*. New Haven: Yale University Press.

Dahl, R. A. 1978: Pluralism revisited. *Comparative Politics*, 10(2).

Dahl, R. A. 1985: *A Preface to Economic Democracy*. Cambridge: Polity Press.

Duncan, G. and Lukes, S. 1963: The new democracy. In Steven Lukes (ed.), *Essays in Social Theory*, London: Macmillan.

Frankel, B. 1979: On the state of the state: Marxist theories of the state after Leninism. *Theory and Society*, 7(1–2).

Giddens, A. 1981: *A Contemporary Critique of Historical Materialism*, vol. I. London: Macmillan.

Hall, S. et al. 1978: *Policing the Crisis*. London: Macmillan.

Hamilton, A. et al. 1945: *The Federalist or the New Constitution*. New York: Heritage Press.

Held, D. 1987: *Models of Democracy*. Cambridge: Polity Press.

Jessop, B. 1977: Recent theories of the capitalist state. *Cambridge Journal of Economics*, 1(4).

Keane, J. 1984: Introduction. In C. Offe, *Contradictions of the Welfare State*, London: Hutchinson.

Krouse, R. W. 1983: Classical images of democracy in America: Madison and Tocqueville. In G. Duncan (ed.), *Democratic Theory and Practice*, Cambridge: Cambridge University Press.

Lehmbruch, G. 1979: Consociational democracy, class conflict, and the new corporatism. In P. C. Schmitter and G. Lehmbruch (eds), *Trends toward Corporatist Intermediation*, New York: Sage.

Lively, J. 1975: *Democracy*. Oxford: Basil Blackwell.

Lukes, S. 1974: *Power: A Radical View*. London: Macmillan.

McLennan, G. 1984: Capitalist state or democratic polity? Recent developments in Marxist and pluralist theory. In G. McLennan, D. Held and S. Hall (eds), *The Idea of the Modern State*, Milton Keynes: Open University Press.

Martin, A. 1975: Is democratic control of capitalist economies possible? In L. Lindberg, R. R. Alford, C. Crouch and C. Offe (eds), *Stress and Contradiction in Modern Capitalism*, Lexington, Mass.: Lexington Books.

Miliband, R. 1969: *The State in Capitalist Society*. London: Weidenfeld & Nicolson.

Nagel, J. H. 1975: *The Descriptive Analysis of Power*. New Haven: Yale University Press.

Offe, C. 1975: The theory of the capitalist state and the problem of policy formation. In L. Lindberg, R. R. Alford, C. Crouch and C. Offe (eds), *Stress and Contradiction in Modern Capitalism*, Lexington, Mass.: Lexington Books.

Offe, C. 1979: The state, ungovernability and the search for the 'non-political'; paper presented to Conference on the Individual and the State, Center for International Studies, University of Toronto (3 February); repr. in C. Offe, *Contradictions of the Welfare State*, London: Hutchinson, 1984.

Offe, C. 1984: *Contradictions of the Welfare State*. London: Hutchinson.

Offe, C. and Ronge, V. 1975: Theses on the theory of the state. *New German Critique*, 6; repr. in C. Offe, *Contradictions of the Welfare State*, London: Hutchinson, 1984.

Panitch, L. 1977: The development of corporatism in liberal democracies. *Comparative Political Studies*, 10(1).

Pateman, C. 1970: *Participation and Democratic Theory*. Cambridge: Cambridge University Press.

Poulantzas, N. 1972: The problem of the capitalist state. In R. M. Blackburn (ed.), *Ideology in Social Science: Readings in Critical Social Theory*, London: Fontana.

Poulantzas, N. 1973: *Political Power and Social Classes*. London: New Left Books.

Poulantzas, N. 1975: *Classes in Contemporary Capitalism*. London: New Left Books.

Poulantzas, N. 1980: *State, Power, Socialism*. London: Verso/New Left Books.

Schattschneider, E. F. 1960: *The Semi-Sovereign People: A Realist View of Democracy in America*. New York: Rinehart & Winston.

Schmitter, P. C. 1974: Still the century of corporatism? *Review of Political Studies*, 36(1).

Schmitter, P. C. 1979: Modes of interest intermediation and models of societal change in Western Europe. *Comparative Political Studies*, 10(1).

Truman, D. B. 1951: *The Governmental Process*. New York: Knopf.

Weber, M. 1972: *From Max Weber*, eds H. H. Garth and C. W. Mills. New York: Oxford University Press.

Winkler, J. T. 1976: Corporatism. *Archives européennes de sociologie*, 17(1).

3

Legitimation Problems and Crisis Tendencies

The writings of Jürgen Habermas on advanced capitalist societies represent an important contribution to political and social theory.* They have helped to direct our understanding of the organizational principles of society away from old dogmas – dogmas asserting, for instance, that the state is merely 'a system of coercion to support the dominant class' or that it is 'a coalition balancing all legitimate interests'. Since the advantages of Habermas's work over less sophisticated approaches have been emphasized elsewhere, I shall focus this essay, first, on a brief account of his work on the development of capitalist societies and, second, on a number of problems which, I think, weaken its utility and scope (see Frankel, 1979; Held, 1980, parts 2 and 3).

Habermas's first major study, *Strukturwandel der Öffentlichkeit* (1962) (Structural Transformation of the Public Sphere) is a historical inquiry into the formation and disintegration of the 'public sphere': a realm of social life where matters of general interest can be discussed, where differences of opinion can be settled by rational argumentation and not by recourse to established dogma or customs. Habermas traces the emergence of the public sphere from the eighteenth-century forums of public discussion – clubs, cafés, newspapers and journals of all kinds – which were at the forefront of the European literary and political Enlightenment. Such forums nurtured debate about the role of tradition and established a base of opposition to feudal authority. With the growing division between the state and civil society, a division which followed the expansion of market economies, the public sphere flourished. Merchants, traders and others with property and education became actively concerned about the government of society, recognizing that

---

* This is an expanded and revised version of an essay which was first published under the title, 'Crisis tendencies, legitimation and the state', in John B. Thompson and David Held (eds), *Habermas: Critical Debates* (London: Macmillan, 1982), pp. 181–95.

the reproduction of social life was now dependent upon institutions which exceeded the bounds of private domestic authority.

The public sphere was thought by many of its leading participants to anticipate and articulate the interests of the community, the 'general interest'. The pursuit of this interest involved, in their view, both the freeing of civil society from political interference and the limiting of the state's authority to a range of activities supervised by the 'public'. The 'public' was, of course, predominantly the bourgeoisie; the earliest modern constitutions reflected their political aspirations and victories. Yet the goal of free speech and dis- cursive will-formation was, Habermas maintains, never fully realized in the politics of capitalist societies. With the development of large-scale economic and commercial organizations, and with the increase in state activity to stabilize the economy, the realm of the public sphere was gradually restricted and compressed. Powerful organizations strove for a political compromise with one another and with the state, excluding the general public from their negotiations wherever possible. A symptom of these developments was a change in the nature of journalism: from an occupation stimulated by con- viction to one motivated essentially by commerce. The extension of the principles of commodity exchange to more and more areas of life undercut the autonomy of forums potentially critical of the status quo. The classical idea of 'public opinion' was undermined. 'Public-relations work' and 'public-opinion research' replaced discursive will-formation.

The dissolution of the public sphere has important implications for the legitimation of contemporary capitalist society. The latter requires a form of legitimation which ensures sufficient latitude for state intervention to secure both private utilization of capital and mass loyalty to the system. In 'Technology and science as "ideology" ' (1968) (which can be found in *Toward a Rational Society*) Habermas argues that this requirement is met to a consider- able extent by science and technology. Since the late nineteenth century there has been a growing interdependence of science, technology and production: science and technology have become a leading productive force. Economic success appears to depend on the progress of technical innovation. Thus the problems facing capitalist economies (resource allocation, unemployment, economic stagnation) are defined as technical problems soluble only by experts, and politics assumes a singularly 'negative character'. It becomes orientated towards the avoidance of risks and dangers to the system – 'not, in other words, toward the *realization of practical goals* but toward the *solution of technical problems*' (Habermas, 1971, p. 103). The idea of political decision- making based on general and public discussion is replaced by a 'technocratic consciousness'. Occasional plebiscitary decisions about alternative sets of leaders appear to be the only mode of government appropriate for advanced industrial societies.

These developments, Habermas argues, have created a new constellation of economics and politics: 'politics is no longer only a phenomenon of the super-structure' (Habermas, 1971, p. 101). The expansion of the state leads to an ever greater involvement of administrators and technicians in social and economic affairs. It also leads, in conjunction with the fusion of science, technology and industry, to the emergence of a new form of ideology: ideology is no longer simply based on notions of just exchange but also on a technocratic justification of the social order. A perspective emerges in which political decisions seem, as Habermas puts it, 'to be determined by the logic of scientific–technical progress' (Habermas, 1971, p. 105). Politics becomes the sphere for the technical elimination of dysfunctions and the avoidance of problems that might threaten 'the system'.

Towards a new model of crisis

In his more recent works, *Legitimation Crisis* (1976) and *Communication and the Evolution of Society* (1979a), Habermas seeks to reformulate some of his earlier ideas and to analyse in greater detail changes in contemporary society. He does this in the context of the development of a theory of social evolution. Part of this project involves the identification of (1) the 'possibility spaces', that is, the potential avenues of development, which a society's 'core structures' create; and (2) the crisis tendencies to which such structures are vulnerable. Although Habermas is concerned to investigate pre-civilization (primitive communities) and traditional societies, his main focus hitherto has been on modern capitalism. He explores, in particular, the way 'advanced' (or, as he sometimes calls it, 'late' or 'organized') capitalism is susceptible to 'legitimation crisis' – the withdrawal from the existing order of the support or loyalty of the mass of the population as their motivational commitment to its normative basis is broken. It is his contention that the seeds of a new evolutionary development – the overcoming of capitalism's underlying class contradiction – can be uncovered in this and other related crisis tendencies (Habermas, 1976, part II).

Habermas first provides an analysis of liberal capitalism which follows Marx closely (Habermas, 1976, ch. 4). He explicates the organizational principle of this type of society – the principle which circumscribes the 'possibility spaces' of the system – as the *relationship of wage-labour and capital*. The fundamental contradiction of capitalism is formulated as that between social production and private appropriation, that is, social production for the enhancement of particular interests. But, as Habermas stresses, a number of questions have to be posed about the contemporary significance of Marx's views. Have events in the last hundred years altered the mode in which the fundamental contradiction of capitalism affects society's dynamic? Has the logic of crisis changed from the path of crisis growth, unstable accumulation, to something fundamentally different? If so, are there consequences for patterns of social struggle? These questions informed Habermas's early writings. However, the way he addresses them from *Legitimation Crisis* onwards represents a marked elaboration of his earlier views.

The model of advanced capitalism Habermas uses follows many well-known recent studies (cf., for example, Schonfield, 1965; O'Connor, 1973; Offe, 1984). He begins by delineating three basic sub-systems, the economic, the political–administrative and the socio-cultural. The economic sub-system is itself understood in terms of three sectors: a public sector and two distinct types of private sector. The public sector, that is, industries such as armaments, is orientated towards state production and consumption. Within the private sector a distinction is made between a sector which is still orientated towards market competition and an oligopolistic sector which is much freer of market constraints. Advanced capitalism, it is claimed, is characterized by capital concentration and the spread of oligopolistic structures.

Habermas contends that crises specific to the current development of capitalism can arise at different points. These he lists as follows:

Point of origin (sub-systems)	System crisis	Identity crisis
Economic	Economic crisis	—
Political	Rationality crisis	Legitimation crisis
Socio-cultural	—	Motivation crisis

His argument is that capitalist societies today are endangered from at least one of four possible crisis tendencies. It is a consequence of the fundamental contradiction of capitalist society (social production versus private appropriation) that, other factors being equal, there is either: an economic crisis because the 'requisite quantity' of consumable values is not produced; or a rationality crisis because the 'requisite quantity' of rational decisions is not forthcoming; or a legitimation crisis because the 'requisite quantity' of 'generalized motivations' is not generated; or a motivational crisis because the 'requisite quantity' of 'action-motivating meaning' is not created. The expression 'the requisite quantity' refers to the extent and quality of the respective sub-system's products: 'value, administrative decision, legitimation and meaning' (Habermas, 1976, p. 49).

The reconstruction of developmental tendencies in capitalism is pursued in each of these dimensions of possible crisis. For each sphere, theorems concerning the nature of crisis are discussed, theories which purport to explain crisis are evaluated, and possible strategies of crisis avoidance are considered. 'Each individual crisis argument, if it proves correct, is a sufficient explanation of a possible case of crisis.' But in the explanation of actual cases of crises, Habermas stresses, 'several arguments can supplement one another' (Habermas, 1976, pp. 49–50).

At the moment, in Habermas's opinion, there is no way of cogently deciding questions about the chances of the transformation of advanced capitalism. He does not exclude the possibility that economic crises can be permanently averted; if such is the case, however, contradictory steering imperatives, which assert themselves in the pressure of capital utilization, produce a series of other crisis tendencies. That is not to say economic crises will be avoided, but that there is, as Habermas puts it, no 'logically necessary' reason why the system cannot mitigate the crisis effects as they manifest themselves in one sub-system. The consequences of controlling crises in one sub-system are achieved only at the expense of *displacing and transforming* the contradictions into another. What is presented is a typology of crisis tendencies, a logic of their development and, ultimately, a postulation that the system's identity can only be preserved at the cost of individual autonomy, that is, with the coming of a totally administered world in which dissent is successfully repressed and crises are defused. Since Habermas regards legitimation and motivation crises as the distinctive or central types of crisis facing advanced capitalist societies, I should like to give a brief *résumé* of them.

Increased state activity in economic and other social realms is one of the major characteristics of contemporary capitalism. In the interests of avoiding economic crisis, government and the state shoulder an increasing share of the costs of production. But the state's decisions are not based merely on economic considerations. While on the one hand the state has the task of sustaining the accumulation process, on the other it must maintain a certain level of 'mass loyalty'. In order for the system to function, there must be a general compliance with the laws, rules, etc. Although this compliance can be secured to a limited extent by coercion, societies claiming to operate according to the principles of liberal, representative democracy depend more on the existence of a widespread belief that the system adheres to the principles of justice, equality and freedom. Thus the capitalist state must act to support the accumulation process and at the same time act, if it is to protect its image as fair and just, to conceal what it is doing. If mass loyalty is threatened, a tendency towards a legitimation crisis is established.

As the administrative system expands in late capitalism into areas traditionally assigned to the private sphere, there is a progressive demystification of the nature-like process of social fate. The state's very intervention in the economy, education, etc., draws attention to issues of choice, planning and control. The 'hand of the state' is more visible and intelligible than 'the invisible hand' of liberal capitalism. More and more areas of life are seen by the general population as politicized, that is, as falling within its (via the government's) potential control. This development, in turn, stimulates ever greater demands on the state, for example for participation and consultation over decisions. If the administrative system cannot fulfil these demands within the potentially legitimizable alternatives available to it, while at the same time avoiding economic crisis, that is, 'if governmental crisis management fails . . . the penalty . . . is withdrawal of legitimation' (Habermas, 1976, p. 69). The underlying cause of the legitimation crisis is, Habermas states rather bluntly, the contradiction between class interests: 'in the final analysis . . . . *class structure* is the source of the legitimation deficit' (Habermas, 1976, p. 73). The state must secure the loyalty of one class while systematically acting to the advantage of another. As the state's activity expands and its role in controlling social reality becomes more transparent, there is a greater danger that this asymmetrical relation will be exposed. Such exposure would only increase the demands on the system. The state can ignore these demands only at the peril of further demonstrating its non-democratic nature.

So far the argument establishes only that the advanced capitalist state might experience legitimation problems. Is there any reason to expect that it will be confronted by a legitimation crisis? It can be maintained that since the Second World War, Western capitalism has been able to buy its way out of its legitimation difficulties (through fiscal policy, the provision of services, etc.). While demand upon the state may outstrip its ability to deliver the goods, thus creating a crisis, it is not necessary that this occurs. In order to complete his argument, therefore, and to show – as he seeks to – that 'social identity' crises are the central form of crises confronting advanced capitalism, Habermas must demonstrate that needs and expectations are being produced (on the part of at least a section of the population) which will 'tax the state's legitimizing mechanisms beyond their capacity'.

Habermas's position, in essence, is that the general development of advanced capitalism, and in particular the increasing incursion of the state into formerly private realms, has significantly altered the patterns of motivation formation. The continuation of this tendency will lead, he contends, to a dislocation of existing demands and commitments. Habermas analyses these issues, not under the heading 'legitimation crisis' (a point I shall come back to later), but under the heading 'motivation crisis'. 'I speak of a motivation crisis when the socio-cultural system changes in such a way that its output becomes dysfunctional for the state and for the system of social labor' (Habermas, 1976, p. 75). This crisis will result in demands that the state cannot meet.

The discussion of the motivation crisis is complex. The two major patterns of motivation generated by the socio-cultural system in capitalist societies are, according to Habermas, civil and familial–vocational privatism. Civil privatism engenders in the individual an interest in the output of the political system (steering and maintenance performances) but at a level demanding little participation. Familial–vocational privatism promotes a family-orientated behavioural pattern centred on leisure and consumption on the one hand, and a career interest orientated towards status competition on the other. Both patterns are necessary for the maintenance of the system under its present institutions. Habermas argues that these motivational bases are being systematically eroded in such a way that crisis tendencies can be discerned. This argument involves two theses: (1) that the traditions which produce these motivations are being eroded; and (2) that the logic of development of normative structures prevents a functionally equivalent replacement of eroded structures.

The motivational patterns of advanced capitalism are produced, Habermas suggests, by a mixture of traditional pre-capitalist elements (for example the old civic ethic, religious tradition) and bourgeois elements (for example possessive individualism and utilitarianism). Given this overlay of traditions, thesis (1) can itself be analysed into two parts: (a) that the pre-bourgeois components of motivational patterns are being eroded; and (b) that the core aspects of bourgeois ideology are likewise being undermined by social developments. Habermas acknowledges that these theses can only be offered tentatively (Habermas, 1976, pp. 81–4).

The process of erosion of traditional (pre-bourgeois) world-views is argued to be an effect of the general process of rationalization. This process results in, among other things, a loss of an interpretation of the totality of life and the increasing subjectivizing and relativizing of morality. With regard to thesis (1b), that the core elements of bourgeois ideology are being undermined, Habermas examines three phenomena: achievement ideology, possessive individualism and the orientation towards exchange value (Habermas, 1976, pp. 84–92). The idea of endless competitiveness and achievement-seeking is being destroyed gradually as people lose faith in the market's capacity to distribute scarce values fairly – as the state's very intervention brings issues of distribution to the fore and, for example, the increasing level of education arouses aspirations that cannot be coordinated with occupational opportunity. Possessive individualism, the belief that collective goals can only be realized by private individuals acting in competitive isolation, is being undermined as the development of the state, with its contradictory functions, is (ever more) forced into socializing the costs and goals of urban life. Additionally, the orientation to exchange value is weakening as larger segments of the population – for instance, welfare clients, students, the criminal and sick, the unemployable – no longer reproduce their lives through labour for exchange value (wages), thus 'weakening the socialization effects of the market'.

The second thesis – that the logic of development of normative structures prevents a functionally equivalent replacement of eroded traditions – also has two parts. They are (a) that the remaining residues of tradition in bourgeois ideology cannot generate elements to replace those of destroyed privatism, but (b) that the remaining structures of bourgeois ideology are still relevant for motivation formation. With regard to (a), Habermas looks at three elements of the contemporary dominant cultural formation: scientism, post-auratic or post-representational art, and universalistic morality. He contends that in each of these areas the logic of development is such that the normative structures no longer promote the reproduction of privatism and that they could only do so again at the cost of a regression in social development, that is, increased authoritarianism which suppresses conflict. In each of these areas the changing normative structures embody marked concerns with universality and critique. It is these developing concerns which undermine privatism and which are potentially threatening to the inequalities of the economic and political system.

But the undermining of privatism does not necessitate that there will be a motivation crisis. If the motivations being generated by the emerging structures are dysfunctional for the economic and political systems, one way of avoiding a crisis would be to 'uncouple' (an obscure notion in Habermas's writings) the socio-cultural system from the political–economic system so that the latter (apparently) would no longer be dependent on the former (Habermas, 1976, pp. 90, 117ff.). To complete his argument Habermas must make plausible the contention that the uncoupling process has not occurred and that the remaining structures are still relevant for some type of motivation formation, that is, thesis (2b). His claim is that evidence from studies of adolescent socialization patterns (from Kenniston and others) and such phenomena as the women's movement indicate that a new level of consciousness involving a universalistic (communicative) ethic is emerging as a functional element in motivation formation. On this basis he argues that individuals will increasingly be produced whose motivational norms will be such as to demand a rational justification of social realities. If such a justification cannot be provided by the system's legitimizing mechanisms on the one hand, or bought off via distribution of value on the other, a motivation crisis is the likely outcome – the system will not find sufficient motivation for its maintenance.

Habermas's conclusion, then, is that, given its logic of crisis tendencies, capitalism cannot maintain its present form. If Habermas's argument is correct, then capitalism will either evolve into a kind of 'Brave New World' or it will have to overcome its underlying class contradiction (cf. essays 4 and 5 of this volume for an alternative scenario, which places more emphasis on the indeterminacy of politics). To overcome capitalism's underlying class contradiction would mean, Habermas holds, the adoption of a new principle of organization. Such a principle would involve a universalistic morality embedded in a system of participatory democracy, that is, an opportunity for discursive will-formation. What exact institutional form the new social formation might take Habermas does not say; nor does he say, in any detail, how the new social formation might evolve.

In the remainder of this essay, I should like to indicate a number of areas in which Habermas's formulations lead to difficulties. The areas of concern I want to single out particularly are: the relation between legitimation and motivation crises; the analysis of components of culture and social order; the boundary conditions of crisis tendencies; and questions relating to political transformation and the role of critical theory.

Legitimation and motivation crises

The novelty of Habermas's conception of crisis theory lies both in his emphasis on different types of crisis tendencies and on his formulation of the idea of crisis displacement. I do not wish to question that these notions constitute a significant contribution to the understanding of social crises: the disclosure of a relation between economic, political and socio-cultural phenomena is a vital step in overcoming the limitations of economistic theories of crisis, and of theories that place a disproportionate emphasis on the role of ideas alone in social change. Nevertheless, I do not think that Habermas's focus on legitimation and motivation crises is satisfactory.

In the first instance, difficulties arise because the distinction between legitimation and motivation crises is, at best, obscure. Habermas's formulation of these crisis tendencies oscillates between seeing them as distinct and conceiving of them as a single set of events. The latter position is consistent with the absence of a clear differentiation between the 'scarce resources' to which the two types of crisis are, respectively, linked – 'generalized motivations' and 'action-motivating meaning'. As he elaborates them, legitimation and motivation crises are thoroughly enmeshed: a legitimation crisis is a crisis of 'generalized motivations', a crisis which depends on the undermining of traditional 'action-motivating meaning'; a motivation crisis is a crisis that issues in the collapse of mass loyalty. I believe the source of this ambiguity lies in an inadequate conception of the way societies cohere – that is, in a problematic emphasis on the centrality of shared norms and values in social integration and on the importance of 'internalization' in the genesis of individual identity and social order.

For Habermas, social integration refers to 'the system of institutions in which speaking and acting subjects are socially related'. Social systems are conceived here as '*life-worlds* that are symbolically structured'. From this perspective one can 'thematize the normative structures (values and institutions) of a society' (Habermas, 1976, p. 4).[1] Events and states can be analysed from 'the point of view of their dependency on functions of social integration (in Parsons's vocabulary, integration and pattern maintenance)' (pp. 4–5). A society's capacity for reproduction is directly connected, Habermas contends, to successful social integration. Disturbances of a society endanger its existence only if social integration is threatened; that is, 'when the *consensual foundations* of normative structures are so much impaired that the society becomes *anomic*' (p. 3; my emphasis). Although Habermas acknowledges the difference between dominant cultural value systems and meaning structures generated by individuals in their everyday lives when he criticizes Parsons for not distinguishing 'institutional values' and 'motivational forces', he himself fails to utilize these distinctions adequately in his substantive analysis of capitalism (cf., for example, 1970, pp. 181–2; 1976, pp. 75–6).

It is crucial to preserve at all levels of social theory the distinction between dominant normative prescriptions – those involved in procuring legitimation – and the 'frames of meaning' and motives of people in society. Any theory that blurs the boundaries between these, as does Habermas's crisis theory, needs to be regarded with scepticism (see Giddens, 1979, especially pp. 85–7, 101–3). For, as I argue below, social integration, when tied to the generation of a shared sense of 'the worthiness of a political order to be recognized' (legitimacy), is not a necessary condition for every relatively stable society.[2] Clearly, some groups have to be normatively integrated into the governing political culture to ensure a society's reproduction. But what matters most is not the moral approval of the majority of a society's members – although this will sometimes be forthcoming, for instance during wars – but the approval of the dominant groups. Among the latter, it is the politically powerful and mobilized, including the state's personnel, that are particularly important for the continued existence of a social system.[3] Habermas does acknowledge this on some occasions, but he does not pursue its many implications (cf. Habermas, 1976, p. 22). His failure to do so can be explained, I think, by his use of 'unreconstructed' systems concepts and assumptions (cf. McCarthy, 1978, p. 379). Many ideas and assumptions from systems theory – in combination with concepts from action theory, structuralism and genetic structuralism – are intermingled in his work in a manner which is often unsatisfactory and difficult to disentangle.[4] These notions do not provide a suitable framework for the analysis of social cohesion and legitimation: for theories concerned with social stability must be developed without ties to the 'internalized value–norm–moral consensus theorem' and its residues (cf. Giddens, 1979, p. 87). What is required here is a more adequate theory of the production and reproduction of action.

Components of culture and social order

The notion of legitimation crisis presupposes that the motivation of the mass of the population was at one time constituted to a significant extent by the normative structures established by powerful groups.[5] But Habermas, in my view, overestimates the degree to which one may consider the individual as having been integrated into society, as well as the extent to which contemporary society is threatened by a 'legitimation–motivation' crisis.

If one examines the substantial number of studies debating the nature of the social cohesion of capitalist societies, one thing emerges with clarity: patterns of consciousness, especially class consciousness, vary across and within specific cultures and countries (see, for example, Mann, 1973; Giddens, 1977). To the extent that generalizations can be made, they must take account of 'the lack of consensus' about norms, values and beliefs (excepting perhaps a general adherence to nationalism).[6] Moreover, they must recognize that a 'dual consciousness' is often expressed in communities and work-places (cf. Mann, 1970). This implies a quite radical interpretation of many everyday events – often linking dissatisfactions with divisions between the 'rich and poor', the 'rulers and ruled' – and a relatively 'conservative' (defined below), privatistic interest in dominant political parties and processes. Many institutions and processes are perceived and hypostatized as 'natural', 'the way things have been and always will be'; but the language used to express and account for immediate needs and their frustration often reveals a marked penetration of ideology or dominant interpretative systems.

Although there is evidence of dissensus and various levels of class-consciousness, it is clear, none the less, that this rarely constitutes revolutionary consciousness. There is a fairly widespread 'conservatism' about conventional political processes; that is, seeming compliance to dominant ideas, a high interest in the system's output combined with low interest in political input (participation), and often no clear-cut conception of an alternative to the existing order. The question is: what does this 'conservatism' mean? What does it entail? Does it reflect normative integration, depoliticization, a combination of these, or something different again?

While Habermas argues that the legitimacy of the political order of capitalist society is related to 'the social–integrative preservation of a normatively determined social identity', I would argue that stability is related to the 'decentring' or fragmentation of culture, the atomization of people's experiences of the social world. Fragmentation acts as a barrier to a systematic conception of the structure of social practices and possibilities. The political order is acknowledged not because it is regarded as 'worthy' but because of the adoption of an instrumental attitude towards it; compliance most often comprises pragmatic acquiescence to existing institutions. In certain places in his writings Habermas appears to recognize the importance of these points, but he does not accommodate them adequately.[7] By presupposing that the cultural system once generated a large stock of unquestioned values and norms – values which are now regarded as threatened by increased state intervention – his analysis detracts from a systematic appraisal of the processes of 'atomization' and of 'pragmatic' adaptation. I should like to discuss briefly the importance of the latter phenomenon by indicating the significance of precisely those things that are least considered by Habermas – they include the social and technical division of labour (social and occupational hierarchies, the splits between unskilled and skilled and physical and mental labour), the organization of work relations (relations between trade unions, management and state), and the 'culture industry' (the creation of mass-entertainment industries).

Working-class consciousness, along with the consciousness of other social classes and groups, is impregnated by the work process. Analyses by Marcuse, as early as 1941, and more recently by Braverman (1974), point to the significance of understanding the way in which the rationalization and standardization of production fragments tasks. As tasks become increasingly mechanized, there are fewer and fewer chances for mental and reflective labour. Work experiences are increasingly differentiated. Knowledge of the total work process is hard to come by and rarely available, particularly for those on the shopfloor. The majority of occupations (despite the possibility of a greater exchange of functions) tend to become atomized, isolated units, which require for their cohesion 'coordination and management from above'. With the development of the division of labour, knowledge and control of the whole work process are ever more absent from daily work situations. Centralized control mechanisms and private and public bureaucracies then appear as agencies which are necessary for, and guarantee, 'a rational course and order' (Marcuse, 1941, pp. 430–1). With the fragmentation of tasks and knowledge, the identity of social classes is threatened. The social relations which condition these processes are reified: they become ever harder to grasp.

A number of factors have, furthermore, conjoined to reduce the receptivity of many people to critical thinking. Aronowitz has pointed to the way the debilitating impact of the technical division of labour is compounded by social divisions based on ethnicity, race and sex (1973, p. 408).[8] Social and occupational hierarchies combine to undermine attempts to create solidarity. Moreover, organized opposition is all too often ineffective because the representatives of these forces – although they have not lost the 'title of opposition' – are vulnerable to incorporation. This has been the fate of trade-union leaders in many countries. Trade unions have been transformed into mass organizations with highly bureaucratized leadership structures, concentrating on 'economistic' issues and acting as barriers to the expression of rank-

and-file protest about, among other things, lack of control of the work process (cf. Aronowitz, 1973, ch. 4; Mann, 1973, especially chs 2 and 3). Although the exact effects of these processes constitute an empirical question, there are strong reasons to believe that they further remove from the mass of people a chance to understand and affect the institutions that impinge upon their lives.

Factors such as differentiated wage structures, inflation, crisis in government finances and uneven economic development – factors which often disperse the worst effects of economic crisis on to groups such as consumers, the elderly, the sick, schoolchildren – are all part of a complex series which combine to make the fronts of class opposition repeatedly fragmented, less comprehensible (cf. Habermas, 1976, pp. 38–9). The 'culture industry', furthermore, reinforces this state of affairs. The Frankfurt school's analysis indicates the potency of the system of 'diversions' and 'distractions' which the culture industry generates. As Adorno showed in study after study, while the culture industry offers a temporary escape from the responsibilities and routines of everyday life, it reinforces the structure of the world people seek to avoid: it strengthens the belief that misfortunes and deprivations are due to natural causes or chance, thus promoting a sense of fatalism and dependence.[9]

The analysis above is, of course, incomplete and, in many ways, partial and one-sided. The point, however, is to stress the significance of a complex of institutions and developments which seemingly fragment society and people's comprehension of it. Reference to these processes helps to explain, I believe, the research findings which indicate that many people's beliefs and values are characterized by a high degree of ambivalence, as well as the 'conservative' component of dual consciousness. The structural conditions of work and of many other activities atomize individuals' experience and 'draw off', and/or fail to allow access to, knowledge of the work process as a whole and of the organizational principles of society. This constitutes a crucial barrier to knowledge of dominant trends on the one hand, and to potential solidarity on the other. The 'conservative' aspects of dual consciousness comprise in many cases pragmatic acquiescence to existing institutions. Pragmatic acquiescence is involved because all men and women, who seek the maintenance of their own lives, have to act 'rationally'; that is, they have to act 'according to the standards which insure the functioning of the apparatus' (Marcuse, 1941, p. 424). Few alternatives to current institutional arrangements are perceived, and it is recognized that participation in the status quo is necessary for comfort and security. Accordingly, frames of meaning utilized to articulate needs and account for everyday life couched often in terms of problems of powerlessness and insufficient resources frequently diverge from more conservative interpretative schemes employed to make sense of traditional political institutions which stress the latter's inescapability (see essay 4 for a fuller discussion of these themes).[10]

Modern capitalist society's stability is linked, I believe, to this state of affairs

– to what has been aptly referred to as the 'lack of consensus' in the crucial intersection of concrete daily experiences and the values and interpretative schemes articulated in relation to dominant institutions (see Mann, 1970, pp. 436–7). Stability is dependent on the atomization or 'decentring' of knowledge of work and politics. I suspect that modern society has never been legitimated by the mass of the population for any substantial period of time. This does not mean, of course, that the political and economic order is permanently vulnerable to disintegration or revolution. The reasons for this should be apparent; the order does not depend for its reproduction on strongly shared normative ideals.

It is because of considerations such as these that I do not find convincing Habermas's view that civil and familial privatism are dependent for their efficacy on pre-capitalist traditions. A preoccupation with one's own 'lot in life', with the fulfilment of one's own needs, is both a product of, and an adaptive mechanism to, contemporary society. The social and technical division of labour, in a society orientated towards the maximization of profit, is, it seems, a sufficient condition for atomization, isolation and privatism. It is for these reasons also that I do not find convincing Habermas's belief that the forces undermining achievement ideology, the orientation to exchange, etc., have further delegitimizing effects. A more plausible position is that, in the context of an atomized society, changes of this kind enhance an already widespread scepticism about the virtue of existing political institutions, a cynicism and a pragmatic–instrumental orientation. Furthermore, at the empirical level there is no ready evidence to support Habermas's contention of the potentially imminent realization of a communicative ethics – the highest stage of the human being's 'inner cognitive logic'. Contemporary changes in normative structures have, at best, a very ambiguous relationship to what Habermas defines as the original goals of the public sphere – discursive will-formation, universality and critique.[11] On the available evidence (and in the light of there being no substantial evidence in his own work), there does not seem to be a sufficient basis to locate the emergence of a principle of organization of a 'post-modern' society.

But to disagree with Habermas's conception of the vulnerability of contemporary Western society is not to deny, of course, that the system is faced with severe challenges – challenges to the basis on which rights and obligations are structured. The question to ask, however, is not under what conditions will there be a legitimation crisis (although, it must be added, this question remains relevant to the state's personnel and to dominant groups generally), but under what conditions can the 'cognitive penetration' of the order be radically extended? Or, to put the question in the terminology used hitherto, under what conditions can pragmatic, fragmented consciousness be overcome and a grasp of the social order (the organizational principles determining the allocation of 'value' and 'meaning' and alternatives to them) be rendered possible? Answers to this question depend less, I believe, on factors affecting social identity and more on economic and political crisis tendencies in the advanced capitalist societies. The issues discussed below are only some of those that require analysis; they are not intended as a direct response to the question just raised.

The boundary conditions of system crises

System crises (economic and rationality) can, on Habermas's account, be potentially contained (although it does not follow that they will be). Containment occurs, however, only at the cost of increasing legitimation pressures on the state: the state is the interface at which the tensions of both system integration and social integration meet. Habermas's argument rests, of course, on the claim that organized capitalism can control its potential system crises. Can this claim be supported?

Most of Habermas's remarks on system crises centre upon considerations of the nation-state; that is, the focus is on the changing relation between the state and economy within an ideal–typical capitalist country. His discussion of past and present economic tendencies pays little, if any, attention to developments of international capitalism. He raises important considerations in connection with the law of value; but the referent and context is usually that of the nation-state. It is crucially important to explore the development of capitalism in one country in the context of international political economy. The capitalist world was created in dependence on an international market and is ever more dependent on international trade. Before one can conclude that economic crises can be contained (on either a national or an international level), the relationship between economic crises in the nation-state and crisis tendencies in the international market must be better analysed and explained. These issues deserve a much more substantial treatment than Habermas gives them. Without an analysis of them, Habermas's conception of the logic of crisis development can be questioned, for the political–economic constraints on capitalist development appear much less open to control and manipulation than Habermas suggests.

In his recent work on the development of the modern state, Poggi has emphasized the significance of 'the highly contingent, inherently dangerous' nature of the international system of nation-states (1978, ch. 5). Wallerstein's (1974) analysis of the 'European world economy' indicates the importance of comprehending economic interconnections between nation-states which are beyond the control of any one such state.[12] Disproportionate economic development and uneven development generally within and between advanced industrial societies and Third World countries have serious implications for any conception of the logic or dynamic of crisis – implications which should centre attention on the primacy of struggles over who is on the centre and periphery, who controls what resources, and over a host of other basic differences in material interests.

Furthermore, although Habermas recognizes the significance of analysing different types of state activity, the nature of crisis management, and the organizational logic (rationality) of the administrative apparatus, he does not stress the need for a differentiated analysis of state forms, party structures and the relation of government and party structures to socio-economic structure. This also has consequences for an analysis of crisis tendencies; for it is precisely these things, analysed in the context of international conditions and pressures, that have been shown to be crucial determinants in key cases of political and 'social-revolutionary' crisis.[13] No analytic account of crisis tendencies can claim completeness without examining these phenomena.

Political transformation and critical theory

One of the most distinctive features of the Marxist tradition – a tradition with which Habermas closely identifies – is a concern to draw from an examination of 'what exists' an account of 'what exists in possibility'. Inquiry into historical conditions and processes is linked to a desire to reveal political potentialities. In the third and final part of *Legitimation Crisis*, Habermas focuses directly on the problem of analysing potentiality. He argues that a critique of ideology, concerned both with the existing pattern of distorted communication and with how things could be otherwise, must take as its starting-point the 'model of the suppression of generalizable interests' (see Habermas, 1976, pp. 111–17). The model permits a comparison of the normative structures of a society with those which hypothetically would be the case if norms were arrived at, *ceteris paribus*, discursively (p. 113). Linked to a number of assumptions about the conditions under which conflict breaks out, the model establishes the basis for what Habermas calls 'the advocacy role' of critical theory.

The advocacy role consists of 'ascertaining generalizable, though nevertheless suppressed, interests in a representatively simulated discourse between groups that are differentiated . . . from one another by an articulated, or at least virtual, opposition of interests' (p. 117). Using such indicators of potential conflict as discrepancies between claims and demands, and politically permitted levels of satisfaction, one can, Habermas maintains, indicate the nature of ideological repression and the level of generalizable interests possible at a given historical point. In the final analysis 'the theory serves to enlighten its addressees about the position which they occupy in an antagonistic social system and about the interests of which they could become conscious as objectively their own' (Habermas, 1974, p. 32; modified translation).

The following questions – frequently put to those in the tradition of critical theory – are pertinent: To whom is critical theory addressed? How, in any concrete situation, can critical theory be applied? Who is to be the instigator or promoter of enlightenment? It is clear that a discussion of these issues is important if Habermas is to argue successfully that the organization of enlightenment at the social level can be fashioned after critical theory. Yet, as these issues are only discussed in Habermas's writings at a most abstract level, it is difficult to draw any specific political conclusions from his advocacy model and crisis argument. Within the terms of reference of his work on modern capitalist societies we remain very much in the dark as to political processes and events. The practical implications of his theory are left undeveloped.

Habermas might reply to this charge by saying that at the present time it is extremely difficult to draw any definite political conclusions from the state of contemporary advanced capitalist countries. He might say, moreover, that while aspects of his analysis undermine the traditional faith of orthodox Marxists, other aspects suggest the importance of social struggles over gender, race, ecology and bureaucracy, as well as over the nature and quantity of state goods and services and over economistic issues. With both of these points I would agree. However, in the context of what seems to be widespread scepticism (or cynicism) about politics – understood as traditional party politics – and the success of 'cold war' attitudes (and, of course, Stalinism itself) in discrediting socialist ideals, this does not seem enough. There is a need, greater than ever I believe, to establish the credibility of socialism, to develop concrete proposals for alternative ways of organizing society and to show how these can be connected to wants and demands that crystallize in people's experience of dominant social relations (cf. Frankel, 1979, pp. 232-9). In a fascinating interview for *Rinascita*, the weekly journal of the Italian Communist Party, Habermas himself appears to express sympathy for this enterprise.[14] But it is hard to see how his own investigations of advanced capitalism connect in a direct way with this project.

Notes

1   By contrast, Habermas speaks of system integration 'with a view to the specific steering-performances of a self-regulated *system*. Social systems are considered here from the point of view of their capacity to maintain their boundaries and their continued existence by mastering the complexity of an inconstant environment'

(1976, p. 4). Both perspectives, 'life-world' and 'system', are, Habermas stresses, important.

2   Habermas explicates this concept of legitimacy in Habermas (1979c, pp. 178–205). My argument owes a good deal to Mann (1975) and Giddens (1979, ch. 2).

3   But even a crisis of legitimacy among some of these groups, it should be stressed, can leave a social system quite stable so long as the system's coercive organizations remain effective; see Skocpol (1979a).

4   Habermas has stressed the necessity for unifying systems-theoretic perspectives with insights from other approaches. But he has not, as yet, formulated an integrated framework for inquiry. This task appears to be the topic of his current research. But until it is published the methodological framework of his work will remain unclear. Cf. Habermas (1970, pp. 164–84; 1979b,d, especially pp. 125, 169).

5   Habermas argues that with the development of the liberal–capitalist social formation the economic sub-system took over certain socially integrative tasks, i.e. integration was accomplished in part through exchange relations. But although he emphasizes the importance of understanding the ways in which social integration achieved through norms and values is replaced by a system integration operating through exchange (and the ideology of the exchange of equivalents), he also emphasizes how the loyalty and support of the proletariat to the political order is dependent upon pre-capitalist traditions; see Habermas (1976, pp. 20–6; 1979c, p. 190).

6   See Mann (1975, p. 276). A strong case can be made that the only groups highly committed to dominant ideologies are those that created them, i.e. the dominant classes and groups; see Abercrombie and Turner (1978).

7   See Habermas's early work, especially (1962) and (1971), for important analyses of the expansion of instrumental reason into everyday life. *Toward a Rational Society* (1971) is a considerable aid to understanding the impersonal nature of domination.

8   Although Aronowitz focuses on factors that have affected the American working class, his analysis has more general implications.

9   For a more detailed analysis of Adorno's views see Held (1980).

10   The mode in which the latter are understood can be traced back, in part, to schooling, learning to labour, and to the culture industry – to socialization processes which embody ideas and theories about life which do not coincide with many people's own accounts of the 'realities of working life'; cf. Willis (1977).

11   It might be objected that Habermas's case could be made stronger by reference to his theory of social evolution and his theory of the logic of development of normative structures. But these theories cannot, in my view, be drawn upon until they are more fully elaborated.

12   Habermas recognizes the importance of this issue for understanding 'the *external aspect* of the new [modern] state structures', but he does not explicate their relevance for the logic of crisis tendencies.

13   See Skocpol (1979b). The significance of analysing state forms – focusing, in particular, on the changing relation between parliament and administrative branches – has recently been stressed in the debate over the development of corporatism; see, e.g., Jessop (1979).

14   A translation of this interview has appeared in *New Left Review*, 115 (May–June 1979).

References

Abercrombie, N. and Turner, B. S. 1978: The dominant ideology thesis. *British Journal of Sociology*, 29(2).

Aronowitz, S. 1973: *False Promises: The Shaping of American Working Class Consciousness*. New York: McGraw-Hill.

Braverman, H. 1974: *Labor and Monopoly Capital: The Degradation of Work in the Twentieth Century*. New York: Monthly Review Press.

Frankel, B. 1979: The state of the state after Leninism. *Theory and Society*, 7.

Giddens, A. 1977: *The Class Structure of the Advanced Societies*. London: Hutchinson.

Giddens, A. 1979: *Central Problems in Social Theory*. London: Macmillan.

Habermas, J. 1962: *Strukturwandel der Öffentlichkeit*. Neuwied: Luchterhand.

Habermas, J. 1970: *Zur Logik der Sozialwissenschaften*. Frankfurt: Suhrkamp.

Habermas, J. 1971: *Toward a Rational Society: Student Protest, Science, and Politics*, tr. J. J. Shapiro, London: Heinemann.

Habermas, J. 1974: *Theory and Practice*, tr. J. Viertel, London: Heinemann.

Habermas, J. 1976: *Legitimation Crisis*, tr. T. McCarthy, London: Heinemann.

Habermas, J. 1979a: *Communication and the Evolution of Society*, tr. T. McCarthy, London: Heinemann.

Habermas, J. 1979b: Historical materialism and the development of normative structures. In *Communication and the Evolution of Society*, tr. T. McCarthy, London: Heinemann.

Habermas, J. 1979c: Legitimation problems in the modern state. In *Communication and the Evolution of Society*, tr. T. McCarthy, London: Heinemann.

Habermas, J. 1979d: Toward a reconstruction of historical materialism. In *Communication and the Evolution of Society*, tr. T. McCarthy, London: Heinemann.

Held, D. 1980: *Introduction to Critical Theory*, London: Hutchinson.

Jessop, B. 1979: Corporatism, parliamentarism and social democracy. In P. Schmitter and G. Lehmbruch (eds), *Patterns of Corporatist Intermediation*, Beverly Hills: Sage.

McCarthy, T. 1978: *The Critical Theory of Jürgen Habermas*. Cambridge, Mass.: MIT Press.

Mann, M. 1970: The social cohesion of liberal democracy. *American Sociological Review*, 35.

Mann, M. 1973: *Consciousness and Action Among the Western Working Class*. London: Macmillan.

Mann, M. 1975: The ideology of intellectuals and other people in the development of capitalism. In L. N. Lindberg, R. R. Alford, C. Crouch and C. Offe (eds), *Stress and Contradiction in Modern Capitalism*, Lexington, Mass.: D. C. Heath.

Marcuse, H. 1941: Some social implications of modern technology. *Studies in Philosophy and Social Science*, 9.

O'Connor, J. 1973: *The Fiscal Crisis of the State*. New York: St Martin's Press.

Offe, C. 1984: *Contradictions of the Welfare State*. London: Hutchinson.

Poggi, G. 1978: *The Development of the Modern State*. London: Hutchinson.

Schonfield, A. 1965: *Modern Capitalism*. London: Oxford University Press.

Skocpol, T. 1979a: State and revolution: old regimes and revolutionary crises in France, Russia, and China. *Theory and Society*, 7.

Skocpol, T. 1979b: *States and Social Revolutions: A Comparative Analysis of France, Russia and China*. Cambridge: Cambridge University Press.

Wallerstein, I. 1974: *The Modern World-System*. New York: Academic Press.

Willis, P. 1977: *Learning to Labour: How Working Class Kids Get Working Class Jobs*. Westmead: Saxon House.

4

Power and Legitimacy

In this essay I explore questions about power and legitimacy and discuss them in relation to the politics of Britain since the Second World War.* The essay is divided into a number of sections. After an initial statement of some key theoretical issues, I consider two sets of arguments. The first set is about the nature of the post-war years of social 'consensus' (the 'end of ideology' and 'one-dimensional society' theses). The second set concerns the growing 'crisis' of the state and the erosion of its legitimacy from the late 1960s ('government overload' and 'legitimation crisis' theories). In examining each position I try to advance beyond the main competing perspectives by means of a combination of empirical inquiry and theoretical argument. In so doing, I also recount the story of the post-war years in particular periods (1945–early 1970s, mid-1970s–1980s). I conclude by looking at some central issues of power and legitimacy today. The argument which runs through the essay is that while the British state form remains a representative democratic system it has come to depend more and more in the post-war years on institutions of administration, constraint and coercion to ensure stability. This is the result, I believe, of multiple conflicts which have roots in economic, political and cultural domains.

The issues

The decade and a half following the Second World War has been characterized by many as an age of consent, faith in authority and legitimacy. The long war appeared to have generated both a tide of promise and hope for a new era and

* This is a revised version of an essay which first appeared under the title 'Power and legitimacy in contemporary Britain' in Gregor McLennan, David Held and Stuart Hall (eds), *State and Society in Contemporary Britain* (Cambridge: Polity Press, 1984), pp. 299–369. © The Open University, 1984, D209: *State and Society*.

substantial changes in the relationship between state and society. The coronation of Queen Elizabeth II in 1952 – at least two million people turned out in the streets, over 20 million watched on television, nearly 12 million listened on radio – reinforced the impression of a social consensus, a post-war social contract. As one historian put it, 'the coronation was associated in many people's minds, however vaguely, with the idea of a new Elizabethan age in which through the Commonwealth, if not through the Empire, Britain would still retain a glorious place in the world' (Marwick, 1982, pp. 109–10). The monarchy signalled tradition and stability while parliament symbolized accountability. People seemed to identify with each other in and through the state: the patriotic allegiance of all citizens seemed to have been won.

During these early post-war years political commentators from right to left of the political spectrum remarked on the high degree of compliance to the central institutions of British society: private property, welfare, parliament and the monarchy. On the Labour 'front benches' (the place where the party leadership sits in parliament) socialism was regarded ever less as a 'class movement'; and the front benches of the Conservative party affirmed that the 'class war' was obsolete. In the early 1950s Anthony Eden declared the Conservative objective as 'a nation-wide property-owning democracy' while in the late 1950s Harold Macmillan was sufficiently confident to make 'You've had it good. Have it better. Vote Conservative' the slogan for the 1959 general election. Reflecting mournfully on Labour's failure to win, Hugh Gaitskell declared: 'the changing character of labour, full employment, new housing, the new way of life based on the telly, the fridge, the car and the glossy magazines – all have had their effect on our political strength'. Moreover, the belief in 'free enterprise', a 'do-it-yourself' world, moderated and contained by the interventionist state, was reinforced by the political excesses of the right (Fascism and Nazism in central and southern Europe) and the left (Communism in Eastern Europe). The Cold War was an immense pressure confining all so-called 'respectable' politics to the centre ground.

Commenting on this period in British politics A. H. Halsey wrote: 'Liberty, equality, and fraternity all made progress.' Full employment, growing educational and occupational opportunity marked it as a time 'of high net upward mobility and of slowly burgeoning mass affluence. The tide of political consensus flowed strongly for twenty years or more' (1981, pp. 156–7). The existence of this consensus – suggesting that the modern British state was widely regarded as a legitimate order – was strongly supported in the now famous work, *The Civic Culture*, by Gabrial A. Almond and Sidney Verba. *The Civic Culture*, conducted in the late 1950s and early 1960s, was the first nation-wide sample survey of political attitudes in Britain carried out by academics. The study indicated that the British had a highly developed sense of loyalty to their system of government, a strong sense of deference to the independent authority of government and state, attitudes of social trust and confidence, and a deep commitment to moderation in politics.

Before proceeding any further it might be useful to clarify a 'family' of potentially very ambiguous concepts: consensus, consent, compliance and legitimacy. The meaning of this 'family' of concepts has been much discussed in philosophical and sociological literature.[1] An example might help to illustrate some of the problems. Citizens *obey* the commands laid down by rules or laws (concerning, for example, traffic regulation, sending children to school, respecting the property of employers, not 'taking the law into their own hands'). They *comply* with rules; they *consent* to them. In following the rule of law, they affirm a belief in legality. According to some political and social analysts, such a belief entails that the polity or political institutions are accepted, that is, *legitimated*. But the difficulty with *this* concept of legitimacy is that it fails to distinguish between different grounds for obeying a command, complying with a rule, agreeing or consenting to something. We may obey or comply because:

1   There is no choice in the matter (*following orders*, or *coercion*).
2   No thought has ever been given to it and we do it as it has always been done (*tradition*).
3   We cannot be bothered one way or another (*apathy*).
4   Although we do not like the situation – it is not satisfactory and far from ideal – we cannot imagine things being really different and so we 'shrug our shoulders' and accept what seems like fate (*pragmatic acquiescence*).
5   We are dissatisfied with things as they are but nevertheless go along with them in order to secure an end; we acquiesce because it is in the long-run to our advantage (*instrumental acceptance* or *conditional agreement/consent*).
6   In the circumstances before us, and with the information available to us at the moment, we conclude it is 'right', 'correct', 'proper' for us as an individual or member of a collectivity: it is what we genuinely *should* or *ought to* do (*normative agreement*).
7   It is what in ideal circumstances – with, for instance, all the knowledge we would like, all the opportunity to discover the circumstances and requirements of others – we would have agreed to do (*ideal normative agreement*).

These distinctions are analytical: in real life, of course, many different types of agreement are often fused together; and what I am calling 'ideal normative agreement' is not a position anyone is likely to attain. But the idea of an ideal normative agreement is interesting because it provides a benchmark which helps us assess whether those whose acquiescence to rules and laws is, for instance, pragmatic *would* have done as they did *if* they had had better knowledge, information, etc., at the moment of their action. I will not make direct use of this particular idea until the conclusion of the essay.

It is important to be aware for analytical purposes of the continuum of types of obeying, complying, consenting and agreeing. The types are represented on the scale below:

Coercion,		apathy		instrumental	ideal normative
or following orders				acceptance	agreement
			pragmatic		normative
	tradition		acquiescence		agreement
1	2	3	4	5	6	7

I shall reserve the term legitimacy for types 6 and 7 on the scale; that is, legitimacy implies that people follow rules and laws because they think them right, correct, justified – worthy. A legitimate political order is one that is normatively sanctioned by the population.

It is worth pointing out that category 5 on the scale is ambiguous; it could be taken to imply a weak form of legitimacy. But because compliance and consent is instrumental or conditional I shall not take it to mean this; for when acceptance is instrumental it means that the existing state of affairs is only tolerated, or compliance granted, in order to secure some other desired end. If the end is not achieved the original situation will not be more agreeable – in all probability it will be much less so.

A legitimate state or a repressive regime?

Political analysts thinking about the extraordinary turmoil of the twentieth-century industrial capitalist world – two colossal wars, the Russian Revolution, the depression of the 1930s, the rise of Fascism and Nazism – were impressed by the high degree of compliance to the dominant institutions of society and the striking absence of mass movements demanding revolutionary transformation of the political and social order in the years after the Second World War. American, British and continental political scientists and sociologists working in the late 1950s and early 1960s attempted to develop explanations of this state of affairs. One prominent group, arguing within the framework of a pluralist theory of power, developed the 'end of ideology' thesis. It is a thesis which was markedly in tune with views expressed during the late 1950s and early 1960s in the media, in the main political parties, in official political circles, and in many of the organizations of the labour movement. Another much smaller group expressed a radically dissenting view: they offered an interpretation of events which found little, if any, sympathy in the main institutions of state, economy and culture, although it had a major impact on students and the new radical protest movements of the 1960s. This second group, arguing within a modified Marxist framework, analysed the so-called 'end of ideology' as the realization of a highly repressive order: 'the one dimensional society'.[2]

By the 'end of ideology' Lipset, the best known exponent of this position, means a decline in the support by intellectuals, labour unions and left-wing political parties for what he calls 'red flag waving'; that is, the socialist project defined by Marxism–Leninism (Lipset, 1963). The general factors which explain this situation are the demise of Marxism–Leninism as an attractive ideology in light of its record as a political system in Eastern Europe, and the resolution of the key problems facing Western industrial capitalist societies. More specifically, Lipset argues that, within Western democracies, 'the ideological issues dividing left and right have been reduced to a little more or a little less government ownership and economic planning', and that it 'really makes little difference which political party controls the domestic policies of individual nations'. All this reflects, he suggests, the fact that 'the fundamental political problems of the industrial revolution have been solved: the workers have achieved industrial and political citizenship; the conservatives have accepted the welfare state; the democratic left has recognized that an increase in overall state power carries with it more dangers to freedom than solutions for economic problems' (Lipset, 1963, pp. 442–3).

Arguing along parallel lines to Almond and Verba, Lipset affirms that a fundamental consensus on general political values – in favour of equality, achievement and the procedures of democracy – confers legitimacy on present political and social arrangements. Accordingly, the Western democracies, particularly of Britain and the USA, will enjoy a future defined by progressive stability, convergence in the political views of economic classes, parties and states, and the steady erosion of conflict.

Butler and Stokes, focusing particularly on changes in Britain, have made analogous arguments (Butler and Stokes, 1974, pp. 193–208). One of their central themes is the declining relevance of social class to politics. Economic prosperity in the post-war years has brought within the reach of mass markets new types of goods and services, while the welfare state has substantially reduced the remaining 'pockets of poverty'. Differences between the living standards and social habits of working-class and middle-class people have diminished; and social mobility has 'added to the bridges over the class divide'. Accordingly, the 'electorate's disposition to respond to politics in class terms has been weakened'. This process of (apparent) class dealignment led Butler and Stokes to affirm a drift to the 'centre ground' in British politics. While the subsequent evidence of 'volatile' electoral behaviour (a point I shall come back to later) is also examined by them, there is little, if anything, in their work to suggest that the legitimacy of the state might be in doubt.

The theorists of the 'end of ideology', or the end of class politics, offer an interpretation of post-Second-World-War political life which Marcuse, who made famous the thesis of the 'one dimensional society', completely rejects (Marcuse, 1964). Yet curiously, as I have already noted, there is a common starting-point: an attempt to explain the appearance of political harmony in Western capitalism in the post-war years.

Marcuse's analysis begins by pointing to a multiplicity of forces which are combining to aid the management and control of the modern economy. First, he notes the spectacular development of the means of production – itself the result of the growing concentration of capital, radical changes in science and technology, the trend toward mechanization and automation, and the progressive transformation of management into ever larger private bureaucracies. Second, he emphasizes the increasing regulation of free competition – a consequence of state intervention which both stimulates and supports the economy and leads to the expansion of public bureaucracy. Third, he describes a reordering of national priorities by international events and the permanent threat of war – created by the Cold War, the so-called 'threat of communism', and the ever present possibility of nuclear catastrophe. In short, the prevailing trends in society are leading, Marcuse contends, to the establishment of massive private and public organizations which threaten to engulf social life.

A crucial consequence of this state of affairs is what Marcuse calls 'depoliticization': the eradication of political and moral questions from public life by an obsession with technique, productivity and efficiency. The single-minded pursuit of production for profit by large and small businesses, and the state's unquestioned support for this objective in the name of economic growth, sets a highly limited political agenda: it creates a situation in which public affairs become concerned merely with debating different means – the end is given, that is, more and more production. Depoliticization results from the spread of 'instrumental reason'; that is, the spread of the concern with the efficiency of different means with respect to pre-given ends.

This state of affairs is further reinforced, according to Marcuse, by the way the cultural traditions of subordinate classes, regions and minorities (racial and ethnic groups) are swamped by the mass media producing 'packaged culture'. The mass media is shaped to a significant extent by the concerns of the advertising industry with its relentless drive to increase consumption. The effect, he argues, is 'false consciousness'; that is, a state of awareness in which people no longer consider or know what is in their real interests. The world of massive public and private bureaucracies pursuing profitable production corrupts and distorts human life. The social order – integrated by the tight interlock between industry and the state – is repressive and profoundly 'unworthy'; yet, most people do not recognize it as such. Marcuse does analyse counter-trends to this state of affairs but his general emphasis – at least in his book *One Dimensional Man* – is on the way the cult of affluence and consumerism (in modern industrial capitalist society) creates modes of behaviour that are adaptive, passive and acquiescent. Against the portrayal of the political order as one based on genuine consent and legitimacy, Marcuse emphasizes the way it is sustained by ideological and coercive forces. People have no choice or chance to think about what *type* of productive system they would like to work in, what *type* of democracy they would like to participate in, what *kind* of life they would like to create for themselves. If they wish for comfort and security they have to adapt to the standards of the economic and political system. They have to go to work, get ahead, and make the best use of the opportunities with which they are presented; otherwise, they find themselves poor and marginal to the whole order.

The post-war years: 1945–early 1970s; problems with the theories of the end of ideology and one-dimensionality

The details of these theories are not as important as their overall general claims. For despite their many differences – differences which centre on whether the legitimacy of the political order is genuine or contrived – they both emphasize (1) a high degree of compliance and integration among all groups and classes in society, and (2) that the stability of the political and social system is reinforced as a result. I shall argue that both these claims are false by, first, examining some pertinent research findings and, second, by sketching the mounting difficulties faced in the 1960s and early 1970s by the British state and the political system more generally.

The post-war consensus re-examined

An intriguing place to begin is Almond's and Verba's influential study, *The Civic Culture* (1963), which, as I noted earlier, was the first work of its kind on the British political system. According to Almond and Verba, 'the state of feeling of political emotion in a country is perhaps the most important test of the legitimacy of its political system' (Almond and Verba, 1963, p. 100). If a political regime is to survive in the long-run 'it must be accepted by citizens as the proper form of government per se' (p. 230). Democracy, according to these authors, is accepted in this sense 'by elites and non-elites' (p. 180). Almond and Verba arrive at this conclusion by taking as a suitable index for the measurement of legitimacy what individuals report as a source of pride in their country (pp. 102–3, 246). But a number of things need to be noted.

First, only a minority, 46 per cent, of the British respondents expressed pride in their governmental, political institutions (p. 102). Second, and rather more importantly, Almond's and Verba's measure of legitimacy is very crude; for it fails to distinguish between the different possible meanings of pride and their highly ambiguous relation to legitimacy. For instance, I can express pride or pleasure in parliamentary democracy without in any way implying that it operates now as well as it might, or that it is the proper or best or most acceptable form of government. I can express pride in something while wishing it substantially altered. Almond and Verba do not investigate possibilities like this. Third, Almond and Verba seem so anxious to *celebrate* Western democracies of the British type that they misinterpret their own data. Michael Mann (1970) and Carole Pateman (1980) have shown that a careful reading of the data presented in *The Civic Culture* shows that not only is the degree of common value commitment in Britain fairly minimal but that according to the only (and indirect) measure of social class used – the type of formal education of the respondent – working-class people frequently express views which Almond and Verba think 'reflect the most extreme feeling of distrust and alienation' (1963, p. 268). Almond and Verba fail to explain the systematic differences in political orientation of social classes and, cutting across these, of men and women which their own data reveal (Pateman, 1980, pp. 75–80).

That value consensus does not exist to a significant extent in Britain (and the United States) is confirmed by Mann (1970) in a survey of a large variety of empirical materials based on research conducted in the late 1950s and early 1960s. He finds that middle-class people (white-collar and professional workers), on the whole, tend to exhibit greater consistency of belief and agreement over values than do the working class (manual workers). In so far as there are common values held by the working class they tend to be hostile to the system rather than supportive of it. There is more 'dissensus' between classes than there is 'consensus'. Further, if one examines 'political efficacy', that is, people's estimation of their ability to influence government, note-worthy differences are also recorded among classes: the middle class tend to assert far greater confidence than their working-class counterparts. Consider-able distance from, and distrust of, dominant political institutions is indicated among working-class people (Pateman, 1973; 1980). Strong allegiance to the liberal-democratic system and to 'democratic norms' appears to be correlated directly to socio-economic status.

It should be stressed that much of the research on value consensus is ambiguous and difficult to interpret; I will offer a fuller discussion of it later. What matters here and what we can say with confidence is that any claim about widespread adherence to a common value system needs to be treated with the utmost scepticism. But what of the immediate post-war years? Might not Lipset and the others at least find some supporting evidence for their claims during these years? The argument presented so far should lead one to be cautious about this as well.

It is hard to characterize with precision the political atmosphere of the immediate post-war years; surprisingly little detailed social history has been written about the period. In Britain, no doubt, a mixture of joy about the war's end, resignation to difficult economic circumstances and hope for the future intermingled in complex ways across social groups and classes. As the multiple restraints of war were relaxed popular radical sentiments became more clearly demarcated: newspaper commentators at the time, as well as historians and sociologists writing later, have emphasized how high people's expectations were and how these were marked, especially among the mass of working people, with egalitarian ideologies and a sense that things would soon get markedly better (Ryder and Silver, 1977; Middlemas, 1979; Halsey, 1981). Among the soldiers returning from war these aspirations were especially high (Middlemas, 1979, pp. 360–1). There were few illusions about the prevalence of class in Britain prior to and after the war (see Marwick, 1982, p. 48). That British society had been and was a class society, does not appear to have been in question.

If there was a widespread 'consensus' or 'common value system' adhered to by the working classes in Britain during the immediate post-war years it seems better interpreted in terms of what I called earlier 'instrumental consent': in this case, general compliance to dominant political and economic institutions linked directly to an expectation of a qualitatively new and more egalitarian life. As the Postal Censor noted in a (1941) report on working-class and lower-middle-class aspirations for the future, they were 'looking forward confidently to a post-war levelling of class distinction and redistribution of wealth' (quoted in Middlemas, 1979, p. 361). 'Deep scepticism' about government propaganda along with signs of popular 'dangerous' radicalism noted by Mass Observation (a private research organization) as early as 1940 certainly seems to have lived on – perhaps because of the memories of the 1930s. There was a general sense that the 'rights and dignity' of ordinary people would be fully acknowledged in the period to come (cf. Morgan, 1984; Thompson, 1984).

A sense of allegiance to Britain, tied to patriotism generated during the war, was also undoubtedly strong. But the post-war Labour government, and the Conservatives after them, were constantly anxious to emphasize that the state in Britain was the symbol of common values, justly attracting the allegiance of its citizens. Utilizing techniques of 'public information presentation', 'public relations exercises' and 'public opinion management' developed before and during the war, governments went to extraordinary lengths to try to manage opinion, to reinforce acceptance of the state's authority, and to create 'consensus' (see Scannell, 1984). There seems little doubt that governments judged these efforts necessary – further interesting evidence of the unsteady state of consent.

The grounds for allegiance to the nation-state are, of course, complex. But one key factor should not go unmentioned. Victory in war against Nazi Germany had confirmed the importance of some of the freedoms that can be enjoyed in a political democracy like Britain. The Labour Party seemed the 'natural heir' to the institutions which nourish such freedoms *and* to the aspirations which sought an extension of 'liberty, equality and fraternity'. The election of the Labour Party in 1945 confirmed a desire for a programme of change that might slowly establish a socially undivided nation. Labour politicians and later Conservative governments claimed to diagnose adequately the deficiencies in British 'old ways' and promised to rectify them.[3] In so doing they further enhanced expectations of change.

There is an important implication of such high hopes and aspirations: if political and social changes are not undertaken, or if changes are found inadequate, or if they fail perpetually, the scope for disappointment and disillusionment with government and perhaps the state more generally is great. Instrumental consent claims within it this possibility.

In short, neither a system of 'shared values' nor of 'ideological domination' simply conferred legitimacy on the British political system in the post-war years from 1945 to the 1960s. The situation was far more complicated. The complications can be highlighted further by examining the second major point of overlap between the theorists of the 'end of ideology' and 'one dimensionality', that is, the focus on the stability of the political and social order. For the biggest difficulty faced by all this literature on consensus, be it voluntary or contrived, is the sequence of events which followed its publication. With the prosperity of the post-war years it appeared that many, if not all, of the interests of social groups, elites and classes could be accommodated in the politics of the expanding welfare state. Prosperity helped sustain the illusion that the acquiescence of the mass of people meant legitimacy of the political and social order. A simple rosy picture of post-war political harmony and stable prosperity is heavily compromised, however, by a whole variety of economic, political and cultural developments.

The economy

The post-war revival of foreign trade provided almost ideal conditions for successive government attempts to manage economic growth and to redeem the promise of steadily increasing affluence. The idea of a managed economy working at full capacity with adequate provision for the welfare of all citizens seemed to fit reasonably well with the actuality of the immediate post-war years; increased prosperity and expanding opportunities were enjoyed by many. Although British industry had been damaged and severely disrupted during the war, the position of many of Britain's future major competitors (for instance, Germany, France and Japan) appeared much worse; and there was still a supply of relatively cheap raw materials from the empire, as well as special 'protected' markets for British goods. Britain's long commercial and trading history placed it in what seemed a strong international position.

The favourable economic conditions of the early 1950s, which made full employment, price stability and growth all seem possible simultaneously, soon, however, began to melt away. In practically all spheres the performance of the British economy was outstripped by its major competitors. Investment levels were chronically low, profitability was in decline, productivity poor, real wages – while slowly increasing – fell behind those of many other industrial capitalist countries. The terms of trade worsened, there were periodic currency crises, and markets were lost. A series of deepening political–business or 'stop-go' cycles – involving seemingly endless booms followed by sharp downturns in economic activity – became a marked feature of political and economic life. Indicators of worsening economic difficulties were steadily declining rates of growth, progressively rising levels of unemployment and inflation and steadily declining company profits.[4] While problems of unemployment and inflation, among other things, were to become testing problems facing *all* Western capitalist states from the 1970s, the particularly sharp decline of the British economy relative to its competitors is unmistakable (Glyn and Sutcliffe, 1972; Jessop, 1980; Bornstein et al., 1984).

One of the distinctive features of the British economy is its extensive and deeply rooted overseas commitments which helped give Britain such a preeminent position in world trade throughout the nineteenth century. The City of London flourished in this context and became one of the world's leading financial centres. It is worth stressing certain aspects of the City's economic and political position, for it is crucial to understanding British politics and the place of the state in social and economic life (Rubinstein, 1976; Nairn, 1977; Ingham, 1982).

The significance of the City as an economic centre dates from the preindustrial expansion of world trade. The City's commercial and banking activities developed partly through the financing of this trade and partly through the financing of the state itself, for instance, its armies and overseas exploits. From the outset, the City was oriented to the international economy, to the financing of commerce and debt. This orientation was reinforced, Geoffrey Ingham has shown, by several nineteenth-century developments all of which led to the rapid expansion of London's management of international mercantile and monetary transactions. Thus, the City's main interest became the 'buying and selling of money (in all forms); of stocks and shares; of commodities and commercial services such as insurance' (Ingham, 1982, pp. 219–20). This had major consequences for domestic industry in Britain and for employment prospects as well. Ingham refers to a 'disjuncture' of practices and interests between the City and domestic industry. On the one hand, the City is oriented toward short-term gains from a high volume and fast turnover of commercial transactions while, on the other hand, industry works for profitability on a longer time-scale, since its investments take time to implement and mature. This disjuncture, moreover, has always showed itself in two ways:

> First, in the low level of long-term external finance for productive industry [that is, loans and credit available from sources other than productive industry itself], and secondly, the political implementation and defence of policies designed to maintain London as an open, unrestricted market place with a currency strong enough to be a basis for international mercantile and banking transactions. (Ingham, 1982, p. 220)

The influence of those in political life who still believe in the durability of the British state with its old world role (concerned with, for instance, the maintenance of a strong pound, defence of foreign investments and high expenditure on arms and military material) and City interests (concerned with, among other things, a strong pound to maintain the value of overseas investments, high interest rates to increase income levels and the free flow of capital for investment abroad) remains considerable and combines to help sustain the City's powerful position in British politics and economics.

The twentieth-century erosion of Britain's world economic and political position has had very uneven effects on different sections of the economy. While the output of Britain's industrial 'workshops', especially after the Second World War, became less and less significant in world manufacturing, the City of London retained a leading role. It is clear that the interests of the City – of banking, commerce and overseas trade generally – are not necessarily those of British domestic industry; and, in fact, British economic policy from the mid-1950s to the early 1970s was caught in a vicious circle – trying to satisfy first one then the other of these interests and, in the end, satisfying neither adequately. The point has been well put by Jessop:

> since this attempt required a free flow of capital for portfolio and industrial investment overseas and entailed heavy expenditure on foreign aid to maintain the overseas sterling area, production of arms and military material, and defence of foreign investments, markets and vital sources of supply, governments were forced to concentrate their efforts on increasing the reserves and eliminating the deficit on visible trade. However, since the state was also operating in the context of the post-war settlement between capital and labour, it could not pursue these policies to the point where full employment and welfare expenditure were

threatened. The overall effect of these complex structural and political constraints on the conduct of the government's policy was continual oscillation
between deflation and reflation triggered in turn by sterling crises and rising
unemployment. (Jessop, 1980, pp. 31–2)

Financial and overseas interests have been able, within the Treasury and the
Bank of England in particular, to sustain concerns with sterling, currency
reserves and balance of payments over and against increased public expenditure, full employment and economic growth (see P. Hall, in Bornstein et al.,
1984). Moreover, the complex (and often contradictory) pressures facing the
state from the City and much domestic industry have not eased with time,
although their form, as we will see later, has undergone change.

The steady decline in the fortunes of British industry was one of the key
factors facing British politicians from the late 1950s. Although a variety of
economic packages were presented by Conservative and Labour governments
in the 1960s and early 1970s, a sense of the steady deterioration of the British
economy was more marked by the early 1970s than it had been at the start of
the 1960s.

Industrial conflict and strikes

The theorists of the end of ideology and one-dimensionality, while they did
not predict the end of all industrial conflict, certainly provided an inadequate
framework for its comprehension. Far from waning or, as some put it, 'withering away', strikes remained a persistent and much-discussed feature of British
industrial relations. From the late 1950s to the 1970s, while strike-rates varied,
strikes were one of a variety of indicators of the low level of trust between both

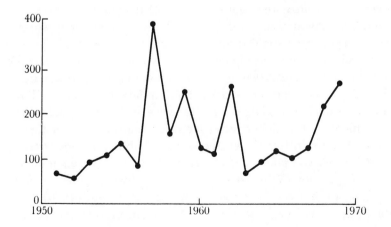

Figure 4.1   The volume of strikes (days 'lost' per 1,000 workers) in the UK (*Source*:
Hibbs, 1976, p. 1041).

POWER AND LEGITIMACY

parties of industry (Fox, 1974). The data on strike volume (days 'lost' per 1,000 wage- and salary-workers) is represented in figure 4.1 above. After 1968 there was a marked increase in strike activity, especially during the Edward Heath government's attempt in the early 1970s to restructure industrial relations legislation. This can be gleaned from the data presented in table 4.1.

Table 4.1   UK strike activity, 1967–1973/4

	1967	1968	1969	1970	1971	1972	1973	1974
Number of strikes	2116	2378	3116	3906	2228	2497	2873	2922
Number of workers involved (1,000s)	734	2258	1665	1801	1178	1734	1528	1626
Number of days lost (1,000s)	2787	4690	6846	10,980	13,551	23,909	7197	14,750

Economically active population 1971: 25,715,000, Population Census.

Source: *Year Book of Labour Statistics, 1977*, ILO. © 1977, International Labour Organization, Geneva.

One of the most significant features of strike activity is the way it is related to the state of the economy. In a variety of interesting studies Douglas Hibbs has shown how strike volume varies with, among other things, the demand for labour (Hibbs, 1976; 1978). Hibbs's analyses affirm what the historian Eric Hobsbawm has called 'the common sense of demanding concessions when conditions are favourable' (1952). As Hibbs explains: 'the working class exercises considerable sophistication in the use of the strike weapon. The pronounced inverse relationship between the volume of industrial conflict and the rate of unemployment demonstrates that on the whole strikes are timed to capitalise on the strategic advantages of a tight labour market' (Hibbs, 1976, p. 1057). Not only are strikes related to levels of unemployment – the lower unemployment is, the higher the strike-rates tend to be – but they are also related to changes in real wages and profits. Hibbs concludes that far from being simple 'reactive phenomena', strikes can be interpreted in no other way than as an expression of the struggle for power between social classes over the distribution of resources, especially over national income (1978).

Hibbs's analyses show how class conflict is an inextricable feature of the cyclical movements of the economy. The crises faced by the state's 'economic managers' (in government, the Treasury, etc.) are in part both a symptom of this conflict and a crucial obstacle to strategies for its resolution. The attempts by Conservative and Labour governments alike in the 1960s and early 1970s to reform the industrial relations system met with little, if any, success. The period under review in this part of the essay ended, as is well known, with the fall of the Heath government at the hands of, among others, the British miners.

Of course, strikes are only one of the more obvious manifestations of intense social conflict. In some sense they are the tip of the iceberg: resistance to changing work practices, absenteeism, high labour turnover, industrial sabotage are among a range of other symptoms. But perhaps one of the most remarkable features of the 1950s and 1960s was the growth of unofficial strikes and the shop stewards movement. This was not simply a result of changes on the side of management, although changes in the organization of production – its progressive rationalization and centralization – undoubtedly played a part. The biggest trade unions had got progressively bigger in the inter-war and post-war years. Increased size did not make the representation of local concerns and interests easier. Middlemas goes so far as to say that the biggest of the unions were engaged in a 'cult of size' and that this 'turned what had once been manageable institutions into sprawling, precarious empires vulnerable both to unofficial shop-floor revolt and employer's counter-attacks' (Middlemas, 1979, p. 392). Certainly, the growth of massive trade unions went hand in hand with another trend: those excluded from the formation of wage and other policies at the national level asserted their independence on the shopfloor.

Throughout the 1950s unofficial stoppages increased and a marked trend developed toward superimposing local wage agreements on to national settlements. The attempt to control wages and especially local 'wage drift' (the difference between actual earnings and officially agreed rates at national or industry level) with incomes policies in the 1960s only further alienated rank-and-file workers. The prices and incomes policies of the Labour government in the middle and late 1960s had short-run successes, but each small success seemed to be followed by a crescendo of wage increases. Labour Party attempts in the late 1960s to reform the 'unofficial movement' of the shopfloor (elaborated in *In Place of Strife*) – to make this movement more amenable to control by trade-union officials and government alike – foundered, as did the Conservative attempt that followed (the Industrial Relations Act 1971). Traditional management prerogatives, the policy-making capacity of government as well as the very rule of law were under challenge (Hyman, 1972; Lane, 1974; Middlemas, 1979; Jessop, 1980). The fragility of tripartite negotiations or 'corporatist arrangements' was clear: they were arrangements amongst formal leaderships who often perhaps shared more in common with each other than they did with their constituencies.

State expenditures and fiscal crisis

The post-war reconstruction involved the state in the finance of permanently high levels of expenditure (see G. Thompson, 1984). By the early 1970s total public expenditure rose to over 50 per cent of gross national product (GNP) and the British state began to face a series of escalating deficits (see Gough, 1975). In the wake of the 'post-war settlement', the attempt to maintain full employment and to meet extensive welfare obligations imposed on the state rapidly escalating costs. In the context of the overall deterioration in Britain's economic performance the problems of meeting these costs through taxation and borrowing became ever more acute. The result was the mushrooming 'fiscal crisis' of the state; that is, the tendency of state expenditures to outrun revenues (O'Connor, 1973).

The fiscal crisis of the British state is a symptom of a multiplicity of difficulties: foremost among these are problems which derive from the attempts to sustain a highly regulated economy with maximum employment possibilities while simultaneously meeting the demands and interests of, among others, domestic industry, the export sector, financial centres like the City and the various sectors of the labour movement. The pervasive dissensus between classes, the fragile nature of much working-class political consent, the risk that industrial conflict might spill over directly into challenges to government, law and the state, provided enormous pressures on successive governments to expand the range of the activities of state agencies. This was reflected not only in successive governments' expenditure on health, education and social security, but in a variety of direct financial aids (for example cheap energy from the nationalized industries), tax allowances and budgetary assistance to industry (Gough, 1975). A series of government attempts to advance the rationalization and reorganization of industry through, among other things, the introduction of planning experiments, was also a prominent feature of the time.

But the mounting pressures on state expenditure did not just derive from the immediate circumstances of the post-war years. Britain's past global role and politicians' seeming reluctance to adjust to 'second division' status meant continually high levels of military and related expenditures compared, for instance, to other European countries and Japan (Cambridge Political Economy Group, 1974). While at one time such policies had clearly been essential to the maintenance of overseas trade, markets and financial dealings, they were arguably at least – as they still are now – anachronistic, and another heavy burden on Treasury resources. Finally, it is worth mentioning the increase in expenditure on the police and judiciary, an item that has continued to grow especially rapidly – one more indicator perhaps of social and political tension.

Electoral scepticism and party politics

Rising standards of living throughout most of the 1950s, 1960s and early 1970s provide a somewhat paradoxical background to the deepening shadow of economic crisis and political difficulties. Successive governments accepted the credit for improvements in standards of living and, at every election, the political parties assumed the burden of responsibility for high aspirations (Moss, 1982, p. 151). But the responsibility assumed by these political agents has, as Middlemas aptly put it, 'contrasted unfavourably with the actual inability of the state . . . to accomplish its declared job of delivering a consistently better future' (Middlemas, 1979, p. 424). It is far easier to assess actual political performance when pretensions and promises are so clearly advertised.

There is evidence of growing scepticism and disenchantment with traditional party politics throughout the period 1945–early 1970s. The two major parties together attracted an ever smaller proportion of the total vote, while the share of third-party votes increased. All winning parties had the support of only a minority, support which dropped to not more than one-third of the electorate (a level at which it has remained ever since). Although electoral trends are hard to interpret accurately, these trends – along with huge swings in by-elections in the 1960s, the mixed fortunes of the Scottish and Welsh Nationalists, the marked decline of Labour votes in traditional Labour strongholds – combined to suggest growing disillusionment, uncertainty and volatility in support for the dominant parties. Electoral studies appeared to confirm this suggestion (Butler and Stokes, 1974). The politics of the centre-ground, 'Butskellism', or what one might call the politics of 'crisis avoidance', appeared throughout the 1960s and early 1970s to be less and less attractive to voters.

By the middle of the 1960s Harold Wilson's Labour Party claimed the mantle of 'the natural party of government'. Pursuing policies preoccupied with establishing 'national unity', Wilson sought (as did James Callaghan and Denis Healey in the late 1970s) to hold together the rapidly eroding centre-ground of British politics. Labour became ever more the party of the status quo: the party of the regulatory state, the declining mixed economy – 'tightened belts' – and the massive inequalities which persisted in all spheres of life (see Panitch, 1976). It was on this ground that it was so easily out-manoeuvred by the Conservatives under Edward Heath in 1970 (and later by Margaret Thatcher) under anti-'big state', anti-bureaucratic, anti-corporate, anti-union banners – banners suggesting the possibility of radical change on behalf of the individual, the family and law and order.

While the declared ideologies of the major parties began to polarize in the late 1960s, the political achievements of both remained firmly on the centre-ground. Edward Heath's famous U-turn in 1972 seemed to be just more evidence that party programmes meant relatively little in practice and that all governments 'changed direction' in office. In this context, widespread scepticism and cynicism about party politics is not perhaps too difficult to understand.

The authority of the state in question? 1968 and after

Increasing unemployment and inflation, the general decline in the performance of the economy compared to major competitors, rising levels of official and unofficial industrial conflict, challenges to the 'rule of law' during such conflict, mounting fiscal difficulties meeting the costs of the welfare interventionist state, growing signs of disillusionment with the two dominant parties, electoral scepticism in the face of the claims of politicians: all of these were signs indicating that within and underlying the state and the political system there were deeply structured difficulties. While the state had become immensely complex, it remained in general much less monolithic and much less capable of imposing clear direction than Marcuse had suggested, and less legitimate than the theorists of the end of ideology had thought. By the end of the 1960s few denied that dissensus was rife: the certitude and confidence of the middle-ground (and largely of the middle and upper classes) was slipping away; and the instrumental consent of segments of the working class seemed to be giving way to progressive disillusionment and conflict.

The 1968–9 period was something of a turning-point (Hall et al., 1978). The anti-Vietnam-war movement, the student movement and a host of other political groups associated with the New Left began to alter the political pace: it was a time of astonishing political polarization. Demands for peace, the end of imperialism, resistance to racism, the extension of democratic rights to industry, sexual freedom, the liberation of women, were just some of the issues which produced unparalleled scenes of protest in (post-war) London and took France to the edge of revolution in May 1968. The new movements seemed to define themselves against almost everything that the traditional political system defended. They defined the system as rigid, regimented, authoritarian and empty of moral, spiritual and personal qualities. A mass rebellion against one-dimensionality which Marcuse had thought possible but unlikely in 1964 (the year *One Dimensional Man* was published), appeared on the verge of development.

Widespread dissent was met by, among other things, the 'heavy hand' of state power: violent clashes involving riot police were frequently reported in the press. These conflicts were interlaced with further pressures on the state: the revival of nationalist movements in Wales and Scotland and, of course, the intensification of struggle in Northern Ireland. 'The Break-up of Britain', the title of one well-known book about the period, certainly seemed imaginable (Nairn, 1977).

Moral panics

The developments from the late 1950s to the early 1970s had a profoundly unsettling effect on the standard-bearers of 'traditional' morality: those who in government, the media, independent (public) schools, among other places, saw themselves as the arch-defenders of the best of '*the* British way of life'. Tracing the history of this defence from its earliest manifestations, Stuart Hall and others have argued in a provocative work that it begins

> with the unresolved ambiguities and contradictions of affluence, of the post-war 'settlement'. It is experienced, first, as a diffuse social unease, as an unnaturally accelerated pace of social change, as an unhingeing of stable patterns, moral points of reference. It manifests itself, first, as an unlocated surge of social anxiety . . . Later, it appears to focus on more tangible targets: specifically, on the anti-social nature of youth movements, on the threat to British life by the black immigrant, and on the 'rising fever chart' of crime. Later still – as the major social upheavals of the counter-culture and the political student movements become more organized as social forces – it surges, in the form of a more focused 'social anxiety', around these points of disturbance. It names what is wrong in general terms: it is the permissiveness of social life. Finally, as the crisis deepens, and the forms of conflict and dissent assume a more explicitly political and a more clearly delineated class form, social anxiety also precipitates in its more political form. It is directed against the organized power of the working class: against political extremism; against trade union blackmail; against the threat of anarchy. (Hall et al., 1978, p. 321)

This analysis is important, for it reminds us how extraordinarily complex are the patterns of political and social change and reaction. The political events of the late 1960s and early 1970s cannot simply be characterized by the emergence of radical movements. Reaction to them was also strong and this reaction was not simply located in 'the establishment', in the centres of 'patrician culture'.[5] Scepticism about politics, the demise of the centre-ground in party affairs, fear about 'lack of direction', can become the basis of a call for 'new leadership', the firm application of 'law and order', the affirmation of the 'need for control' of all those who threaten the status quo. The anxieties of many – from all sorts of class, occupation and social position – can become a foundation for a massive defence of the state against all kinds of perceived threats, and the basis of a new 'strong state'.

It is time to take stock of the argument so far. Neither the theories of the 'end of ideology' nor 'one-dimensionality' can account adequately for the relation between state and society, the instability of the economy and government policy, and the persistence and escalation of tension and conflict which emerged in the post-war years. The joint preoccupation of these theories with compliance, consensus and integration of social groups into the political order led them to overlook the different meanings of compliance and integration and the *conditional* nature of much acquiescence. Mass acquiescence to dominant institutions in the post-war years by no means entailed the mass legitimation of the British state. That this is so is amply borne out by the palpable lack of political and social stability in the 1960s and early 1970s. While this certainly did *not* add up to a major revolutionary attack upon the state, it constituted a severe test of the very foundation of the political order. A crisis of the state *seemed* to be developing.

What exactly was the nature of the crisis? How were its dimensions to be analysed? What were its origins and causes? Were the strengths and limits of state power really exposed?

Contrasting accounts of the crisis of the state: overloaded state or legitimation crisis?

What is a crisis? A distinction must be drawn between, on the one hand, a partial crisis (or phase of limited stability) and, on the other, a crisis which might lead to the transformation of a society. The former refers to such phenomena as the political–business cycle – involving booms and recessions in economic activity – which have been a chronic feature of the British economy. The latter refers to the undermining of the core or organizational principle of a society; that is, to the erosion or destruction of those societal relations which determine the scope and limits to change for, among other things, political and economic activity (see essay 3). A crisis of this second type – which I shall refer to as a 'crisis with transformative potential' – involves challenges to the very core of the political and social order.

In marked contrast to those political analysts of the 1950s and early 1960s who talked about 'integration', 'consensus', 'political stability', etc., those thinking about the late 1960s and 1970s were struck by almost the opposite. The work of recent political science and political sociology reflects preoccupations with 'British decline', 'a breakdown in consensus', 'the crisis of the state'. This section will set out briefly the arguments of two contrasting theories of crisis – theories which try to make sense of the events of the 1960s and early 1970s. The contrast is, again, between writers arguing from the premises of a pluralist theory of politics, and authors arguing from the premises of Marxist theory. Both groups of writers, it is worth stressing, are staunch 'revisionists'; that is, they have modified substantially the theories which they take as their starting-points.

The first group – arguing from pluralist premises – can be referred to as theorists of 'overloaded government'; the second group – arguing from Marxist premises – develop a theory of 'legitimation crisis'. The writers who discuss 'overloaded government' include Brittan (1975 and 1977), Huntingdon (1975), Nordhaus (1975), King (1976) and Rose and Peters (1977). The theory of 'legitimation crisis' has been developed by, among others, Habermas (1976) and Offe (1984) (cf. essays 2 and 3).[6] For the purposes of this essay it is unnecessary to follow all the details of these writers' analyses, nor do we have to follow the differences in emphasis between, say, King (1976) and Brittan (1975). It will be enough to present broad general summaries of the two positions. I shall leave their appraisal until later.

It should be emphasized that both these contrasting accounts of the crises facing the modern state focus on the possibility of 'crisis with transformative potential'. But while theorists of overload are clearly warning of this as a danger and/or menace to the state (and suggest measures of containment and control), the theorists of 'legitimation crisis' see this as presenting both difficult political dilemmas and potentiality for decisive, progressive, radical change. It is also noteworthy that overload theorems have been influential in party political circles and much discussed in general ways in the media. Theories of legitimation crisis have remained by and large the province of some left-wing political analysts, although they have gained influence in more general academic circles recently.

To help comprehension of the arguments I have set out the key steps of each in diagram form: figures 4.2 and 4.3. I shall go over each of these steps briefly, connecting some of the major points to illustrations from British politics.

The overloaded government

1a A pluralist starting-point: the theorists of the overloaded state frequently characterize power relations in terms of fragmentation – power is shared and bartered by numerous groups representing diverse and competing interests, for example business organizations, trade unions, parties, ethnic groups, students, prison officers, women's institutes, defenders of blood sports, etc. Hence, political outcomes are determined by democratic processes and pressures; governments try to mediate and adjudicate between demands.

1b The post-war market society plus the early successes of Keynesian economic policy generated rising mass affluence and the general prosperity of the post-war years, for example booms in consumer goods, new housing, spread of television and entertainment industries.

2 Accordingly, expectations increased, linked to higher standards of living, for example annual increments in income and welfare, availability of schooling and higher education.

3 Aspirations were reinforced by a 'decline in deference' or respect for

authority and status. This is itself a result of, among other things, growing affluence, 'free' welfare, health and education which undermines private initiative and responsibility, and egalitarian and meritocratic ideologies which promised much more than could ever be achieved realistically.

4   In this context, groups press politicians and governments hard to meet their particular aims and ambitions, for example higher wages (most employed groups), protection of jobs in declining industrial sectors (some trade unions), high interest rates (banks), low interest rates (borrowers, including domestic industry), low prices (consumer groups), higher prices (some business organizations).

5   In order to secure maximum votes politicians too often promise more than they can deliver, and sometimes promise to deliver contradictory and therefore impossible sets of demands: competition between parties leads to a spiral of ever greater promises.

6   Thus, aspirations are reinforced; political parties are seen by the general population as competing means to the same end, that is, better standards of living.

7   In government, parties all too often pursue strategies of appeasement for fear of losing future votes. 'Firm action', for example, to set the economy on the 'right path' or deal with 'young offenders' is postponed or never taken.

8   Appeasement strategies and the pursuit of self-interest by administrators lead to ever more state agencies (in health, education, industrial relations, prices and incomes, etc.) of increasingly unwieldy proportions. 'Faceless' bureaucracies develop which often fail to meet the ends for which they were originally designed.

9   The state is ever less able to provide firm effective management faced as it is with, for instance, the spiralling costs of its programmes. Public spending becomes excessive and inflation just one symptom of the problem.

10   As the state expands it progressively destroys the realm of individual initiative, the space for 'free, private enterprise'.

11   A vicious circle is set in motion (go back to circle 4 on figure 4.2 and carry on around), which can be broken only by, among other things, 'firm', 'decisive' political leadership less responsive to democratic pressures and demands.

Legitimation crisis of the state

In contrast to the theory of overloaded government, I shall now set out legitimation crisis theory. Its main elements are as follows:

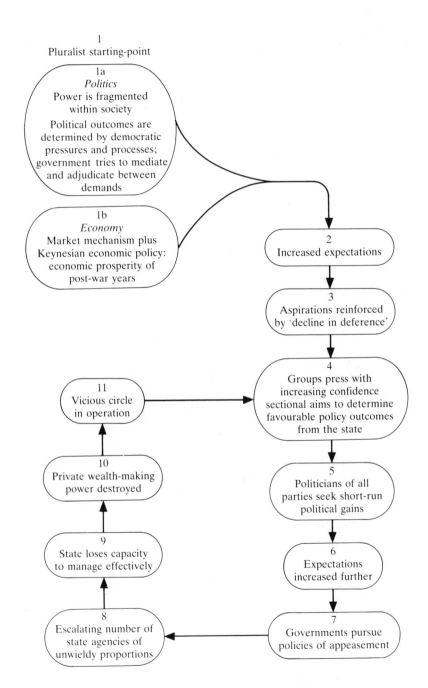

Figure 4.2 Overloaded government: crisis of liberal welfare state.

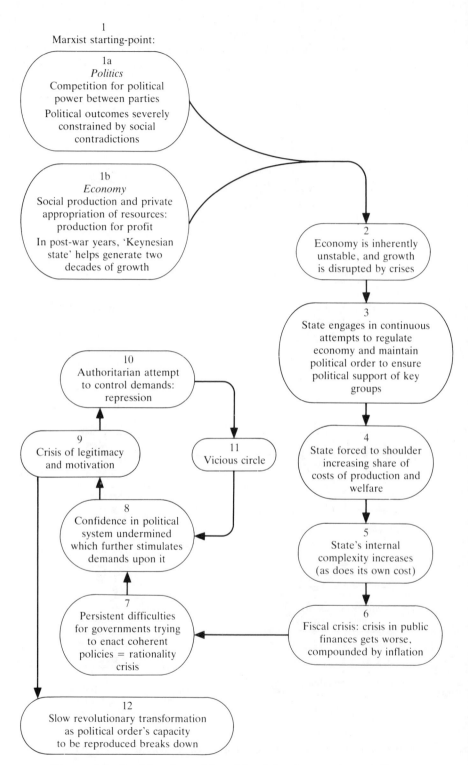

Figure 4.3 Legitimation crisis: crisis of the democratic capitalist state.

1a A Marxist starting-point: while political parties compete for office through the formal rules of democratic and representative processes, their power is severely constrained by the state's dependence on resources generated to a very large extent by private capital accumulation. The state has thus a general 'interest' in facilitating processes of capital accumulation: hence it takes decisions which are compatible in the long-run with business (capitalist) interests. At one and the same time, the state must appear neutral between all (class) interests so mass electoral support can be sustained.

1b The economy is organized through the private appropriation of resources which are socially produced (that is, produced via a complex web of interdependence between people). Production is organized for profit maximization. The 'Keynesian state' in the immediate post-war period helped to sustain two decades of remarkable prosperity.

2 But the economy is inherently unstable: economic growth is constantly disrupted by crises. The increasingly extensive effects of changes within the system (high rates of unemployment and inflation at the troughs and peaks of the political–business cycle) and/or the impact of external factors (shortages of raw materials as a result of international political events, for instance) have had to be carefully managed.

3 Accordingly, if the economic and political order of contemporary societies is to be maintained, extensive state intervention is required. The principal concerns of the state become sustaining the capitalist economy and managing class antagonisms (through agencies, for example, of welfare, social security and law and order). The state must constantly act to ensure the acquiescence and support of powerful groups, especially the business community and trade unions.

4 In order to avoid economic and political crises governments take on responsibility for more and more areas of the economy and civil society, for example the rescue of industries in trouble. Why? Because a bankruptcy of a large firm or bank has, among other things, implications for numerous apparently sound enterprises, whole communities, and hence for political stability.

5 In order to fulfil their increasingly diversified roles, governments and the state more generally have had to expand their administrative structures (for example enlargement of the civil service), thus increasing their own internal complexity. This growing complexity, in turn, entails an increased need for cooperation and, more importantly, requires an expanding state budget.

6 The state must finance itself through taxation and loans from capital markets, but it cannot do this in a way which will interfere with the accumulation process and jeopardize economic growth. These con-

straints have helped to create a situation of almost permanent inflation and crisis in public finances.

7   The state cannot develop adequate policy strategies within the systematic constraints it encounters; the result is a pattern of continuous change and breakdown in government policy and planning (for example stop-go policy, the fluctuating use of incomes policy). Habermas and Offe refer to this as a 'rationality crisis' or a 'crisis of rational administration'. The state, controlled by a Conservative government, cannot drastically reduce its costs and spending for fear of the power of unions to cause large-scale disruption; the state, controlled by Labour, cannot efficiently pursue strong socialist policies, because business confidence would be undermined and the economy might be drastically weakened. Hence, governments of different persuasions come and go, and policy chops and changes.

8   The state's growing intervention in the economy and other spheres draws attention to issues of choice, planning and control. More and more areas of life are seen by the general population as politicized, that is, as falling within its (via the government's) potential control. This development, in turn, stimulates ever greater demands on the state, for example, for participation and consultation over decisions.

9   If these demands cannot be fulfilled within available alternatives, the state may face a 'legitimation and motivation crisis'. Struggles over, among other things, income, control over the work-place, the nature and quality of state goods and services, might spill beyond the boundaries of existing institutions of economic management and political control.

10   In this situation, a 'strong state' may emerge: a state which places 'order' above everything else, repressing dissent and forcefully diffusing crises. Authoritarian states smashed most forms of opposition in the late 1930s and 1940s in central and southern Europe. One cannot rule out such attempts occurring again – or, much more likely, representative governments using progressively more 'strong arm' tactics.

11   If one of the two scenarios in point 10 occurs, a vicious circle may be set in motion. Move back to circle 8 (figure 4.3) and carry on around.

12   However, the fundamental transformation of the system cannot be ruled out: it is unlikely to result from *an* event, an insurrectional overthrow of state power; it is more likely to be marked by a process – the continuous erosion of the existing order's capacity to be reproduced and the progressive emergence of alternative socialist institutions (for example state agencies taking more industry into public ownership, state organization of ever more resources according to need not profit, extension of work-place and community democracy).

Crisis theories: initial assessment

How are we to assess these two contrasting theories of mounting political crisis? There are many significant differences between the theorists of over-loaded government and legitimation crisis, some of which I shall discuss in a moment. None the less, they also appear to share a common thread. First, governmental, or more generally state, power is the capacity for effective political action. Second, state power depends ultimately on the acceptance of the authority of the state (overload theorists) or on legitimacy (legitimation crisis theorists). Third, state power (measured by the ability of the state to resolve the claims and difficulties it faces) is being progressively eroded. The state is increasingly hamstrung or ineffective (overload theorists, points 7–9) or short on rationality (legitimation crisis theorists, point 7). Fourth, state power is being undermined because its authority or legitimacy is declining progressively. For overload theorists the 'taut and strained' relationship between government and social groups can be explained by increased expectations, excessive demands related to, among other things, the decline in deference. Legitimation crisis theorists, in turn, focus on the way increased state intervention undermines traditionally unquestioned values and norms and politicizes ever more issues, that is, opens them up to political debate and conflict.

Although the emphasis of Offe's and Habermas's work is more explicitly on legitimation, both overload and legitimation crisis theorists claim that state power is being eroded in the face of growing demands and claims: in one case these demands are regarded as 'excessive', in the other they are regarded as the practically inevitable result of the contradictions within which the state is enmeshed. But, on both views, state power and political stability alter with changes to the pattern of values and norms.

While these theories offer a number of important insights, they also raise some fundamental questions: is the authority or legitimacy of the state eroding to the point where we are justified in talking about a mounting political crisis with transformative potential? Is state power eroding in the manner depicted? Is the state increasingly vulnerable to political and social turmoil?

I have three fundamental objections to the 'common thread' which runs through overload and legitimation crisis theory. First, there is no clear empirical evidence to support the claim of a progressively worsening crisis of the state's authority or legitimacy. Second, it is not obvious that state power is eroding. Both overload and legitimation crisis theorists tend to treat the state as an 'empty' box through which things pass. This fundamentally under-estimates, in my view, the state's own capabilities and resources which derive from, for example, its administrative and coercive apparatuses. Finally, while particular *governments* may be vulnerable when citizens fail to confer legitimacy, the *state* itself is not necessarily more vulnerable to collapse or disintegration. The question of the vulnerability of the contemporary British state needs to be looked at again carefully.

Accordingly, in the remainder of this section, I shall explore at greater length issues about forms of political orientation. In the next section I shall relate the discussion to contemporary British politics and argue that recent developments can only be properly understood in light of the way the modern British state developed in the context of both national and international pressures. I will then draw together many of the points made hitherto and present a model to help illuminate the way the political order coheres. The final section will offer a few brief concluding remarks.

Schism, antagonism and legitimacy

Many authors have been critical about claims that value consensus, or a common system of political attitudes and beliefs, is widespread in Britain: there is more 'dissensus' between classes than there is 'consensus'. But while the degree to which the political and social order is regarded as 'worthy', as legitimate, is to a significant extent related to class, the research on these issues has not been extensive, studies often leave a lot to be desired, and the evidence is not always without its ambiguities. With this in mind, I shall review the findings of a few key works.[7]

Some of the central issues have been explored by Abercrombie et al. (1980). They argue that there is little historical evidence to support the view that there is either a common value system, or a one-dimensional ideology, or widespread legitimation. 'Bourgeois individualism', the secular ideology of a rising entrepreneurial class in the seventeenth and eighteenth centuries, did not diffuse downwards to the emergent class of wage-workers. Their compliance in the series of changes that led to the ascendancy of capitalistic enterprise was secured, first of all, by their forcible expropriation from the land and then by the economic necessity of having to find paid employment. So far as contemporary capitalism is concerned, the authors accept the view of Mann and others that the bulk of the working class holds beliefs less coherent in character and, in some respects, substantially divergent from those of the middle and upper classes. Affirmative perspectives on the state and economy, they contend, secure the coherence of governing elites and classes. Clearly, some groups have to be integrated into the governing political culture to ensure a society's reproduction; what matters most – and what generally can be demonstrated – is the moral approval of existing institutions by dominant groups.

Examining the evidence from research based on interviews and ethnographic studies suggests, the authors further argue, that much more weight should be given to the autonomy of working-class cultural traditions than many authors have done – traditions which *tend* to emphasize the virtues of collectivism and community over and against 'bourgeois individualism' ('getting ahead') and the naked pursuit of private property ('the drive to accumulate') (Abercrombie et al., 1980, pp. 140ff.). The evidence on attitudes to liberal–democratic institutions is less clear-cut, but the fairly consistent findings of the 1960s and 1970s they note include:

1 Between half and three-quarters of working-class respondents to surveys suggest that 'big business has too much power in society', there is 'a law for the rich and another for the poor' and 'the upper classes are hostile to working-class interests'.
2 Between two-fifths and one-half of working-class respondents did not think they had or could have 'any influence on government'.
3 Only one-third thought that the British political system 'works for the interest of most of the people most of the time'.

These findings suggest that there is a majority of working-class people who deny that liberal democracy works as its advocates say it should – as, for instance, pluralists claim it does (Abercrombie et al., 1980, p. 148). Noteworthy as this is, however, it only covers a fairly narrow range of issues which concern politics and the state.

Focusing more broadly on the latter, Dennis Kavanagh argues that the picture of political consent in Britain presented in textbooks – emphasizing the pervasiveness of the qualities of 'consensus, pragmatism, gradualism, tolerance, limited partisanship and deference' – is anything but borne out by his survey of recent evidence uncovered in political science (Kavanagh, 1980, pp. 124–76). He reports the findings under a number of headings, the most significant aspects of which I have summarized briefly below:

1 *On pride in the system of government.* Widespread disaffection is noted. For instance, the large-scale *Attitudes Survey* conducted for the 1970 Royal Commission on the Constitution reported a 'general feeling of dissatisfaction' with the 'system of running Britain'. Nearly half (49 per cent) favoured some change while 'only 5 per cent thought things could not be improved'.
2 *On partisanship between parties.* The evidence to the mid-1970s shows growing disillusionment with the two dominant parties; voters saw ever fewer differences between them. In 1951 only 20 per cent polled by Gallup thought the parties 'much of a muchness', by 1974 the figure was 45 per cent (although this figure is, I suspect, much lower again today).
3 *On trust in government.* While the 'totally cynical' about government and the political system amount to only between 10 and 15 per cent of those studied, on none of four conventional political science measures of trust in

government does 'a majority offer a "trusting" response' in a recent work (see Marsh, 1978).

4 *On a sense of belonging to a national community.* The sense of belonging to a 'British community' is weak outside England. Most Scots and Welsh people identify with their own respective nationalities, while people in Northern Ireland divide their loyalties between Ulster and Ireland (Rose, 1974). The political movements in Northern Ireland amount, of course, to the severest challenge to the authority of the British government.

5 *On influencing government.* In 1969 over 60 per cent of those sampled in an extensive study felt that government paid 'not much' attention to what ordinary people think (Butler and Stokes, 1974).

Relating such findings to phenomena such as the demise in support for the two major parties, demands for devolution, increased political violence, etc., Kavanagh asks whether the British political system is faced with a growing crisis of legitimacy (Kavanagh, 1980, p. 152). He stresses that it is important to distinguish attitudes to the state generally from attitudes to particular groups of leaders; and while much dissatisfaction is related to the latter, he believes that general political consent is unstable. Two reasons are given (p. 170). First, 'no great popular confidence exists' in political institutions (although the absence of a pronounced desire for 'radical change' is also noted). Second, traditional bonds, indicated by electoral voting patterns, are waning between class, party and nationality. The evidence highlights, Kavanagh contends, that people's relationships to party, government and the state are becoming ever more instrumental; that is, consent or loyalty is tied increasingly to the promise and actuality of better political and economic performance. Support for the political status quo is *conditional*.

Unlike Kavanagh I do not think that the phenomenon of extensive instrumental consent is new, but his review of the pertinent evidence certainly bears out the widespread nature of such attitudes. It also bears out something else that parallels Mann's findings: while legitimacy is not extensively conferred most people do not have a clear-cut conception of what alternative institutions they desire. Hence, there is reason to suspect that the distance, remoteness or even alienation people experience in connection with dominant political and economic institutions might be the basis of further political uncertainty and volatility in the future. Before concluding this section, I want to spend a moment reviewing a study conducted in 1978 by Louis Moss.

Moss's study – based on extensive interviews with over 1,300 people in England and Wales – is perhaps the most elaborate survey of opinion on government yet conducted. Its results provide additional evidence for the claims presented so far about the prevalence of dissensus between classes, high levels of ambivalence about dominant political institutions, low levels of trust, acceptance and legitimacy, and hopes for change marked by a seeming absence of clear political direction. The advantage of Moss's study is that it focuses in more detail on the various institutions of government and state. I shall just mention a few of the pertinent findings.

Beginning with the rather diffuse (but intriguing) category of 'trust in government', the study reveals that only 24 per cent thought they could 'trust government to do what is right most of the time' (Moss, 1982, p. 64). Comparative data from the University of Michigan are interesting; for they reveal that 37 per cent of those sampled in the USA in 1974 felt they could 'trust government'. It is noteworthy that this US figure was recorded *after* the retreat from Vietnam and *after* the Watergate scandal! What people understand by 'government' and 'trust' here is very uncertain, but the British figure is none the less remarkably low. The data reported in table 4.2 add further dimensions to the question of trust. Moss's comments on the findings are apposite:

Table 4.2   Branches of government, trust and interests

When you hear the word 'government', which one of these comes first to your mind? Which of these would you say is most important in deciding what is to be done? Which would you trust most to look after your interests?

	(a) Comes first to mind (%)	*(b)* Most important (%)	*(c)* Most trusted (%)
1 MPs	14.7	14.1	18.1
2 Political parties	22.2	9.2	3.7
3 Parliament	37.3	28.0	10.6
4 Government ministers	17.6	30.3	8.2
5 Civil servants	2.3	6.7	4.0
6 Local councillors	4.2	8.5	35.1
7 Don't know	1.7	3.0	7.6
8 None	—	0.4	12.9
	1,331	1,335	1,335
	(%)	(%)	(%)
2 and 3 Parties and parliament	59.5	37.2	14.3
4 and 5 Government ministers and civil servants	19.9	37.0	12.2
1 MPs	14.7	14.1	18.1
6 Local councillors	4.2	8.5	35.1

Source: Moss, 1982, p. 68.

'Parties and parliament become less important as one moves from [column] (a) to (b) and from (b) to (c). Whilst nearly 60 per cent of the sample see them as the corporate embodiment of the public face of government, less than one fifth of the sample put their trust in them as a guardian of their personal interests' (Moss, 1982, p. 69). The central representative function of British democracy seems not very highly regarded.

It is interesting that while local councillors are not thought of as very significant in the determination of political outcomes, they are conceived – in relative terms – as more 'reliable' to look after people's interests (see table 4.2 again). This and other aspects of the study bear out what might have been expected from earlier studies, that there is a clear preference for what is local: people claim to understand better local affairs and generally believe 'local representatives' are more aware of 'ordinary people's needs' – even if it is admitted that such representatives are powerless to do anything about them. These results are related to social class: the 'higher up the stratification hierarchy' one goes the more one tends to find both 'increased trust in general' *and* increased 'trust' in the central institutions of the state.

The government system based in London was widely conceived as distant and remote from 'ordinary people', and was widely reported as ineffective. Over 50 per cent of the sample claimed they did not understand the system of government 'very well'. A majority of the sample (58 per cent) thought that government had little, or at best mixed, effect on their lives. Perhaps not surprisingly nearly 40 per cent sampled were either 'rather uninterested' or 'not interested at all' in the 'affairs of government in London'. But general interest in 'London government affairs', concern for who wins the next election (because it is believed it will make a considerable difference), claims to knowledge about politics are all related to class. It seems that, as Moss puts it, 'those who feel more assured of their place in the social scene (higher socio-economic groups) are much more consistently favourable to the institutions. Presumably this may help to explain, too, their greater certainty about the electoral system' (p. 177). Finally, Moss found a substantial proportion (over 40 per cent) in favour of 'substantial changes' to the system of government but a great deal of ambivalence about what sort of change was desirable. Even those against substantial change often expressed markedly negative views about many of the institutions of liberal democracy. This all seems, as Moss maintains, 'a poor return for the constant barrage of argument, assertion and denial to which the electorate is exposed' (p. 99).

It is interesting to note in passing that while Moss's study neglected what is clearly one of the most important aspects of the British state – the monarchy – the evidence collected by earlier studies fits well with some of the themes of his work. If surveys of public opinion restrict themselves to general questions about support for the monarchy, they find that the overall level of support is high by practically any criterion, although it is especially high among top socio-economic groups and among Conservative voters. However, if attention is turned from the monarchy as a general symbol to particular aspects of it, a more complicated picture emerges. As Jessop put it, summarizing earlier findings: 'one third of the population believe royalty have too many privileges [and] one half believe the Royal Family has too much money . . . Furthermore, agreement with these criticisms is strongest among the subordinate classes and among Labour voters' (Jessop, 1974, pp. 89–90). Disagreement between classes and ambivalence about the monarchy is revealed when attitudes to it are examined in a little depth.

Summary: statement of the argument so far

There are many limits to the value of survey data: caution is required in its interpretation. But the various studies reviewed here are from a wide variety of research traditions and all rather significantly report fairly similar findings. I want to summarize the most important points now and connect them to the general concerns of the essay.

The evidence reviewed highlights further the inadequacy of the terms of reference of both the end of ideology and one-dimensionality perspectives. There is a striking absence of powerful consensual values (with the exception perhaps of a diffuse adherence to nationalism in England and, among some groups, in Northern Ireland) which might confer widespread legitimacy. There is also a striking absence of one-dimensionality: the extent to which the state, parliament and politics are regarded as 'worthy' is to a significant extent related to class. Having said this, it should be noted that the widespread scepticism, cynicism, distrust and detachment of many men and women does not amount to pervasive evidence of revolutionary views either.

Pragmatic acquiescence or instrumental orientations and conditional consent appear common among the working classes, as does a 'dual' or 'divided' consciousness. Is this phenomenon new? And is this relevant evidence of a mounting crisis of the authority of the state (overload theorists) or of legitimacy and motivation (legitimation crisis theorists)? There does not seem much evidence to support these views. (1) As I argued earlier, instrumental attitudes are not new: it is doubtful whether in the post-war years legitimacy was conferred as widely as is often thought. (2) While dissensus and conflict are rife, it is not apparent that a massive protest potential has *grown* demanding increased participation in political decision-making and developing extensive criticism of the existing economic and political order. (3) The pervasive scepticism and detachment of many men and women in their attitude to traditional forms of politics has not given way to any clear demands for alternative kinds of institutions: there is a clear absence of images of alternatives, except among rather marginal groups. But, what of the signs of conflict, the severe challenges to the way resources and rights are distributed outlined in earlier sections of this essay (pp. 108–18)?

In a nutshell, it is *not* that the end of ideology has been 'reversed', or a one-dimensional world has collapsed, or the authority of the state is suddenly in decline because demands have become excessive, or legitimacy is now undermined; rather, it is that the cynicism, scepticism, detachment of many people today fails sometimes to be offset by sufficient comforts and benefits as the economy and successive governments run into severe difficulties. The often expressed distrust has been, and can be, translated into a range of actions. The possibilities for antagonistic stances against the state – prefigured or anticipated in people's distrust of politicians, respect for the local and the common sense of ordinary people, rejection of 'experts' – are there, as indeed are germs of a variety of other kinds of political movement which seek to reassert the authority of 'the state'. That there should be antagonism and conflict is not surprising: conditional consent or pragmatic acceptance of the status quo is potentially unstable precisely because it is conditional or pragmatic.

The evidence discussed above when linked to the material on the sustained difficulties of the British economy, on official and unofficial industrial conflict, on the fiscal difficulties of the state, on electoral scepticism, on the variety of political movements stemming from the 1960s (the women's movement, anti-nuclear groups, ecological protests) and on the tensions of the inner-city areas, does suggest a number of fundamental questions. In the absence of marked consensual values how does the political order still hold together? It is clearly not simply legitimacy that provides the 'glue', that 'cements' or 'binds' the polity. On what does the 'cohesion' of the political system depend then?

The 1980s: the state at the intersection of international and national pressures

In this section I want to explore further the strength and vulnerability of the contemporary British state. I shall pursue the question of social compliance and state power but in closer relation to recent developments. Three points (which will be expanded upon throughout the section) are of particular importance to the analysis:

1   The processes which shaped the formation of the modern British state created a situation which can be characterized as one both of structural weakness (primarily as a result of the extraordinary decline in Britain's world position as a political and economic power) and of growing political strength (primarily as a result of the expansion of institutions of administration, constraint and coercion to contain, in part, the multiple economic and social difficulties linked to decline).

2   Economic crisis (indicated by unemployment, inflation, fiscal difficulties and trade deficits) and the failure hitherto of political strategies to resolve it (for example the demise of James Callaghan's and Denis Healey's Social

Contract during the 'winter of discontent' (a period of intense industrial conflict), 1978–9, or the marked decline of British manufacturing capacity under Margaret Thatcher's Conservatives) considerably increases the number of those who experience the worst effects of these problems. As the prospects for prosperity look uncertain and the political and economic system fails to 'deliver the goods' and 'deliver on promises', the potentiality of enhanced political conflict grows.

3   While there are extensive pressures and demands on the polity (as suggested by theorists of overload and legitimation crisis), the resources of state power generate sufficient scope to ensure that actual political outcomes (particular policies, coalitional arrangements and so on) are not simply determined by socio-economic forces.

Parliamentary politics from the mid-1970s was marked by Labour's attempt, after the fall of Edward Heath's government in 1974, to reforge the centre-ground in British politics and to mobilize a fresh coalition among powerful trade unions and business groups. The results of this 'corporatist strategy' are well known. Labour's claim to be able to establish a unique relation with both trade unions and industry was heavily compromised by the sustained strikes of 1978–9. At the time of writing it seems very improbable that the Thatcher governments' almost 'anti-corporatist' strategy – the marginalization of the representatives of trade unions and, to a lesser extent, of manufacturing organizations – will do anything other than reverse for a short period Britain's economic and political difficulties including: crisis in public finances, inflation, unemployment, trade imbalances, crisis of inner-city areas and the overt sense of hopelessness and frustration among Britain's youth, especially among young blacks (Hall, 1979). The question is, how is this state of affairs to be explained? How are we to understand the trends in British politics and the contemporary position of the state?

Let me go back for a moment to theories of overload and legitimation crisis. In general terms, I think Habermas's and Offe's analysis of the way the state is enmeshed in conflict is correct; as is their analysis of some of the pressures that can create a 'crisis of rational administration' (see pp. 122–4, points 1–7). But it follows from my argument in the previous section that I do not find convincing their subsequent focus on legitimation, and the spread of a legitimation crisis. While, in contrast, the theorists of overload are right to point to the many different *kinds* of groups pressing their demands on government, I find neither their starting point (pluralist premises) nor their diagnosis of problems of state power and conflict satisfactory (see essays 1 and 2). Pluralism does not provide an adequate framework to explain the development and constraints on the state in Britain: the segments of the dominant class which have markedly shaped economic policy, and the class conflict over national income, among other things. The model sketched by Habermas and Offe rightly suggests the necessity of a very different starting point to pluralist premises, while the evidence presented in the previous section highlights the significance of classes to the dynamics and instability of political life. However, I do not wish to discuss these two theories of crisis at greater length now. For I want to make a more fundamental criticism of them both and suggest that they are (1) too general and abstract and (2) inadequate in their attempts to relate developments within a nation-state to international conditions and pressures. I want to try to substantiate this by arguing that one can only really begin to advance our understanding of the contemporary British state if we grasp the political, economic and cultural structures which have developed over the long term. It is by following the state's development at the intersection of national and international pressures that we can proceed most fruitfully.

Structural weaknesses of the British state

The development of the modern British state led to a position of what we might call 'double dependence': on material resources generated at home through the largely privately controlled processes of manufacturing, trading and banking as well as on those resources generated from overseas activities. This relationship of double dependence – from which the state derives its income – contributed directly to economic vulnerability in the post-war years. Britain's rapid demise as a world power has led to special difficulties. While severe political and economic problems faced *all* Western nation-states from the mid-1970s, those in Britain became especially acute. For too long Britain's supremacy rested on the might of an empire while all around it the economic and political map was changing. As new nations asserted their independence and as competition between 'advanced' industrial societies increased, the senior personnel of the British state continued to retain faith in its seemingly natural greatness. The cost of 'patrician hegemony' – that is, of an influential section of the dominant class still imbued with the values of tradition, loyalty, empire, etc. – rapidly increased, no matter which party was in power (Nairn, 1981, pp. 365ff.). The very conditions which led to the early successes of the British state – extensive overseas commitments and a cohesive upper class – now were the basis of its rapid decline (in comparison with many other European countries). The British state is hamstrung by a profound structural weakness: dependence on changing overseas conditions to which an influential sector of the economy is still oriented, but which does not today provide the basis for general prosperity and employment.

The constraints and conflicts in which the state is enmeshed and which generate 'crises of rational administration' in Britain are, then, not merely those which derive from conditions internal to the nation-state: the division between the owners and controllers of industry and labour, electoral struggle, social conflicts of various kinds, etc. Rather, they are also the result of the constitution of the modern British state at the intersection of international and national conditions. But the political outcomes of this crisis are far from clear.

Party politics and international status

As the sun set over Britain's empire and competition among industrial nations intensified throughout the post-war years, politicians of nearly all persuasions placed hopes in general economic rejuvenation on strategies geared to the maintenance of Britain's international status either as an independent power, or in junior partnership with the United States or latterly with Europe (see Coates, 1984).[8] These strategies helped sustain the illusion that the decline in Britain's world position could be checked. By the late 1970s and early 1980s it was clear, however, that nothing of the sort had been achieved.

Successive Labour governments have, moreover, attempted to transform state–economy relations through strategies involving rationalizing, centralizing and modernizing industry. But whatever good intentions Labour politicians may have had, the entrenched interests of the most powerful state agencies along with a segmented or divided economy proved insuperable obstacles to their policies for change. Margaret Thatcher easily outmanoeuvred the Labour government in the 1979 elections: the Labour government had become the party of the status quo, of existing institutional arrangements, of cuts in social expenditure and of the stagnating economy (Held and Keane, 1984). The reasons for the decline in electoral support for the Labour party are, of course, complicated (and controversial). In 1979 Labour's room to manoeuvre was severely hampered both in parliament (the uneasy coalition with the Liberals) and in the economy (deteriorating international economic circumstances). But the government, I think, compounded the difficulties it faced by insisting on a tough 5 per cent pay norm (phase 4 of the Social Contract) after a long period of income restraint. The resulting 'winter of discontent' alienated many Labour supporters and provided extraordinary political ammunition to Labour's opponents.

Margaret Thatcher came to office promising something new and yet warning that her policy mix – aiming to redraw the boundaries between state and economy (pulling the former as much as possible out of the affairs of the latter) and reasserting the authority of the law – would take time to work. I shall return a little later to some aspects of this strategy. But one thing, above all, is remarkable: it provided an impetus, in conjunction with North Sea oil, to well-established trends (Nairn, 1981, pp. 389ff.; P. Hall, 1984, pp. 34ff.). Within a short period of time in office, the Conservatives abolished all foreign exchange controls, which meant that money could flow in and out of the economy at will. This opened vast new opportunities for the City that were quickly taken advantage of; for example investment overseas rapidly increased. Accordingly, British banks and financial institutions were in an even stronger position to manage the resources of, among others, the wealthy, multinational corporations and other countries (for example some of the OPEC nations). The effects on domestic industry included a loss of potential investment and further difficulties exporting (due, for instance, to the high value of sterling and/or fluctuating exchange rates). The problems facing the British political economy were immediately compounded: unemployment, deflation, industrial bankruptcy, high prices – but these were some of the best years ever for the City and banks. As a result, the industrial decay of large areas of Scotland, Wales, Northern Ireland and the north of England accelerated, as it did in some parts of the south, particularly inner-city areas.

Is growing political and social conflict inevitable under these circumstances?

Dispersing the effects of political and economic crisis and the limits of such strategies

As long as governments and states are able to secure the acquiescence and support of those collectivities who are crucial for the continuity of the existing order (for example City interests, vital industries, unions with workers in particularly powerful economic positions), 'public order' can be sustained and is likely to break down only on certain 'marginal' sites. What can be called 'strategies of displacement' (developing ideas in Offe, 1984; see essay 2) are crucial here; that is, strategies which disperse the worst effects of economic and political problems on to vulnerable groups while appeasing those able to mobilize claims most effectively. I am *not* arguing that politicians or administrators necessarily desire or intend to displace the worst effects of economic crisis on to some of the least powerful and most vulnerable of society. But if politics is the 'art of the possible', or if – to put it in the terms used hitherto – governments will generally try to ensure the smoothest possible continuity of the existing order (to secure support, expansion of economic opportunities, enhanced scope for their policies), then, they will see little option but to appease those who are most powerful and able to mobilize their resources effectively. Successive governments have pursued strategies involving both appeasement and the uneven dispersal of the effects of economic crisis. As the crisis and difficulties facing the British economy have become worse, these strategies have come more to the fore (Bornstein et al., 1984).

Many of those who for one reason or another are most vulnerable have suffered the worst effects of the crisis of the British political economy. They include: the young (whose opportunities have decreased); blacks (whose employment prospects, housing and general conditions of living are becoming ever more difficult); the disabled and sick (who have suffered a deterioration of services due to public sector cuts); the unemployed and poor (who have vastly increased in numbers) and those who live in regions particularly hard hit, for instance, certain major areas in South Wales, the north of England and Northern Ireland. It is perhaps not surprising that some of these groups become restless and active in 'street' and other forms of protest. The extensive riots in British cities in 1981 were just one symptom of feelings of hopelessness and frustration. It is in contexts such as these that Thatcher's Conservative governments and many branches of the mass media, in particular, have sought to pin the responsibility for some of the present difficulties on the 'scrounger and the welfare state'. Stuart Hall has pointed out that their stories

> have been heavily embroidered with epithets drawn from the stock of populist demonology: the workshy, the feckless poor, the surly rudeness, the feigned infirmities, the mendacity, lack of gratitude, scheming idleness, endless hedonism and 'something for nothing' qualities of 'Britain's army of dole-queue swindlers'. So the Welfare State has been constructed in the media as a populist folk-devil: Britain's undeserving poor, the great majority of whom, if the *Mail* and the *Sun* are to be believed, spend most of their days, between signing on, lolling about on the Costa Brava. (Hall, 1979, p. 6)

Apart from the fact that proven fraud accounts for only a tiny proportion of claims for Supplementary Benefit (less than 0.5 per cent in recent years), this attempt to blame particular individuals or types of individual for their plight and thus to define Britain's problems essentially as problems of motivation, lack of self-restraint and discipline misses entirely the deep structural roots of Britain's protracted economic and political difficulties. Further, it is a definition of the problem which, I think, fewer and fewer people will find compelling in the long term. Why?

The difficulty for this 'definition' is, in fact, that the number of people affected by economic stagnation and the short-fall on successive government promises has increased as has the range of people affected: unemployment has soared during the last decade (see p. 152) and remains (despite recent decreases) a fundamental matter affecting many occupations; officially defined poverty has spread (according to Townsend, 12 million people in Britain live on or near the poverty line); young people from all social classes have found educational opportunities diminishing; women have found themselves often the first to be sacked, shunted to part-time work, and have had the scope of their potential activities radically reduced; more and more regions of the country have been subject to decline and urban difficulties (see, for example, Breugel, 1979; Townsend, 1979; Lewis, 1984; Smith, 1984). While there are many sources of schism dividing groups against one another and undermining the possibility of united opposition to contemporary political and economic arrangements, in the changing circumstances of today it seems that, at the minimum, official political accounts of 'the state of the nation' will be treated with even more scepticism, cynicism and distrust than heretofore. Under these circumstances it is at least possible that British politics will become an arena of greater flux and change.

Social movements, representation and the state

Surveying British politics it is not hard to point to a variety of different types of conflict over wages, work, industry, race, gender, bureaucracy, the environment as well as over the nature and quantity of state goods and services. It is also not difficult to highlight widespread scepticism (or cynicism) about politics – generally understood as traditional party politics. Possibilities for antagonistic stances against governments, the state and 'the system' more generally – prefigured or anticipated in people's distrust of politicians, concern for local issues, etc. – are realized in a variety of actions. The foundation of instrumental consent appears strained.

There are trends which enhance the possibility of a severe political crisis. The favouritism toward certain powerful or dominant groups expressed by corporatist strategies or 'special' bargains erodes the electoral–parliamentary support of the more vulnerable groups, which may be required for governments' survival. More fundamentally, such strategies, especially if successful for a short time, may further erode respect for, and the acceptability of, institutions which have traditionally channelled conflict, for example party systems. Thus new arrangements may backfire, encouraging the formation of opposition movements to the status quo based on those excluded from key established political decision-making processes, for example the jobless, shopfloor workers, those concerned with ecological issues, campaigners for nuclear disarmament (CND), the women's movement activists, and those in the nationalist movements within the 'United' Kingdom (Offe, 1980). Many of these latter groups have their origins in the 1960s and earlier. Some of them have continued to grow. Their significance lies not only in their growth – E. P. Thompson claimed that by 1983–4 CND had become the biggest mass movement in Europe since 1848 – but in their attempt to forge a new participatory politics, involving as many of their members as possible in, among other things, the crucial processes of decision-making.

Moreover, the attempts by successive governments to ensure the acquiescence, if not support, of powerful groups (especially key trade unions) are threatened by the failure of these governments to meet declared political and economic objectives and to manage crises successfully. Labour's 1976–8 Social Contract became ever more a vehicle for the management of sustained deflation rather than for, as promised, greater social justice and economic growth. Thatcher's Conservative governments have broken with any such general arrangements, relying on the vulnerability and timidity of employees faced by mass unemployment. Nevertheless, even Thatcher's governments have made a series of promises: her mix of policies was presented as the only way forward in economic and social terms. The distance between promise and actual performance has persisted: opportunities in education, health and welfare have in general decreased, inequalities have been exacerbated and sustained growth in the manufacturing industries is still elusive.

While there is widespread scepticism about conventional politics, there is also, however, considerable uncertainty about alternatives to the status quo; Cold War attitudes and, of course, Stalinism have discredited certain socialist ideas in the eyes of many. As I argued earlier, while legitimacy is not extensively conferred, there is considerable uncertainty not only about what kinds of institutions there might be but also about what general political *directions* should be taken. Thus there is reason to believe that the scepticism and remoteness many people feel in relation to dominant political institutions might be the basis of further political disaffection in the future. As possibilities for antagonistic stances against the state are realized, so too are the germs of a variety of other kinds of political movements, for example movements of the 'new' right. Anxiety about directionless change can fuel a call for the re-establishment of tradition and authority. This is the foundation for the appeal by the 'new' conservatives – or the New Right – to the people and the nation, to many of those who feel so acutely unrepresented.

The New Right and strategies for state legitimation

The New Right is, in general, committed to the view that political life, like economic life, is – or ought to be – a realm of individual freedom and initiative (see essays 5 and 6). Only individuals can judge what they want and, therefore, the less the state interferes in their lives the better for them. Accordingly, a *laissez-faire* or free market society is the key objective along with a 'minimal state'. The political programme of the New Right (or neo-liberals) includes: the extension of the market to more and more areas of life; the creation of a state stripped of 'excessive' involvement both in the economy and in the provision of opportunities; the curtailment of the power of certain groups to press their aims and goals (for instance, trade unions); the construction of a strong government to enforce law and order.[9]

The Thatcher governments' advocacy of the 'rolling back of the state' has been on grounds similar to those of the New Right and of some of the theorists of overloaded government: individual freedom has been diminished because of the proliferation of bureaucratic state agencies attempting to meet the demands of those involved in group politics. The Thatcher governments have been committed to the classic liberal doctrine that the collective good (or the good of all individuals) can be properly realized in most cases only by private individuals acting in competitive isolation and pursuing their sectoral aims with minimal state interference. This commitment to the market as the key mechanism of economic and social regulation has a significant other side in the history of liberalism: a commitment to a 'strong state' to provide a secure basis upon which, it is thought, business, trade and family life will prosper (see essay 1).

It is essential to the Thatcher governments' strategy of expanding the realm of non-state activities that the politics of the post-war settlement be fundamentally altered. The three Thatcher governments have sought to break with the dominant trend in post-war decades toward a regulated mixed economy, a welfare interventionist state. The strategy is predicated both on an aversion to state intervention and control, and on a belief that the state has neither the management capability nor the responsibility to ensure the general performance and effectiveness of the economy and its related institutions. Thatcher's Conservatives, and the New Right more generally, have sought to attack the claim that the state and government are inextricably linked to the *direct* creation of expanding economic opportunities and social welfare.

The political success of the Thatcher regime to date (confirmed by its re-election in 1983 and 1987) has rested, I believe, in large part on the uncoupling or separation of the instrumental or performative dimension of the state, that is, the state as an instrument for the delivery of goods and services, from consideration of the state as a powerful, prestigious and enduring representative of the people or nation. Thatcher has sought to draw upon and reinvigorate the symbols and agencies of the latter while systematically attacking the former. The current success of this political project lies, in part, in its direct connection to, and mobilization of, that cynicism, distrust and dissatisfaction with many of the institutions of the interventionist welfare state that has long existed. Her achievement, I believe, is to have recovered the traditional symbols of the British nation-state and made them her own (precisely those symbols associated with Great Britain, the 'glorious past', the empire and international prestige) while separating these from the idea of the state as a capable guarantor of economic and social opportunities. Sociologists and political commentators have often noted a diffuse and general commitment to the idea of the nation, to nationalism, to pride in being British (for example Nichols and Armstrong, 1976). There is good reason to think that this diffuse commitment has been – after some decades of relative dormancy – reactivated (at least in England) and brought once again to the foreground of British politics. How long this selective revival of symbols can be sustained is an open question. The argument in this essay suggests that this new attempt to legitimize the state's authority rests on a fragile economic base. Whether this fragility will have a direct political consequence is, however, another matter.

Unfortunately, it is hard to test properly the interpretation of Thatcher's achievements I have just offered because insufficient time has elapsed and insufficient research has been conducted (cf. essay 5; and see Jessop et al., 1988, for a fuller discussion of current debates and findings). Some very rough data are available from recent surveys of public opinion. These data give us no information about how attitudes and beliefs might divide across socio-economic groups and classes and, therefore, have little direct bearing on the kind of argument presented so far. But they do indicate, and this perhaps is noteworthy, that in two time-periods in 1981 and 1983 the only institutions out of ten to register the confidence of a majority of the population consistently were the police, the armed forces and the legal system (Gallup, 1981 and 1983).[10] The Falklands war was no doubt an important factor contributing to the expression of confidence in institutions like the army; it reactivated patriotic sentiment and brought it once again to the centre of British politics. But if my argument above is correct then the effects of the Falklands war have to be understood within the context of a wider political strategy – a strategy to bolster the legitimacy of the state's traditional authority while systematically discrediting its capability to assume direct responsibility for the management of economic and social affairs.

Political compliance and the 'strong' state

There are many factors which ensure compliance with existing institutions; and among these are the formidable resources of state power itself, especially those for the maintenance of 'law and order'. I should like to focus briefly on these resources and, then, in the final part of the essay, I shall place them within a model of the many factors which lead to political and social compliance.

There is evidence to suggest a massive reorganization of the apparatus for maintaining law and order in recent times (see, for example, Jessop, 1980, pp. 62–5). This has involved a further concentration and centralization of state power developing considerable capacities for information storage, surveillance and pre-emptive control of, among other things, industrial conflict and political dissent. The tip of the iceberg involves new legal powers for the police (for example, the Police and Criminal Evidence Act 1984, and the Prevention of Terrorism Act 1984) and the introduction of specialized forces (for instance, Special Patrol Groups, Special Response Units, Anti-Terrorist Squads) all with fairly wide-ranging briefs. There has been, moreover, an increase in cooperation between the police and the military as both have acquired a wide range of weapons for use in civilian disturbances along with highly complex equipment for the surveillance and containment of disputes.

For instance, the police are now able to draw on vast new computer facilities. The police national computer (which can support 21,000 requests for information per hour) has been designed in part to aid the trends towards pre-emptive policing supported by extensive information (State Research, 1982, pp. 107–8). Additional specialized computers include the 'C' division Metropolitan Police computer – the secret national police intelligence unit. It appears that its function is to store 'information on over 1.5 million people many of whom have not committed any crime but are "of interest to the police"' (State Research, 1982, p. 113). The latest MI5 (the largely domestic security agency) computer system is immense: its storage capacity is two and a half times greater than the national police computer and is thought to be capable of storing information on up to 20 million people.

These facts alone might not be so important if it were not for the evidence which further suggests that extensive surveillance ability enables 'security' agencies to extend their control over hitherto ordinary civil and political activities. Of course, some of this capacity aids the protection of citizens from aggressive and violent attacks by groups whose objectives and methods we might all deplore. Additionally, the capacity by no means generates omniscience; and such capacities as do exist are frequently underutilized. On the other hand, increased technological know-how allows potentially what one might call the 'logic' of surveillance to be realized: even allies and friends must be spied upon because one day they too may become enemies (Campbell, 1981, p. 16). Information on the activities of security agencies is, of course, hard to come by and one can never be certain of its reliability. But a survey by Duncan Campbell (1981) suggests that targets of surveillance have included:

1   Leaders of industrial disputes. In 1978, for example, the Grunwick strike committee's phone was tapped and long-range microphones were used by the Special Branch in an attempt to monitor conversations.
2   Embassies. According to an ex-intelligence official all embassies (including the US) are targets of bugging and tapping.
3   Journalists and politicians. Even ministers (for example Judith Hart, in the last Labour government) have had their phones tapped.

As important as the range of monitored activities, are questions about the accountability of the security agencies. Campbell argues provocatively that the 'sovereignty' of these powerful organizations lies with their 'top men' and there is minimum parliamentary control and little accountability even to ministers. This situation is apparently compounded by the extensive interlocking of the British network of surveillance with that of the United States's NSA (National Security Agency). Much of the British network is closely tied into the US operations. But it is, according to Campbell, a *dependent* alliance – an alliance which links British security and, more generally, foreign policy to that of the United States – a link which would perhaps be hard to break, even, for example, for an elected Labour government mandated to ensure more independence in foreign affairs.

A sophisticated system of collecting and storing information is a prime source of state power and directly aids – through the control of communications, 'public' information and planning processes – the containment not only of crime but of all those who are considered civilian dissidents. (The military control of Poland in the 1980s is an example of the extreme application of such power.) These capacities comprise a formidable quantity of human energy and resources assembled and mobilized to help ensure compliance, law and order. For a country which has been held as a model of tolerance and consensus such a state of affairs is perhaps remarkable (cf. Halsey, 1981, ch. 7). It testifies to the claim of the previous section of this essay: tolerance and consensus are far rarer qualities in Britain than many have heretofore claimed. This is clearly recognized, at least, by those who have built up the 'secret' strong state, accumulating the resources to manage subject populations. The apparatuses of coercion and administration have generated considerable capacities to contain opposition.

There are many factors which lead to political compliance. While this section has explored elements of the formation of the modern British state which have exacerbated economic and political difficulties, it has also explored some of the reasons why growing conflict is not inevitable. Strategies of displacement fragment and disperse the worst effects of crisis; new attempts are made to legitimize the authority of government and the state; and formidable resources exist to monitor and potentially to control many aspects of day-to-day life. Accordingly, although public order forces are highly visible in the lives of some groups (such as blacks, immigrants, unemployed youths, prostitutes, workers on picket lines), in certain regions (where industrial and urban decay is advanced, for example parts of Liverpool) and in political activities of various kinds (for instance, demonstrations, marches, civil rights campaigns in Northern Ireland), it remains the case that they can maintain a low profile in most situations. Moreover, a low profile is often more than sufficient as a reminder of the ultimate constraints on civil and political life.

Social compliance and state power: a model

In this section I would like to draw together several strands of the essay and bring out a number of central ideas in a schematic model – a model of social compliance and state power. In order to explain the integration and reproduction of the political order we need to depart from the view that state power and political stability depend only upon things like legitimacy or respect for the authority of the state. Rather, I shall argue, compliance results from a

complex web of interdependencies between people, collectivities and institutions – interdependencies which incorporate relations of power and dependence (Lockwood, 1964; Giddens, 1979). Three themes are of particular
importance: (1) state power is only a part, albeit a very important part, of the
relations of power or the power structure; (2) the resources of state power are
themselves extensive and complex (more so than suggested by the theorists
considered so far); (3) there are many overlapping and interlocking forces
which fragment experience of the political and social world and constitute
major hurdles to any movement seeking fundamental transformations in
political life.

The model I will present here is of a rather different kind from those
presented by the theorists we have discussed so far. Whereas they tend to focus
either on political stability or on political crisis, the model dwells on neither
exclusively. Rather, it focuses on the interrelation between state and civil
society and on the resultant divisions and fragmentation of political and
economic life. It is these divisions which constitute the basis of political
stability today. The model concentrates on a set of elements which bear on the
scope and limits of state action and then considers wider features of civil
society. Taken together these elements delineate a series of trends or tendencies, but without a single clear-cut outcome. For all the elements in the
model are parts of a process in which outcomes depend, above all, on the
contingencies of political conflict.

Economic compulsion   Both Marxists and non-Marxists have recognized the
distinctive elements of constraint and compulsion that emerge when people
are separated from the means (land, technology, techniques, etc.) of production. Weber analysed the way the emergence of modern capitalism
included the formation of a mass of propertyless wage-workers, who have to
sell their labour to owners of capital in order to sustain a livelihood (Weber, in
Giddens and Held, 1982). Marx, of course, wrote at length about the way the
worker is 'forced to sell his [or her] labour-power for a wage in order to live'.
He called this 'the dull compulsion of economic relations'. If we wish to enjoy
some of the comforts of life we have to participate in these relations; for nearly
all working people there is no realistic alternative but to try to earn a living
and comply with working arrangements created largely by others: 'dropping
out', relying upon social security or being super rich are the only immediate
ways out – and the latter only for a tiny minority. These processes in themselves constitute an immense pressure to conformist patterns of behaviour
(Abercrombie et al., 1980, p. 166).

Transfer and concentration of the means of violence   Dependence on employment is
the main basis of the power relation between employers and employees (a
relation which, as I mentioned earlier (pp. 111–13), alters with the state of

the economy). The management or supervision of employees – which is, of course, extensive in all occupations – is not sustained by the immediate threat of the use of physical force, as it frequently was in the past. The 'means of violence' are concentrated in the hands of the state. Anthony Giddens elaborates a version of this idea as follows:

> The monopolisation of the means of violence in the hands of the state went along with the *extrusion of control of violent sanctions from the exploitative class relations involved in emergent capitalism*. Commitment to freedom of contract, which was both part of a broader set of ideological claims to human liberties for which the bourgeoisie fought, and an actual reality they sought to further in economic organisation, meant the expulsion of sanctions of violence from the newly expanding labour market. (Giddens, 1981, p. 180)

With the development of capitalism the state entered into the very fabric of the economy by reinforcing and codifying – through legislation, administration and supervision – its structure and practices. It thus constituted and complemented, as it still does, economic relations.

Partial and dependent state: the depoliticization of property To the extent that private and public spheres are kept distinct, the state can, with certain justification, claim to represent the community or the general interest, in contrast to the world of individual aims and responsibilities. But the opposition between general and particular interests is, as Marx argued, often illusory. The state defends the 'community', and thus its own claim to legitimacy, as if fundamental differences in social class and interest did not largely define central elements of economic and political life. In treating everyone in the same way, according to principles which protect the freedom of individuals and defend their right to property, the state may act 'neutrally' while generating effects which are partial, sustaining the privileges of those with property (see essay 1, pp. 32–3). Moreover, the very claim that there is a clear distinction between the private and public, the world of civil society and the political, is dubious under contemporary social and economic circumstances. A key source of contemporary power – private ownership of the means of production – is ostensibly depoliticized; that is, treated by virtue of the differentiation of the economy and state as if it were not a proper subject of politics. The structure of the economy is regarded as non-political, such that the massive division between those who own and control the means of production, and those who must live by wage labour, is regarded as the outcome of free private contracts, not a matter for the state. But by defending private property in the means of production, the state already has taken a side.

The state, then, is not an independent structure or set of institutions above society, that is, a 'public power' acting straightforwardly for 'the public'. On the contrary it is deeply embedded in socio-economic relations and linked to particular interests. It is also to a significant degree vitally dependent – dependent on the process of capital accumulation which it has, for its own sake, to maintain. Charles Lindblom, who writes from a position closer to pluralism than Marxism, explains the point well (and in a manner compatible with the perspectives of Offe and Habermas).

> Because public functions in the market system rest in the hands of businessmen, it follows that jobs, prices, production, growth, the standard of living, and the economic security of everyone all rest in their hands. Consequently government officials cannot be indifferent to how well business performs its functions. Depression, inflation, or other economic disasters can bring down a government. A major function of government, therefore, is to see to it that businessmen perform their tasks. (Lindblom, 1977, pp. 122–3)

The system of private property and 'dull economic compulsion' is necessarily reinforced by the state, however much various governments may seek to balance this interest with welfare and other policies. For state intervention in the economy has to be broadly compatible with the objectives of powerful economic interests, for example 'the City', financiers, industrialists; otherwise civil society (business and family life) and the stability of the state are put at risk.

Sources of state power: the coercive and administrative apparatus Weber's classic definition of the state placed emphasis upon its capability of monopolizing the legitimate use of violence within a given territory. Weber writes: 'Of course, force is certainly not the normal or only means of the state – nobody says that – but force is a means specific to the state . . . the state is a relation of men dominating men [and, generally, men dominating women], a relation supported by means of legitimate (i.e. considered to be legitimate) violence' (Weber, 1972, p. 78). The state maintains compliance or order within a given territory; in individual capitalist societies this involves crucially the maintenance of the order of property, and the enhancement of domestic economic interests overseas, although by no means all the problems of order can be reduced to these. The state's web of agencies and institutions finds its ultimate sanction in the claim to the monopoly of force, and a political order is only, in the last instance, vulnerable to crises when this monopoly erodes.

The significance of the institutions of force or coercion goes beyond the use of the military against 'national enemies', that is, defensive policing of territories and aggressive exploits overseas. The quelling of the riots in Brixton and elsewhere in the summer of 1981 is just one example of the wide use of such forces to ensure compliance within the nation-state. Further, the police are deployed constantly (and the military occasionally) to manage not only crime but industrial and political dissent as well. In addition, the means for the enforcement of order and law include massive agencies of surveillance. Nobody has documented the dimensions of this source of 'administrative power' better in recent times than Michel Foucault. As he wrote:

> If the economic take-off of the West began with the techniques that made possible the accumulation of capital, it might perhaps be said that the methods for administering the accumulation of men (population) made possible a political take-off in relation to the traditional ritual, costly, violent forms of power, which soon fell into disuse and were superseded by a subtle, calculated technology of subjection. (Foucault, 1977, pp. 220–1)

In discussing forms of subjection it is important to distinguish two connected phenomena: the supervision of the activities of subordinates in organizations of all kinds and the accumulation of information which can be stored by an institution or collectivity (Giddens, 1981, pp. 169ff.). The collection and storing of information about members of a society is a prime resource for those who wield power and it is closely related to the supervision of subject populations; it directly aids the control of a range of activities (as I illustrated in the previous section). The computerization of information adds little that is qualitatively new to these operations, it merely aids them – extending the capacity 'to make tyranny total', as Frank Church commented in his Congressional investigations of the technology available to the US National Security Agency (which has extensive connections to the British secret service).

The state, thus, plays a massive role in enforcing political order through its many agencies. Clearly this role has changed over time: in the early ascendancy of industrial capitalism the direct use of force in economic and political life was probably far more frequent than it is now; but against this must be weighed the fact that the means both of information coordination and supervision are far more sophisticated today than they ever were. At the minimum it seems justified to say that if the political order was more extensively adhered to, there would be less call for such extensive apparatuses of 'enforcement': presumably the latter exist because they are judged by those in power to be necessary. There is a formidable concentration of resources – far more formidable than the theorists of overload and legitimation crises suggest – at the disposal of both the key executive branches of government (the prime minister, the cabinet and its offices) and the permanent senior officials at Whitehall in the national and international networks of surveillance. The resources for the successful exercise of political strategy should not be underestimated.

Capacity and limits of state administration   While the state has an interest in sustaining and encouraging commerce, business, etc., the criteria by which those in state agencies make decisions are distinct from the logic of market operations and the imperatives of profit maximization. Through administrative or legislative organs, policy alternatives can be presented to clients with conflicting interests, thereby creating a possible opportunity for compromise. State managers (those in powerful non-routine jobs) can formulate objectives and alternatives which respond to different pressures and in accordance with a government's strategy for electoral success. Building upon ideas raised in essay 2 (pp. 74–6), it can be said that the power of governments and the pattern of state policy are, leaving aside international conditions and pressures, determined by four interlocking institutional arrangements: by formal rules which set the mode of access to governmental power (free elections, free speech, freedom to organize); by the institutional arrangements which determine the articulation and implementation of state policy (civil services, judiciary, police, etc.); by the capacity of the economy to provide sufficient resources for state policies; and by the constraints imposed by the power of dominant collectivities (for example, the willingness of corporations to invest limits the scope of intervention into the process of accumulation and appropriation of capital, while trade unions can block attempts to erode hard-won social benefits).

The state is not controlled *directly* by the various interest groups (the City, domestic industry, etc.) of the dominant economic class. In pursuing their own interests (the prestige and stability of their jobs, their futures and those of their kin, among other things) the state's managers are likely to have interests which are compatible with those of at least some leading economic factions (Crouch, 1979, p. 140). But, while state managers are in general dependent on the outcomes of the process of capital accumulation, the multiplicity of economic and electoral constraints on policy mean that the state is by no means a straightforward agent of capitalist reproduction. The history of the labour movement is the history of a constant effort to offset some of the disadvantages of the power differential between employees and employers. In response the state has (until recently at least) found it necessary to introduce a variety of policies which increase the social wage, extend public goods, enhance democratic rights, and alter the balance between public and private sectors. Social struggle is thus 'inscribed' into, that is, embedded in, the organization, administration and policies of the state (see Poulantzas, 1978). The state's partiality and dependence is to a degree both masked (hidden) and offset by successive government attempts to manoeuvre within these conflicting pressures.

International constraints and politics   The pressures to which the state responds are international as well as national. International events like the oil crisis of 1973 are only the tip of the iceberg: the capacity and limits of government and state power are related systematically to international circumstances. External developments exercise a decisive influence upon the very constitution of the state. If, as was the case in Britain for well over two hundred years, a country enjoys extensive maritime and military dominance, many domestic conflicts of interest can be resolved temporarily with the help of materials plundered, extracted or exchanged at advantageous prices from colonies and dependent territories. But the erosion of this particular form of power – the speed of which escalated rapidly in the post-war years despite the fact that a key segment of the British economy remained substantially oriented to overseas operations – allows considerably fewer modes of this kind for alleviating conflict.

Today, the integration of Britain into Europe constitutes a crucial limit to state power. For it involves the partial loss of sovereignty to the central institutions of Brussels, as does membership of the North Atlantic Treaty Organization (NATO) and of a host of other international institutions, such as the International Monetary Fund (IMF). These phenomena, along with the internationalization of capital through the growth of multinational corporations and banks, take many decisions out of the hands of domestic institutions (see essay 8 for an exploration of these themes). As a result, opposition, for instance, to decisions to close down factories, to run down industries affecting whole regions, to proliferate nuclear weapons, can founder for want of being able satisfactorily to pin responsibility on to any central authority. The internationalization of economics and politics can, thus, displace national power centres and weaken the scope of protest and possible democratic control.

Displacement strategies of the state The state, in its bid to sustain the continuity of the existing order, favours selectively those groups whose acquiescence and support are crucial: the City, oligopoly capital and some groups of organized labour. The hope is that representatives of these 'strategic groups' will increasingly step in alongside the state's representatives to resolve threats to political stability through a highly informal, extra-parliamentary negotiation process in exchange for the enhancement of their corporate interests (Panitch, 1976; Offe, 1980). These attempts to establish new forms of 'political management' constitute a desire for a kind of 'class compromise' among the powerful – a compromise that is, however, all too often at the expense of vulnerable groups, for example the young, the elderly, the sick, non-unionized, non-white, and those in vulnerable regions, for example areas with 'declining industries no longer central to the economy'.

The capacity of governments to develop successful political strategies and policy alternatives is enhanced by their ability to displace the effects of economic problems on to vulnerable groups while appeasing those able to mobilize claims most effectively. By dispersing the effects of economic crisis unevenly, the basis is weakened for solidarity amongst those who might potentially oppose existing political and economic arrangements.

Further divisions: work and domestic life   The separation of the worlds of work and domestic life, and of the worlds of men and women, is another major source of schism and divided allegiance. The advent of industrial capitalism brings about a split between work-place and domestic life (Marglin, 1974; Giddens, 1981). The main phenomenon which establishes this division is recognition by traders and employers that control over labour can only be effectively achieved (and thereby profits maximized) if workers are located in factories. Thus the system that creates what Marx termed 'dull economic compulsion' also creates a vast split in everyday life between work on the one hand, and home, leisure and relaxation on the other. A private world of individuals and small families – a world in which consumption is paramount – is set off for the first time from the world of social or collective production. This is one (crucial) moment in the demise or fragmentation of community – the atomization and segmentation of life. To the extent that people displace both their hopes and their disappointments from work and political life on to the private sphere – seeking 'freedom', for example, only in patterns of consumption or in sexual encounters – the difficulties posed by political and economic crisis can be partially forgotten. While the 'private sphere' has often radically different connotations for men and women, it can become the only sphere where they attempt, albeit in different ways, to assert and fulfil themselves (Chinoy, 1965; Zaretsky, 1976; Pateman, 1988).

Further sources of schism: the media, formal education and official information agencies
The evidence presented in this essay highlights both the general moral approval of dominant institutions by the politically powerful and mobilized (which is crucial to ensure the reproduction of a political order), as well as the prevalence of value dissensus and of pragmatic acquiescence and instrumental orientations among many working people. It reveals also that a substantial proportion of people claim not to understand the system of government, and claim little or no interest in what the government is doing or in the outcomes of elections. This is indeed, as Moss put it, a 'poor return' for the constant barrage of written materials, discussion and information presented by the media and other institutions. But the impact of the latter should not be under-estimated. Marcuse's provocative work reminds us of the relentlessness of such institutions and their highly affirmative images of the status quo. Mann refers to their power, and especially that of the education system, to produce a divided consciousness. Earlier sections of this essay referred to attempts to create political consent partly through the promulgation of images of national unity and the reinvigoration of the traditional symbols of the British nation-

state. The reporting of the Falklands war is a case in point; through the use of a whole package of rules, conventions and laws pertaining to secrecy (going well beyond the 1911 Official Secrets Act), the government was able to keep a remarkable amount of information to itself, offering only a highly selective impression, and making it very hard to discern exactly what was happening and in whose interest. (A useful account of the rules, conventions and laws pertaining to secrecy can be found in May and Rowan, 1982.)

The power of institutions like the media can be exaggerated. It is clear that values, beliefs and the very framework of thought of many people do not simply reflect the stamp of the production system, the commercial preoccupations of much of the media, and the official agencies of information. But together their fairly relentless presentation of affirmative images constitutes, at the minimum, a systematic inhibition to reflection on alternative institutions, to the development of an oppositional or counter ideology to existing political and economic arrangements (Bottomore, 1980, p. x). There is little in the language and ideas of the media, for example, to encourage the critical views of those in marginal or subordinate positions. It is hardly surprising, therefore, to uncover a dual or divided consciousness and a lack of consensus. The views 'aired' in politics and the media intersect in complex ways with daily experience, local tradition and regional life. Fragmentation of cultural experience is one almost inevitable result.

Conclusion

Political order is not achieved through common value systems, or general respect for the authority of the state, or legitimacy, or, by contrast, simple brute force; rather, it is the outcome of a complex web of interdependencies between political, economic and social institutions and activities which divide power centres and which create multiple pressures to comply. State power is a central aspect of these structures but it is not the only key variable.

The precariousness of 'government' today is linked both to the limits of state power in the context of national and international conditions and to the remoteness, distrust and scepticism that is expressed about existing institutional arrangements, including the effectivity of parliamentary democracy. The institutions of democratic representation remain crucial to the formal control of the state, but the disjuncture between the agencies which possess formal control and those with actual control, between the power that is claimed for the people and their limited actual power, between the promises of representatives and their actual performance, is likely to become more apparent. But in the context of the many factors which fragment opposition movements, it is, of course, hard to predict the balance of political forces in the future: the 'balance' always depends on *political* negotiation and conflict – in other words, on a process which is underdetermined by socio-economic life.

The first section of the essay introduced the notion of an 'ideal normative agreement'; that is, an agreement to follow rules and laws on the grounds that they are the regulations we would have agreed to in ideal circumstances – with, for instance, all the knowledge we would like and all the opportunity we would want to discuss the requirements of others (p. 101). I find this idea useful because it provides a basis for a 'thought experiment' into how people would interpret their needs, and which rules and laws they would consider justified, under conditions of unconstrained knowledge and discussion. It enables us to ask what the conditions would have to be like for people to follow rules and laws they think right, correct, justified – worthy. Surveying the issues and evidence explored in this essay, we can say, I believe, that a state implicated deeply in the creation and reproduction of systematic inequalities of power, wealth, income and opportunities will rarely (the exceptions perhaps being occasions like war) enjoy sustained legitimation by groups other than those whom it directly privileges. Or, more contentiously, only a political order that places the transformation of those inequalities at its centre will enjoy legitimacy in the long run.

Notes

1 The points below owe a good deal to a consideration of Mann (1970) and Habermas (1976).

2 Note that, unless indicated to the contrary, writers in both groups were writing about trends in Western industrial societies generally.

3 The reasons for Labour's failure to consolidate their post-war triumph in the long run are beyond the scope of this essay. Among them I would include the way key Labour politicians helped undermine the popularity of socialist ideas by espousing uncritically the rhetoric of the Cold War and by diverting excessive funds into arms and defence expenditure. Cf. Morgan (1984) and Thompson (1984).

4 This state of affairs is shown in table 4.3, and the progressive rise in unemployment is charted in figure 4.4.

5 By 'patrician culture' I mean, following Nairn (1977 and 1981, pp. 365ff.), adherence to the values of nobility, tradition and grace along with an emphasis upon independent action and private initiative in civil society.

6 Legitimation crisis theory was not developed with special reference to Britain, but to the extent to which it is concerned with general developments in capitalist societies, it can be applied to Britain. The theory of overloaded government was partly developed with reference to Britain, although it as well is often thought to be applicable to many states in advanced liberal-democratic societies.

Table 4.3 Post-war cycles

Post-war cycles	I	II	III	IV	V	VI
Period	1952–7	1958–61	1962–5	1966–70	1971–5	1976–8
Duration	6 yrs	4 yrs	4 yrs	5 yrs	5 yrs	3 yrs
Real GNP rise (%)	16.4	12.1	13.4	11.2	7.5	8.6
Peak unemployment (av % adult in yr)	1.8 (1952)	2.0 (1959)	2.2 (1963)	2.3 (1968)	4.4 (1975)	5.7 (1977–8)
Peak inflation (% RPI rise in yr)	5.3 (1955)	3.4 (1961)	4.7 (1965)	6.4 (1970)	24.1 (1975)	16.1 (1977)
Peak payments deficit (a) (% of GDP)	0.91	1.12	1.29	†	3.6	‡
Average pre-tax company profits (av % for cycle) (b)	15.9	15.4	14.5	12.1	5.5	n.a.

† Masked by 1967 devaluation (a) current account in calendar years.
‡ Distorted by North Sea oil (b) share of company profits in GNP.
Note: Jay's table concerned incomes policy cycles, the table above concerns 'stop-go' cycles (no longer coincident from period V onwards).
Source: Jessop (1980, p. 87; originally adapted from P. Jay, *The Times*, 1 July 1974).

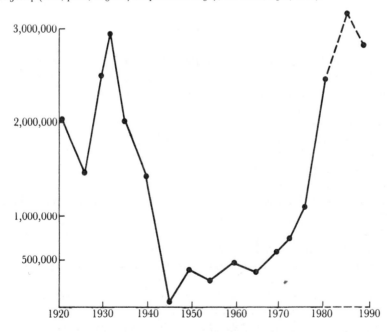

Figure 4.4 Unemployment in the UK, 1921–1988 (*Source*: Halsey, 1981, p. 30. The broken line indicates where the figure has been updated for this volume using data from the *Employment Gazette*).

7   A fuller review can be found in my Open University publication, 'Power and legitimacy in contemporary Britain', in *The State and Society* (unit 23), Milton Keynes, 1984.

8   Accordingly, a high level of military spending has been maintained. 'The Government estimates that it will spend nearly £16 billion in the 1983–4 financial year – including £624 million on maintaining the Falklands garrison and repairing the losses of the South Atlantic war . . . At this rate Britain is spending more than any of her major European allies, whether her military expenditure is considered in absolute terms, as a proportion of national income, or per head of population' (*Guardian*, 7 July 1983).

9   It might be noted that item four of this programme is arguably inconsistent with items one and two. In fact, a tension exists in modern British Conservatism between those who assert individual freedom and the market as the ultimate concern, and those who believe in the primacy of tradition, order and authority, because they fear the social consequences of rampant *laissez-faire* policies. My account of the New Right concentrates on the former group, who have been most influential in current politics.

10 The institutions were the church, the armed forces, the education system, the legal system, the press, trade unions, the police, parliament, the civil service and major companies. The monarchy was not included in the surveys, although 76 per cent of all respondents to a 1981 Marplan opinion poll thought the 'advantages of the Monarchy outweigh the costs'.

References

Abercrombie, N., Hill, S. and Turner, B. 1980: *The Dominant Ideology Thesis*. London: Allen & Unwin.

Almond, G. and Verba, S. 1963: *The Civic Culture: Political Attitudes and Democracy in Five Nations*. Princeton, NJ: Princeton University Press.

Almond, A. and Verba, S. (eds) 1980: *The Civic Culture Revisited*. Boston: Little, Brown.

Beer, S. 1982: *Britain Against Itself*. London: Faber.

Benson, L. 1978: *Proletarians and Parties*. London: Methuen.

Bornstein, S., Held, D. and Krieger, J. (eds) 1984: *The State in Capitalist Europe*. London: Allen & Unwin.

Bottomore, T. 1980: 'Foreword' in N. Abercrombie, S. Hill and B. Turner, *The Dominant Ideology Thesis*. London: Allen & Unwin.

Breugel, I. 1979: Women as a reserve army of Labour: a note on recent British experience. *Feminist Review*, 3.

Brittan, S. 1975: The economic contradictions of democracy. *British Journal of Political Science*, 5(1).

Brittan, S. 1977: Can democracy manage an economy? In R. Skidelsky (ed.), *The End of the Keynesian Era*, Oxford: Martin Robertson.

Butler, D. and Stokes, D. 1974: *Political Change in Britain*. London: Macmillan.

Cambridge Political Economy Group 1974: *Britain's economic crisis*. Nottingham: Spokesman Pamphlet, No. 44.

Campbell, D. 1981: *Phonetappers and the Security State*. London: New Statesman.

Chinoy, E. 1965: *Automobile Workers and the American Dream*. Boston: Beacon.

Coates, D. 1984: The character and origin of Britain's economic decline. In D. Coates and G. Johnston (eds), *Socialist Strategies*, Oxford: Martin Robertson.

Crouch, C. (ed.) 1979: *State and Economy in Contemporary Capitalism*. London: Croom Helm.

Dennis, S. 1983: Education and the European State: evolution, rationalization and crisis. In S. Bornstein, D. Held and J. Krieger (eds), *The State in Capitalist Europe*, London: Allen & Unwin.

Douglas, J. 1976: The overloaded crown. *British Journal of Political Science*, 6(4).

Foucault, M. 1977: *Discipline and Punish*. London: Allen Lane.

Fox, A. 1974: *Beyond Contract: Work, Power and Trust Relations*. London: Faber.

Gamble, A. and Walton, P. 1976: *Capitalism in Crisis*. London: Macmillan.

Giddens, A. 1979: *Central Problems in Social Theory*. London: Macmillan.

Giddens, A. 1981: *A Contemporary Critique of Historical Materialism*. London: Macmillan.

Giddens, A. and Held, D. (eds) 1982: *Classes, Power and Conflict*. London: Macmillan.

Glyn, A. and Sutcliffe, B. 1972: *British Capitalism, Workers and Profit Squeeze*. Harmondsworth: Penguin.

Gough, I. 1975: State expenditure in advanced capitalism. *New Left Review*, 92.

Habermas, J. 1976: *Legitimation Crisis*. London: Heinemann.

Hall, P. (1984) Patterns of economic policy. In D. Held et al. (eds), *States and Societies*, Oxford: Martin Robertson.

Hall, S. et al. 1978: *Policing the Crisis*. London: Macmillan.

Hall, S. 1979: Drifting into a law-and-order society. *The Cobden Lecture* (1979), The Cobden Trust, London.

Hall, S. and Jacques, M. (eds) 1983: *The Politics of Thatcherism*. London: Lawrence & Wishart.

Halsey, A. H. 1981: *Change in British Society*. Oxford: Oxford University Press.

Held, D. and Keane, J. 1984: In a fit state. *New Socialist*, March–April.

Held, D. and Krieger, J. 1983: Accumulation, legitimation and the state. In D. Held et al. (eds), *States and Societies*, Oxford: Martin Robertson.

Hibbs, D. 1976: Industrial conflict in advanced industrial societies. *American Political Science Review*, LXX(4).

Hibbs, D. 1978: On the political economy of long-run trends in strike activity. *British Journal of Political Science*, 8.

Hobsbawm, E. 1952: Economic fluctuations and some social movements since 1800. *Economic History Review*, second ser., 5.

Huntingdon, S. 1975: Post-industrial politics: how benign will it be? *Comparative Politics*, 6.

Hyman, R. 1972: *Strikes*. London: Fontana.

Ingham, G. 1982: Divisions within the dominant class and British 'exceptionalism'. In A. Giddens and G. Mackenzie (eds), *Social Class and the Division of Labour*, Cambridge: Cambridge University Press.

Jessop, B. 1974: *Traditionalism, Conservatism and British Political Culture*. London: Allen & Unwin.

Jessop, B. 1980: The transformation of the state in post-war Britain. In R. Scase (ed.), *The State in Western Europe*, London: Croom Helm.

Jessop, B., Bonnett, K., Bromley, S. and Ling, T. 1988: *Thatcherism: A Tale of Two Nations*. Cambridge: Polity Press.

Kavanagh, D. 1980: Political culture in Great Britain. In G. Almond and S. Verba (eds), *The Civic Culture Revisited*, Boston: Little, Brown.

King, A. 1976: *Why is Britain becoming Harder to Govern?* London: BBC.

Lane, T. 1974: *The Union Makes Us Strong*. London: Arrow.

Lewis, J. 1984: Regional policy and planning. In S. Bornstein, D. Held and J. Krieger (eds), *The State in Capitalist Europe*, London: Allen & Unwin.

Lindblom, C. E. 1977: *Politics and Markets*. New York: Basic Books.

Lipset, S. M. 1963: *Political Man*. New York: Doubleday.

Lockwood, D. 1964: Social integration and system integration. In G. K. Zouschan and W. Hirsch (eds), *Explorations in Social Change*, London: Routledge & Kegan Paul.

Mann, M. 1970: The social cohesion of liberal democracy. *American Sociological Review*, 35. Also in A. Giddens and D. Held (eds) (1982) *Classes, Power and Conflict*, London: Macmillan.

Mann, M. 1973: *Consciousness and Action Among the Western Working Class*. London: Macmillan.

Marcuse, H. 1964: *One Dimensional Man*. Boston: Beacon.

Marglin, S. 1974: What do the bosses do? *Review of Radical Political Economics*, 6(2). Also in A. Giddens and D. Held (eds) (1982) *Classes, Power and Conflict*, London: Macmillan.

Marsh, A. 1978: *Protest and Political Consciousness*. London: Sage.

Marwick, A. 1982: *British Society since 1945*. Harmondsworth: Penguin.

May, A. and Rowan, K. (eds) 1982: *Inside Information: British Government and the Media*. London: Constable.

Middlemas, K. 1979: *Politics in Industrial Society: The Experience of the British System since 1911*. London: André Deutsch.

Morgan, H. O. 1984: *Labour in Power 1945–51*. Oxford: Oxford University Press.

Moss, L. 1982: People and government in 1978; prepared for a joint meeting of Applied Statistics and Social Statistics Committees of the Royal Statistical Society, April 1982.

Nairn, T. 1977 and 1981; 2nd edn: *The Break-up of Britain*. London: New Left Books and Verso.

Nichols, T. and Armstrong, P. 1976: *Workers Divided*. London: Fontana.

Nichols, T. and Benyon, H. 1977: *Living with Capitalism*. London: Routledge & Kegan Paul.

Nordhaus, W. D. 1975: The political business cycle. *Review of Economic Studies*, 42.

O'Connor, J. 1973: *The Fiscal Crisis of the State*. New York: St Martin's Press.

Offe, C. 1980: The separation of form and content in liberal democratic politics. *Studies in Political Economy*, 3.

Offe, C. 1984: *Contradictions of the Welfare State*. London: Hutchinson.

Panitch, L. 1976: *Social Democracy and Industrial Militancy*. Cambridge: Cambridge University Press.

Pateman, C. 1973: Political culture, political structure and political change. *British Journal of Political Science*, 1.

Pateman, C. 1980: The civic culture: a philosophical critique. In G. Almond and S. Verba (eds), *The Civic Culture Revisited*, Boston: Little, Brown.

Pateman, C. 1988: *The Sexual Contract*. Cambridge: Polity Press.

Poulantzas, N. 1978: *State, Power, Socialism*. London: Verso.

Rose, R. 1974: The United Kingdom as a multi-national state. In R. Rose (ed.), *Studies in British Politics*, 3rd edn, London: Macmillan.

Rose, R. and Peters, G. 1977: The political consequences of economic overload. University of Strathclyde Centre for the Study of Public Policy.

Ryder, J. and Silver, H. 1977: *Modern English Society*. London.

Rubinstein, W. D. 1976: Wealth, elites and the class structure of modern Britain. *Past and Present*, 70.

Scannell, P. 1984: A conspiracy of silence. In G. McLennan, D. Held and S. Hall (eds), *State and Society in Contemporary Britain*, Cambridge: Polity Press.

Smith, D. 1984: Education and the European state: evolution, rationalization and crisis. In S. Bornstein, D. Held and J. Krieger (eds), *The State in Capitalist Europe*, London: Allen & Unwin.

Stanworth, P. 1980: Trade, gentility and upper-class education in Victorian Britain. *International Studies of Management and Organization*, X, 1-2.

Stanworth, P. and Giddens, A. (eds) 1974: *Elites and Power in British Society*. Cambridge: Cambridge University Press.

State Research 1982: Computers and the British police. In *State Research*, vol. 29, London: State Research.

Stephens, J. D. 1979: *The Transition from Capitalism to Socialism*. London: Macmillan.

Thompson, G. 1984: Rolling back the state. Economic intervention 1975-82. In G. McLennan, D. Held and S. Hall (eds), *State and Society in Contemporary Britain*, Cambridge: Polity Press.

Thompson, E. P. 1968: *The Making of the English Working Class*. Harmondsworth: Penguin.

Thompson, E. P. 1978: The secret state. In D. Held et al. (eds), *States and Societies*, Oxford: Martin Robertson.

Thompson, E. P. 1980: *Writing by Candlelight*. London: Merlin.

Thompson, E. P. 1984: Mr Attlee and the Gadarene swine. *Guardian*, 3 March 1984.

Townsend, P. 1979: *Poverty*. Harmondsworth: Penguin.

Weber, M. 1972: *From Max Weber*, eds H. H. Gerth and C. W. Mills. Oxford: Oxford University Press.

Young, H. and Sloman, A. 1982: *No, Minister*. London: BBC.

Zaretsky, E. 1976: *Capitalism, the Family and Personal Life*. London: Pluto.

5

Liberalism, Marxism and the Future Direction of Public Policy

On 17 April 1984, people from Docklands in East London mounted a demonstration on the river Thames.* Frustrated by decisions taken by local and central government and by private corporations, the residents of North Woolwich sailed to Westminster in order to present their own plans for the development of Docklands.[1] One local resident explained the sources of their frustration as follows:

> We're talking really here about people's heritages. Well, I was born in Docklands, generations of my family worked in Docklands. Some built the docks, some built the bridges . . . To me it's a whole culture being destroyed by these developers who don't really know what people want – people's needs.

As one docker put it:

> We are losing our work . . . We lost 20,000 jobs in 10 years in one port. They got the best, they drew the best like a vampire would out of a dead body. They drew all the best out of that area and just left it to rot and that's exactly what's happened to the whole of the East End where they sucked out the best they could get out of any particular part and left, without paying any benefit back, without leaving the people of the East End any benefit whatsoever.

Another docker put it this way – 'I mean, it all stems from bad management, bad planning, the lack of consulting with the people that work', or, as a local resident said:

> I don't want to get political . . . but this is only my opinion and what I feel from when I walk around the area and people talk to me, this is why they so often get apathetic, 'cos they always think the money speaks the last word.

---

* This essay, modified for this volume, was first published in Peter Nolan and Suzanne Paine (eds), *Rethinking Socialist Economics* (Cambridge: Polity Press, 1986), pp. 13–34.

Residents and workers mobilized to produce their own alternative for the area – The People's Plan. One of its supporters explained it in these terms:

> The People's Plan . . . started out as an idea of involving people, in getting things for themselves for their own area because all the time you find that people from above, in local government council offices, will make up plans and say, right, this is what we're going to give these people in this area, regardless of whether they want it or not and this was an opportunity to go out and ask people, say to them – 'Look, you live here, it's up to you now. What do you want? What do you see for your area? How do you see it developing?'

The People's Plan demanded that Docklands be developed for 'the benefit of all people living in the area'. It stated their major needs as:

- more control over decisions affecting their lives;
- more jobs, including the generation of small industries and training schemes;
- more houses for rent;
- better schools and childcare facilities;
- more open spaces, parks and recreational facilities.

There are three traditional responses on the Left to initiatives like The People's Plan. Orthodox Marxists are likely to be extremely sceptical about the long-term political significance of such efforts. They might welcome the protest, but they are generally of the view that underpinning them is a 'false' romanticization of community: the protest should be channelled along strictly class-political lines. For the state cannot simply be bargained with or contained by democratic protest; its coercive structures have to be conquered and transcended. Interestingly, social democrats (or 'labourists') are just as sceptical. Again, they might value the initiative, but they tend to believe that all such protests ought to be pursued through the official avenues of local and national politics – after all, many of these channels are themselves the result of successful social democratic struggle. The third group, libertarians (or 'participatory socialists'), would generally welcome the initiative wholeheartedly; for initiatives like The People's Plan prefigure the desirable form an alternative, fully democratic society would take – a society in which the frustrated capacities of working people (frustrated by private capital and the paternalistic state) would no longer be held in check, and people would govern their own affairs directly.

In my view, none of these responses alone is acceptable. Initiatives like The People's Plan raise fundamental questions about the nature of democracy, how democracy might be extended, and the relationship of democracy, liberty and equality. These are, to say the least, fundamental matters; and the traditional responses of the left will no longer, if they ever could, suffice. Why?

The New Right and the Thatcher governments

Part of the answer lies in the 'success' of the New Right (or neo-liberalism). The New Right has, in general, advocated the view that only individuals can judge what they want and, therefore, the less the state interferes in their lives the more freedom they will have to set their own priorities (see Hayek, 1960 and 1982; cf. Nozick, 1974). Accordingly, a *laissez-faire* or free-market society is a key objective along with a 'minimal state' (see essay 6 for a detailed account of these ideas). The governments of Margaret Thatcher (and of Ronald Reagan and George Bush in the United States) have championed the 'rolling back of the state' on grounds similar to those of the New Right: individual freedom depends on reducing the regulations on social and economic affairs. In making the latter a prime task, the Thatcher governments have embraced the classic liberal concerns not only with the establishment of the conditions for individuals to pursue their aims with minimal political interference but also with the creation of a secure basis for the pursuit of prosperity in business, trade and family life. This amounts to a strategy for restricting the scope of the state's action and simultaneously increasing aspects of its power so that it has the resources to ensure political stability (cf. essay 1 pp. 24–5, and essay 4, pp. 139–41).

There are two questions to ask: why has the Thatcher strategy enjoyed a degree of political success; and will this strategy work or fail in the long run?

The political success of the Thatcher governments over the past decade or so is due to many factors including the disarray of the Labour Party and the impact of the Falklands war.[2] However, as a political strategy its success is also related, I believe, to the dwindling popularity of the 'Keynesian welfare state', or what I call 'state-administered socialism'. There are several different variants of state-administered socialism; from the state socialist societies of the East to the traditional social democratic regimes of the West. While there are major differences between these types, which I by no means wish to underestimate, they also have certain elements in common: all can be associated with centrally controlled bureaucratic institutions. The programme of state-administered socialism in Britain, despite its considerable achievements during the post-war years, has lost much of its radical appeal because it fails to recognize the desirable form and limits of state action. This is true, I want to argue, in several related respects.

To begin with, the British model of state-administered socialism – nationalized industry, state-provided health services, households regulated on the model of the patriarchal family through social services and so on – assumed that state power could become the caretaker of existence. Intervening in social life by securing capital investment, reducing unemployment and expanding welfare opportunities, the state tended to assume omniscience over questions of needs and wants. The effect was to encourage the passive consumption of state provision and, in so doing, seriously to undermine people's confidence in directing their own lives. In retrospect, it is hardly surprising that among its unforeseen effects were the generation of a marked distrust of those in charge of the apparatus of government, a deep scepticism about expertise and a general decline in the legitimacy of 'socialism'. It became widely assumed that socialism meant bureaucracy, surveillance, red tape, and state control – not only in the rhetoric of Thatcher (and in the mass media's particular images of Eastern Europe), but also in the actual experience of those in daily contact with certain branches of the welfare state, for example social security offices, social services, housing authorities and city planners.

Furthermore, the shortcomings of state-administered socialism were compounded when successive Labour governments – and those Conservative governments which presided over the expansion of the welfare state – progressively failed to 'deliver the goods', as they inevitably did in the deteriorating circumstances of the international economy and British capitalism, especially after the oil crisis in 1973. This climate of economic crisis undermined the assumption that the state could, in any simple way, secure economic growth, reduce unemployment and expand social welfare. The relative prosperity of the post-war years (especially of the 1950s to the early 1970s) had helped to create the illusion that many, if not all, of the interests of social groups, elites and classes could be accommodated in the politics of the expanding welfare state. Growing resources meant that management and labour, along with administrators of services and their clients, might find scope for manoeuvre and a basis for satisfaction or future satisfaction. By contrast, economic crisis brought sharply into focus the state's incapacity to realize the ideals of welfare socialism, as it dramatized the bureaucratic, hierarchical, inequitable and often repressive character of many state policies.

In addition, state effectiveness has been weakened by the attempt of both Labour and Conservative governments to broaden the regulation and control of social life. This made the state more dependent upon, and vulnerable to, the resistance of powerful social groups (above all, City interests, industrial organizations, certain trade unions) – a trend already strongly evident in the years of the Callaghan government (1976–9). For all these reasons, the 'hand of the state' became more visible while becoming no more capable of progressive and effective reform.

It is, of course, a sadly ironic fact that the difficulties of state-administered socialism have been most successfully popularized by the New Right. While the regressive consequences of the Thatcher regime are not of prime concern here (see essay 4, pp. 139–41), it is important to stress that the difficulties of state-administered socialism have both strengthened Thatcher's hand and highlighted the political vulnerability of certain socialist strategies. This is true in two decisive respects. First, the New Right has tried to capitalize upon the failure of governments to keep many of their promises. It has sought to distance itself from the process of making such promises as well as to discredit many of the important commitments of post-war governments. Secondly, the Thatcher regime has taken the lead in popularizing the demand for less state action. Preoccupied with the need to redraw the boundaries between state and civil society – the realm of privately owned or voluntarily run (non-state directed) activities – it is concerned with segregating spheres of life that have become highly interdependent. In so doing, it has sought to promulgate a highly particular interpretation of social virtues – self-interest, hard work, self-reliance, freedom of choice, private property and distrust of state bureaucracy. According to this so-called 'libertarian' ideology, comprehensive state regulation saps both individual initiative and social resources that make self-organization and 'mutual aid' possible. I wish to argue that such claims have enjoyed a considerable measure of success to date precisely because they connect with and mobilize a considerable amount of cynicism, distrust and dissatisfaction with many of the institutions of the interventionist Welfare State that has long existed. In other words, the success of Thatcher and the New Right is parasitic upon the profound difficulties faced by a bureaucratic, state-administered socialism.

This is by no means to say that most of those who are disenchanted with aspects of the politics of the interventionist Welfare State are neo-liberals (see, for instance, Whiteley, 1981; Taylor-Gooby, 1983 and 1985; Jowell and Airey, 1984; Jowell et al., 1988). Rather, it is to highlight the considerable evidence that points to high levels of ambivalence about dominant political institutions, to low levels of trust, acceptance and legitimacy of bureaucrats, experts and politicians, and to a fairly widespread sense that 'ordinary people's needs' are misunderstood (see essay 4, for a survey of pertinent findings; cf. the participants of The People's Plan). In addition, there is some evidence of marked dissatisfaction, particularly among lower-income groups and women, with their treatment by welfare state institutions, and of a tendency to regard the provision of benefits as excessively rigid, paternalistic and bureaucratic (see LEWRG, 1980; West et al., 1984; and Hyde, 1985).[3]

There are many reasons why the Conservative strategy of redrawing the boundaries between the state and civil society is likely to fail. To begin with, the problems of the British economy – unemployment, flight of capital overseas, the erosion of the manufacturing base – are deeply structured; the present government's policies not only miss many of the roots of Britain's protracted economic and political difficulties, but they also in part exacerbate these difficulties.[4] Furthermore, 'Thatcherism' is incapable of realizing the 'libertarian' values it affirms – above all, those of freedom of choice, mutual aid and self-reliance. A capitalist-directed economy and a progressively more centralized 'strong state' (nurtured through such measures as the Police and Criminal Evidence Act, the Public Order Act, enforcement of strict limits on local government spending (rate-capping) and abolition of the Greater London Council (GLC) and the Metropolitan County Councils) directly contradict its professed anti-bureaucratic, non-hierarchical principles. Only the socialist tradition, it will be argued here, can, in the end, genuinely defend the libertarian ideals of mutual aid, democratic accountability and a restriction on state power.

Whether the New Right's grip on the public imagination can be loosened once and for all depends crucially on the left's capacity to rework and publicly articulate the issues of state and civil society, which 'Thatcherism' has helped to make a public problem. The New Right has contributed to a discussion about the limits of state-administered socialism with which the left must engage. The left, in other words, needs its own critique of state-administered socialism – a critique which embraces both the undesirable elements of the British model and explores the parallels which exist with unacceptable aspects of the state socialist societies. The libertarian appeals of the New Right are a reminder that controversies over who shall inherit the vocabulary of freedom are long overdue; and they are imperative for the survival of democratic socialism.

What form, then, ought state action to take, and how should its limits be defined from a socialist perspective? There is growing consensus on the left that, if the socialist movement is to become once again publicly credible and viable in the long run, it must re-emphasize the old goals of equality *and* liberty. To put the point schematically: the New Right counterposes equality (which it assesses from a wholly negative point of view) against liberty (which it sees as wholly positive), and so concerns itself with minimal state interference in people's existence and the application of 'free' market principles to more and more aspects of life. The 'old' left (whether orthodox Marxist or Labourist) emphasizes the state's capacity to create equality and downplays questions of liberty; hence, it has too often been satisfied with the notion of a 'big state' to impose equality on civil society. The question posed by the growing consensus on the left in favour of equality and liberty is how can 'the state' and 'civil society' be combined to promote equality and liberty? In order to address this question it is worth reflecting on the terms of reference of the two most central traditions of contemporary political thought: liberalism and Marxism.

Liberalism and Marxism

Liberal thinkers have in general tied the goals of liberty and equality to individualist political, economic and ethical doctrines.[5] The individual is, in essence, sacrosanct, and is free and equal only to the extent that he or she can pursue and attempt to realize, with minimum political impediment, self-chosen ends and personal interests. Equal justice can be sustained between individuals if, above all, individuals' entitlement to certain rights or liberties is respected and all citizens are treated equally before the law. Liberalism is preoccupied with the creation and defence of a world in which 'free and equal' individuals can flourish; this is a position maintained alike by, for example, Locke, J. S. Mill and Nozick. By contrast, the thinkers in the Marxist tradition (and in most strands of socialism) defended the desirability of certain social or collective goals. For Marx and Engels to take equality and liberty seriously is to challenge the view that these values can be realized by individuals through essentially private enterprise and the liberal-democratic state. Equality, liberty and justice – recognized by them as 'the great universal ideals' – cannot be achieved in a world dominated by private ownership of property and the capitalist economy. These values, according to them, can be realized only through class struggle, the dictatorship of the proletariat and eventually through the complete democratization of society and the 'withering away of the state'. Only the latter conditions can ultimately guarantee the reduction of all forms of coercive power so that human beings can develop – as free and equal.

The views of liberals and Marxists are, of course, radically different. The key elements of their theories are fundamentally at odds. It is therefore somewhat paradoxical to note that they share a vision of reducing arbitrary power and regulatory capacity to its lowest possible extent. Both liberals and Marxists fear the extension of networks of intrusive power into society, 'choking', to borrow a phrase from Marx, 'all its pores'. They both have traditions of criticizing the bureaucratic, inequitable and often repressive character of much state action. In addition, they are both concerned with the political, social and economic conditions for the development of people's capacities, desires and interests. Put in this general and abstract way, there appears to be a convergence of emphasis on ascertaining the circumstances under which people can develop as 'free and equal'.

To put the point another way, the aspiration of the liberal and Marxist traditions to a world characterized by free and equal relations among mature adults reflects, above all, a concern to ensure the following:

1 The creation of the best circumstances for all humans to develop their nature and express their diverse qualities (involving an assumption of respect for individuals' diverse capacities, their ability to learn and enhance their potentialities).
2 Protection from the arbitrary use of political authority and coercive power (involving an assumption of respect for privacy in all matters which are not the basis of potential and demonstrable 'harm' to others).[6]

3 The involvement of citizens in the regulation of public life (involving an assumption of respect for the dignity and equal worth of human lives).[7]
4 Provision for the consent of individuals in the maintenance, justification and legitimation of regulative institutions (involving an assumption of respect for the authentic and reasoned nature of individuals' judgements);
5 The expansion of economic opportunity to maximize the availability of resources (involving an assumption that when individuals are free from the burdens of unmet physical need they are best able to develop themselves).

There is, in other words, a set of aspirations which liberalism and Marxism have in common. These aspirations can be linked together and stated in the form of a central principle – what I call the 'principle of autonomy'.[8] The principle can be stated as follows:

> *Individuals should be free and equal in the determination of the rules by which they live; that is, they should enjoy equal rights (and, accordingly, equal obligations) in the specification of the framework which generates and limits the opportunities available to them throughout their lives.*

Both liberalism and Marxism give priority to the development of 'autonomy' or 'independence'. But to state this – and to try and articulate its meaning in a fundamental but highly abstract principle – is not yet to say very much. For the full meaning of a principle cannot be specified independently of the conditions of its enactment. Liberalism and Marxism may prioritize 'autonomy', but they differ radically over how to secure it and, hence, over how to interpret it.

The specification of a principle's conditions of enactment is a vital matter; for if a perspective on the most desirable form of the state and civil society is to be at all plausible, it must be concerned with both theoretical and practical issues, with philosophical as well as organizational and institutional questions. In this regard I shall contend that both liberalism and Marxism are mistaken about the conditions under which the principle of autonomy can be enacted. It is, therefore, important to identify and examine these conditions – conditions which cannot, of course, be specified independently of historical and political circumstances. I should like to stress from the outset that the discussion maintains as its backdrop Western capitalist countries and, in particular, Britain. My argument is that the conditions of enactment of the principle of autonomy can be specified adequately only if one draws upon aspects of both liberalism and Marxism, and appreciates the limitations of both overall positions.

The principle of autonomy can only be realized adequately if we take seriously some of the central prescriptions, and thus some of the central arguments, of both liberalism and Marxism. Equality and liberty – the interconnections of which the principle tries to specify – can only be advanced if one appreciates the complementarity of liberalism's scepticism about political power and Marxism's scepticism about economic power. Liberalism's thrust to create a sovereign democratic state, a diversity of power centres and a world marked by openness, controversy and plurality is radically compromised by the reality of the so-called 'free market' – the imperatives of the system of corporate power and multinational corporations, the logic of commercial and banking houses and the economic and political rivalry of the power blocs. If liberalism's central failure is to see markets as 'powerless' mechanisms of coordination and, thus, to neglect the distorting nature of economic power in relation to democracy, Marxism's central failure is the reduction of political power to economic power and, thus, the neglect of the dangers of centralized political power and the problems of political accountability. Marxism's embodiment in East European societies today is marked by the growth of the centralized bureaucratic state; its claim to represent the forces of progressive politics is tarnished by socialism's relation in practice, in the East and also in the West, with bureaucracy, surveillance, hierarchy and state control. Accordingly, liberalism's account of the nature of markets and economic power must be doubted while Marxism's account of the nature of democracy must be questioned.

It is important to take note also of some of the limitations shared by liberalism and Marxism. Generally, these two political perspectives have failed to explore the impediments to full participation in democratic life other than those imposed – however important these may be – by state and economic power. The roots of the difficulty lie in narrow conceptions of 'the political'. In the liberal tradition the political is equated with the world of government or governments alone. Where this equation is made and where politics is regarded as a sphere apart from economy or culture – that is, as governmental activity and institutions – a vast domain of politics is excluded from view: above all, the spheres of productive and reproductive relations. A similar thing can be said about the Marxist conception of politics. Although the Marxist critique of liberalism is of great significance – showing as it does that the organization of the economy cannot be regarded as non-political, and that the relations of production are central to the nature and distribution of power – it is ultimately limited because of the direct connection it draws (even when the state is conceived as 'relatively autonomous') between political and economic life. By reducing political to economic and class power – and by calling for 'the end of politics' – Marxism itself tends to marginalize or exclude certain types of issues from politics. This is true of all those issues which cannot, in the last analysis, be reduced to class-related matters. Classic examples of this are the domination of nature by industry (which raises ecological questions), of women by men, and of certain racial and ethnic groups by others. Other central concerns include the power of public administrators or bureaucrats over their 'clients' and the role of 'authoritative resources' (the capacity to coordinate and control the activities of human beings) which build up in most social organizations.

The narrow conception of 'the political' in both liberalism and Marxism has meant that key conditions for the realization of the principle of autonomy have been eclipsed from view – conditions concerning, for instance, equal rights and obligations in the organization of economic life (essentially unexamined by liberalism) and equal rights and obligations with respect to the household, child-rearing and many aspects of human reproduction (essentially unexamined by liberalism and Marxism). (I am not saying, of course, that no liberal or Marxist has been concerned with these things; rather I am arguing that their perspectives or frameworks of analysis cannot adequately encompass them.) In order to grasp the diverse conditions necessary for the adequate institutionalization of the principle of autonomy, we need a broader conception of 'the political' than is found in either of these perspectives – a conception which emphasizes that politics is about power; that is to say, about the 'transformative capacity' of social agents, agencies and institutions, about the forces which influence and reflect its distribution and use, and about the effect of this on resource use and distribution (see pp. 1–2, 73–4, 246–7 for an elaboration of this broad concept of politics).

If politics is understood in this broad way, then the specification of the conditions of enactment of the principle of autonomy amounts to the specification of the conditions for the participation of citizens in decisions about the use and distribution of resources in relation to affairs that are important to them (that is, us). Thus, rather than striving toward a world in which there is an 'end of politics', we should strive toward a state of affairs in which political life – democratically organized – is an essential part of all people's lives. Can we specify the nature of this state of affairs more precisely? How can 'the state' and 'civil society' be combined to promote equality and liberty, that is, the principle of autonomy?

Re-forming the relation between state and civil society

The principle can be realized, I believe, only by recognizing the need for a process of 'double democratization' (see Held, 1987; Keane, 1988). By double democratization I mean an attempt to re-form the state and civil society through two interdependent processes: the restructuring of state institutions and the expansion of autonomy in civil society. Such an attempt must reject the assumption that the state could ever replace civil society or vice versa. It would defend thereby, on the one hand, the liberal principle that the separation of the state and civil society must be a permanent feature of any democratic political order and, on the other hand, the Marxist notion that this order must be one in which productive property, status and the power to make decisions are no longer subject to private appropriation. The aim would be progressively to equalize the power and, thereby, the capacity of men and women to act in the key realms of political and social life, while recognizing the importance of a diversity of types of power centre.

State institutions must be viewed as necessary devices for enacting legislation, promulgating new policies, containing inevitable conflicts between particular interests, and preventing civil society from falling victim to new forms of inequality and tyranny. Institutions of representative democracy are an inescapable element for coordinating and authorizing these activities, although such institutions would have to be transformed, in ways indicated below, if they are to become both accessible and effective regulators of public life. In this scheme of things, on the other hand, a multiplicity of social spheres – including socially owned enterprises, housing cooperatives, independent communications media and health centres (organized perhaps according to the principles of direct democracy) – must secure enhanced powers to check and control their own projects. That is to say, they must be protected by a legal framework which recognizes the right of their members to control the resources at their disposal, whether these are material or authoritative, without undue interference from the state or political parties. The state and civil society must become the condition for each other's democratization.

Without a secure and independent civil society, goals such as freedom and equality cannot be realized. But without the protective, redistributive and conflict-mediating functions of the state, struggles to transform civil society are likely to become fragmented, or the bearers of new forms of inequality of power, wealth or status. The central issue today is not the old alternative between liberalism or Marxism, reformism or revolution to abolish the state. Rather, it is the question of how to enact the 'double-sided' process of creative reform protected by state action and innovation from below through radical social initiatives.

To analyse the process of democratization as a 'double-sided' process is more than simply an attempt to clarify the framework of the present political discussion about the future of socialism. The limits and forms of desirable state action are also becoming a crucial theme in European discussions of practical socialist policies, a debate which can be illustrated briefly by reference to two new socialist initiatives in the area of investment and the reorganization of social welfare provision.

Since 1975, for instance, extensive discussions have occurred in Sweden about the ways in which a gradual extension of social ownership of productive property can be achieved. One thing to emerge from these discussions was the Meidner Plan. Its details are complex, but the thrust of its programme is to create the means for increasing the level of socially controlled investment (Korpi, 1978). This would be done by formulating an egalitarian, planned wages policy (promoting a direct attack on poverty and low pay while trying to keep wages within limits tolerable to an open economy) and by using increased taxes on profits to create investment funds on a local and regional basis which are citizen-controlled. This proposal seeks to avoid the problem whereby wage restraint leads traditionally to an increased rate of private profit without increasing investment, let alone greater social control over productive resources. In the long run, it also aims to break with the conventional view that state economic planning plus nationalization equals socialism. It is this idea which is important; the proposal itself, of course, needs much further examination.

The second example of new socialist strategy is the Scandinavian proposals to 'lease-back' institutions of social policy to the community. These proposals are a response to the evident increase in concern in the post-war period with bureaucratic and hierarchical state institutions such as planning authorities, schools and housing agencies. At the same time, such proposals attempt to counter directly the New Right strategy of privatization (returning to the private sector control of state services and resources). These proposals suggest that state institutions of social policy can be turned into something more positive and democratic if control of them is reclaimed or leased back to the people who use and service them. Although they would remain publicly funded, the policies of such organizations would be guided neither by capitalist markets nor by state direction, but by criteria of social need generated by producers' and consumers' decisions. As a consequence, the state would guarantee the resources and facilities for childcare, health clinics or schools, while leaving the government of these organizations to local constituencies.

In my view, these policy examples are important not because they can be 'imported' and adopted in a straightforward manner, but because they recognize explicitly the urgent need to deal with the undesirable elements of bureaucratic state regulation and surveillance which have grown so enormously since 1945. However, such policies do not automatically secure more decentralized, horizontally structured egalitarian patterns of social life. Vigorous political initiatives, funding and legal recognition are necessary conditions of their survival and expansion. Thus, the second and equally important prong of a new strategy for socialism becomes crucial: the democratization of state policy-making and administration.

In Britain the need to democratize political institutions has mostly been confined to questions of reforming party leadership, union decision-making and electoral rules. This focus leaves out a whole variety of issues which socialists must address if they are to resume leadership in the battle for democratic political rights. Proportional representation and the internal reform of parties are only two of a wide gamut of necessary considerations. Others must include public funding of elections for all parties meeting a minimum level of support; genuine access to, and equal distribution of, media time; freedom of information (for example, abolition of the Official Secrets Act and the many rules and regulations concerning secrecy); decentralization of the Civil Service to the regions; and the defence and enhancement of local authority power against rigid, centralized state decisions. But none of these strategies for making the polity more democratic will enjoy full success unless a further difficult problem is confronted: can the requirements of democratic public life (openness, controversy, pluralism, universal participation) be reconciled with those domestic and international institutions for maintaining 'law and order' which thrive on secrecy, cunning and the monopoly of the means of violence? This is, to say the least, a pressing problem and one that can only be confronted, I believe, by exploring ways in which the sovereignty of parliament can be established over the state (see essay 6).

Freedom, equality and political strategy

If freedom and equality are to be taken seriously today, the following factors, among others, need emphasis:

(1) All political doctrines which effectively restrict freedom to a minority of the population should be rejected. 'Negative freedom' – the avoidance of political restraint upon action – which much neo-liberal and modern Conservative thought demands, *de facto* subordinates the mass of the population to forces entirely outside their control.

(2) While the concept of 'negative freedom' is not unimportant, liberty means little if it is not positive, the power to choose among alternatives. Freedom comes from having the actual capacity (the health, skills and resources) to pursue different courses of action in political, economic and social life.

(3) In this sense, freedom means that people should enjoy equal rights and, accordingly, equal obligations in the generation and the use of opportunities available to them throughout their lives. Freedom entails the acceptance of obligations which go along with rights – obligations which follow from acceptance of the dignity and equal worth of human lives and of the necessity of the direct and equal involvement of citizens in the regulation of public life.

(4) Freedom must be given a concrete content; it only exists in everyday life as freedoms. An assessment of freedom must be made on the basis of liberties that are tangible, and capable of being used here and now within the realms of both state and civil society. The formal existence of rights is of little value if they cannot be actualized. The question is: How can they be actualized?

Or, to put the point another way: What is to be made of initiatives like The People's Plan? What is wrong with the traditional ways in which the left responds to such initiatives? The orthodox Marxist left has no basis on which to conceptualize adequately the significance of such efforts. It generally fails to see their potential as a way of revitalizing civil society and putting in the hands of citizens the ability to exercise greater control over their own affairs. Orthodox Marxism is, in fact, extremely suspicious of any notion of competing power centres – centres, that is, which might compete with the role of the party – let alone of the idea of an 'autonomous' civil society. The social-democratic left is again suspicious, preferring official and 'professional' means of political intervention. It has neither the conceptual framework nor the practical experience systematically to encourage attempts at non-state planning. The libertarian response is also unsatisfactory. For if the argument in this essay is accepted, experiments in popular planning ought to be interpreted as part of a much more complex set of strategies. It is one thing to argue in general (and vague) terms that initiatives like The People's Plan are prefigurative of an alternative society; but it is quite dangerous to think of them as actually anticipating all the elements of an alternative society. The emphasis of this essay, at least, must be on seeing such initiatives as representing a significant but very partial and incomplete alternative; they are important as a form of resistance, and are suggestive of ways in which citizens and communities might radically reclaim control over aspects of their own lives. However, they must be understood as a small element within a larger framework. A socialism which is viable and worthy of respect must be synonymous with the democratization of the state as well as of society. Socialism must, in addition, involve the maintenance and transformation of the division between the state and society by making state policy more accountable, and by democratically reordering non-state activities. Only if the 'democratic road to socialism' is understood as a double-sided process of this kind can it regain a durable position as a credible and practical political alternative.

Notes

1   This essay brings together a variety of ideas and themes which I have explored in recent work. The material on popular planning is drawn from a case study I did for Open University television (D209/TV12–1/FOU D265R); a significant portion of the rest of the material is adapted from 'Power and legitimacy in contemporary Britain' (1984b, and essay 4 of this volume); 'Beyond liberalism and Marxism' (1984a) and with John Keane, 'Socialism and the limits of state action' (1984). I would like to acknowledge in particular my debt to John Keane. Many of the ideas in the section on 'The New Right and the Thatcher government' and 'Redrawing the boundaries between state and civil society' were discussed in our joint essay; his

ideas were decisive in these developments. But he may not, of course, agree with aspects of their elaboration here.

2   Part of the pressure on the Labour vote can be explained by changes in the occupational structure of Britain and the decline, in particular, of manual labour as a proportion of the overall work-force. The traditional manual working class has been a particularly important element of the Labour vote and its contraction signals difficulties for Labour (cf. Heath et al., 1985; Crew, 1986; Butler and Kavanagh, 1988). But even if there has been a decline in Labour's 'natural constituency', there remain complicated questions to explain. Why, for instance, have Thatcher's Conservatives successfully made inroads into the working-class vote, and why has their support remained relatively stable across a fairly wide spectrum of social groups and classes? The argument below seeks to shed some light on these issues.

3   It needs to be stressed that there is regrettably little empirical work which systematically separates out opinion about aspects of the extent of public expenditure from perceptions of the way public services are (and might be) actually delivered. I would like to thank Fiona Williams for bringing to my attention the few pertinent studies which have been carried out.

4   My view of these roots is set out in essay 4.

5   Unless I indicate to the contrary, I shall use 'liberalism' here to connote both liberalism since Locke and liberal democracy. See my 'Central perspectives on the modern state' (pp. 12–28) for a discussion of these terms; but cf. Dunn (1979, ch. 2).

6   This is, of course, subject to all the same problems as Mill's principle of harm.

7   Mill and Marx (in characteristic nineteenth-century and ethnocentric style) held this to be true for humans in 'advanced stages' of social development: Mill sought to justify at some length the British rule of India and Marx was convinced of the 'progressive' impact of capitalism on countries with less 'advanced' social and economic systems.

8   I have developed and refined my conception of this principle, and its place in modern democratic theory, in *Models of Democracy* (1987), especially ch. 9. In addition, see Beetham (1981) and Cohen and Rogers (1983) whose writings have directly informed the argument set out below.

References

Beetham, D. 1981: Beyond liberal democracy. *Socialist Register*.

Butler, D. and Kavanagh, D. 1988: *The British General Election of 1987*. London: Macmillan.

Cohen, J. and Rogers, J. 1983: *On Democracy*. New York: Penguin.

Crew, I. 1986: On the death and resurrection of class voting; some comments on *How Britain Votes*. *Political Studies*, 24 (4).

Dunn, J. 1979: *Western Political Theory in the Face of the Future*. Cambridge: Cambridge University Press.

Giddens, A. 1979: *Central Problems in Social Theory*. London: Macmillan.

Hayek, F. A. 1960: *The Constitution of Liberty*. London: Routledge & Kegan Paul.

Hayek, F. A. 1982: *Law, Legislation and Liberty*, vol. 3. London: Routledge & Kegan Paul.

Heath, A., Jowell, R. and Curtice, J. 1985: *How Britain Votes*. Oxford: Pergamon Press.

Held, D. 1983: Central perspectives on the modern state. In D. Held et al. (eds), *States and Societies*, Oxford: Martin Robertson.

Held, D. 1984a: Beyond liberalism and Marxism? In G. McLennan, D. Held and S. Hall (eds), *The Idea of the Modern State*, Milton Keynes: Open University Press.

Held, D. 1984b: Power and legitimacy in contemporary Britain. In G. McLennan, D. Held and S. Hall (eds), *State and Society in Contemporary Britain*, Cambridge: Polity Press.

Held, D. 1987: *Models of Democracy*. Cambridge: Polity Press.

Held, D. and Keane, J. 1984: Socialism and the limits of state action. *New Socalist*, March–April.

Held, D. and Leftwich, A. 1984: A discipline of politics? In A. Leftwich (ed.), *What is Politics?* Oxford: Basil Blackwell.

Hyde, M. 1985: The British welfare state: legitimation crisis and future directions; unpublished research project.

Jowell, R. and Airey, C. (eds) 1984: *British Social Attitudes*. London: Gower.

Jowell, R. et al. 1988: *British Social Attitudes: The 1987 Report*. London: Gower.

Keane, J. 1988: *Democracy and Civil Society*. London: Verso.

King, A. 1976: *Why is Britain becoming Harder to Govern?* London: BBC.

Korpi, W. 1978: *The Working Class in Welfare Capitalism*. London: Routledge & Kegan Paul.

LEWRG (London Edinburgh Weekend Return Group) 1980: *In and Against the State*. London: Pluto.

McLennan, G., D. Held and S. Hall (eds) 1984: *State and Society in Contemporary Britain*. Cambridge: Polity Press.

Nozick, R. 1974: *Anarchy, State and Utopia*. Oxford: Basil Blackwell.

Offe, C. 1984: *Contradictions of the Welfare State*. London: Hutchinson.

Taylor-Gooby, P. 1983: Legitimation deficit, public opinion, and the welfare state. *Sociology*, 17(2).

Taylor-Gooby, P. 1985: Attitudes to welfare. *Journal of Social Policy*, 14(1).

West, P., Illsey, R. and Kelman, H. 1984: Public preferences for the care of dependency groups. *Social Science and Medicine*, 18(4).

Whiteley, P. 1981: Public opinion and the demand for social welfare in Britain. *Journal of Social Policy*, 10(4).

6

The Contemporary Polarization of Democratic Theory: The Case for a Third Way

On both the right and left of the political spectrum today a search is underway for new political policies, strategies and institutional arrangements.* In the West the crisis of the welfare state, linked to protracted economic and political difficulties, has forced a rethinking of the relation between the economy and the state, and between the sphere of private initiative and public regulation, across the political spectrum. In the East there has been a growing recognition of deeply rooted problems affecting the entire structure of state-directed rule. With it has come a fundamental questioning of the connections between planning institutions, bureaucracy and market relations, among other things. And in West and East renewed concern about the direction of contemporary politics has given way, most notably, to fresh consideration of the very essence of democracy.[1]

This essay focuses on the renaissance of reflection on possible democratic futures by, first, tracing current controversies; second, setting out a number of unresolved fundamental issues; third, exploring an alternative way of thinking about democracy; and, fourth, elaborating some outstanding questions which require further theoretical and practical inquiry. In tracing contemporary political disputes, the chapter focuses on two of the most prominent 'voices' in current political discourse; those of the New Right and New Left. It is a particularly opportune moment to examine these voices because the twentieth anniversary of May 1968 has just taken place in the context of the political dominance of governments led by champions of the New Right, in the Anglo-American world at least. This circumstance is certainly not without its ironies and clearly offers food for thought, and the occasion for thinking ahead.

* This essay was prepared for publication in Adrian Leftwich (ed.), *New Developments in Political Science* (London: Edward Elgar, forthcoming), although it is published for the first time in this volume.

Current controversies

The New Right (or neo-liberalism as it is sometimes called) is, in general, of the view that political life, like economic life, is – or ought to be – a matter of individual freedom and initiative (see Hayek, 1960; 1976; 1982; Nozick, 1974). Accordingly, a *laissez-faire* or free-market society is the key objective along with a 'minimal state'. The political programme of the New Right includes the extension of the market to more and more areas of life and the reduction of the state's involvement in the economy and in the provision of opportunities.[2] New Right thinkers have insisted that both individual freedom and individual responsibility have been diminished in recent times because of the proliferation of bureaucratic state agencies attempting to regulate and control individuals' activities (see essay 4). In so arguing, they have committed themselves to the classic liberal doctrine that the collective good (or the good of all individuals) can be properly realized in most cases only by people acting in competitive isolation and pursuing their sectoral aims with minimal state interference.

At root, the New Right is concerned to advance the cause of 'liberalism' against 'democracy' by limiting the possible uses of state power. A government can only legitimately intervene in society to enforce *general rules* – rules which broadly protect 'life, liberty and estate'. Hayek, one of the leading advocates of these ideas, is unequivocal about this: a free, liberal order is incompatible with the enactment of rules which specify how people should use the means at their disposal (1960, pp. 231–2). Governments become coercive if they interfere with people's own capacity to determine their objectives. The prime example Hayek gives of such coercion is legislation which attempts to alter 'the material position of particular people or enforce distributive or "social" justice' (p. 231). Distributive justice always imposes on some other's conception of merit or desert. It requires the allocation of resources by a central authority acting *as if* it knew what people should receive for their efforts and how they should behave. The value of individuals' services can, however, only justly be determined by their fellows in and through a decision-making system which does not interfere with *their* knowledge, choices and decisions. And there is only one sufficiently sensitive mechanism for determining 'collective' choice on an individual basis – the free market. When protected by a constitutional state, no system provides a mechanism of collective choice as dynamic, innovative and responsive as the operations of the free market.

The free market does not always operate perfectly; but, Hayek insists, its benefits radically outweigh its disadvantages (1960, 1976; and see Rutland, 1985). A free-market system is the basis for a genuinely *liberal* order; for 'economic freedom is', as Friedman put it, 'an essential requisite for political freedom' (1980, p. 21). In particular, the market can ensure the coordination of decisions of producers and consumers without the direction of a central authority; the pursuit by everybody of their own ends with the resources at their disposal; the development of a complex economy without an elite who claim to know how it all works. Politics, as a governmental decision-making system, will always be a radically imperfect system of choice when compared to the market. Thus 'politics' or 'state action' should be kept to a minimum – to the sphere of operation of an 'ultra-liberal' state (Hayek, 1976, p. 172). An 'oppressive bureaucratic government' is the almost inevitable result of deviation from this prescription.

Thinkers like Hayek, along with the movement of the New Right more generally, have contributed significantly to a discussion about the appropriate form and limits of state action. They have helped once again to make the relationship among state, civil society and subject populations a leading political issue. Conceptions about the proper character of this relationship are perhaps more unsettled now than at any point during the post-war years.

But the New Right, of course, is not the only tradition with a claim to inherit the vocabulary of freedom. The 'New Left' has developed profound claims of its own to this lexicon. It is worth stressing that the New Left did not develop principally as a 'counter-attack' on the New Right. (Indeed the contrary is true.) While the presence of the New Right has in recent times sharpened New Left views, the latter emerged primarily as a result of the political upheavals of the 1960s, internal debates on the left and dissatisfaction with the heritage of political theory, liberal and Marxist.[3] I shall focus the brief discussion below on the work of two people who have contributed, in particular, to the rethinking of left conceptions of democracy: Pateman (1970; 1985) and Poulantzas (1980).

The extent to which individuals are 'free' in contemporary liberal democracies is questioned by the New Left theorists. To enjoy liberty means not only to enjoy equality before the law, important though this unquestionably is, but also to have the capacities (the material and cultural resources) to be able to choose between different courses of action. As Pateman put it, 'the "free and equal individual" is, in practice, a person found much more rarely than liberal theory suggests' (1985, p. 171). Liberal theory – in its classical and contemporary guises – generally assumes what has, in fact, to be carefully examined: namely, whether the existing relationships among men and women, working, middle and upper classes, blacks and whites, and various ethnic groups allows formally recognized rights to be actually realized. The formal existence of certain rights in democratic *theory* and *ideology* is, while not unimportant, of little value if they cannot be exercised in everyday *practice*. An assessment of freedom must be made on the basis of liberties that are tangible, and capable of being deployed within the realms of both state and civil society. The famous cynical comment on equality before the law – 'The doors of the Court of Justice stand open to all, like the doors of the Ritz Hotel' – applies equally to democratic participation *and* access to ordinary amenities. Without a concrete content – as particular freedoms – liberty can scarcely be said to have profound consequences for everyday life. If liberals or neo-liberals were to take these issues seriously, they would discover that massive numbers of individuals are restricted systematically – for want of a complex mix of resources and opportunities – from participating actively in political and civil life. Inequalities of class, sex and race substantially hinder the extent to which it can legitimately be claimed that individuals are 'free and equal'.

Furthermore, the very liberal claim that there can be a clear separation between 'civil society' and 'the state' is, Pateman argues, flawed, with fundamental consequences for key liberal tenets (1985, pp. 172ff.). If the state is separate from the associations and practices of everyday life, then it is plausible to see it as a special kind of apparatus which the citizen ought to respect and obey. But if the state is enmeshed in these associations and practices, then the claim that the state is an 'independent authority' or 'circumscribed impartial power' is radically compromised. In Pateman's judgement (and that of many contemporary Marxists and neo-pluralists), the state is inescapably locked into the maintenance and reproduction of the inequalities of everyday life. Accordingly, the whole basis of its claim to distinct allegiance is in doubt (1985, pp. 173ff; cf. Lindblom, 1977 and Offe, 1984; 1985). This is unsettling for the whole spectrum of questions concerning the nature of public power, the relation betwen the 'public' and the 'private', the proper scope of politics and the appropriate reach of democratic governments.

If the state, as a matter of routine, is neither 'separate' nor 'impartial' with respect to society, then it is clear that citizens will not be treated as 'free and equal'. If the 'public' and 'private' are interlocked in complex ways, then elections will always be insufficient as mechanisms to ensure the accountability of the forces actually involved in the 'governing' process. Moreover, since the 'meshing' of state and civil society leaves few, if any, realms of 'private life' untouched by 'politics', the question of the proper form of democratic regulation is acute. What form democratic control should take, and what the scope of democratic decision-making should be, becomes an urgent matter. However, the 'traditional' left response to these issues needs to be treated with caution. For New Left thinkers generally accept that there are fundamental difficulties with orthodox Marxist theory (cf. Macpherson, 1977).

Poulantzas has tried to develop a position, in common with other New Left thinkers, which moves beyond a rigid juxtaposition of Marxism with liberalism. For Poulantzas, the development of Stalinism and a repressive state in Russia is not just due to the peculiarities of a 'backward' economy – as many

Marxists today still argue – but can be traced to problems in Marx's and Lenin's thought and practice. Marx's and Lenin's belief that the institutions of representative democracy can be simply swept away by organizations of rank-and-file democracy is erroneous. Lenin, above all, mistook the nature of representative democracy when he labelled it simply as 'bourgeois' (cf. Polan, 1984). Underlying this typical Leninist view is a mistaken distrust of the idea of competing power centres in society. Moreover, it was because of distrust of this kind that Lenin ultimately undermined the autonomy of the soviets after the 1917 revolution, and put the revolution on an 'anti-democratic' road. Poulantzas affirms the view that 'without general elections, without unrestricted freedom of press and assembly, without a free struggle of opinion, life dies out in every public institution' (Rosa Luxembourg, quoted by Poulantzas, 1980, p. 283).

Poulantzas argues that the whole relation between socialist thought and democratic institutions needs to be rethought in the light not only of the reality of Eastern European socialism but also of the moral bankruptcy of the social-democratic vision of reform. Social-democratic politics has led to the adulation of 'social engineering', proliferating policies to make relatively minor adjustments in social and economic arrangements. The state has, accordingly, grown in size and power undermining the vision that social-democratic politics might once have had. But what, then, is the way forward? Institutions of direct democracy or self-management cannot simply replace the state; for, as Max Weber predicted, they leave a coordination vacuum readily filled by bureaucracy. Poulantzas emphasizes two sets of changes which he believes are vital for the transformation of the state in West and East into forms of what he calls 'socialist pluralism'. The state must be democratized by making parliament, state bureaucracies and political parties more open and accountable while new forms of struggle at the local level (through factory-based politics, the women's movement, ecological groups) must ensure that society, as well as the state, is democratized, that is, subject to procedures which ensure accountability. But how these processes interrelate Poulantzas does not say, stressing instead that there are 'no easy recipes'.

While the New Left theorists have highlighted a number of fundamental difficulties with liberal accounts of democracy and, in particular, with the New Right position, the New Left conception of democracy as it is and as it could be cannot simply be accepted. Too many fundamental issues are left unaddressed. Little is said, for instance, about how the economy is actually to be organized and related to the state apparatus, how institutions of representative democracy are to be combined with those of direct democracy, how the scope and power of administrative organizations are to be checked, how those who wish to 'opt out' of the political system might do so, how the problems posed by the ever changing international system could be dealt with. Moreover, the arguments pass over the question of how the 'model' could be realized, over the whole issue of transitional stages and over how those who might be worse off in some respects as a result of its application (those whose current circumstances allow them to determine the opportunities of others) might react and should be treated.

Furthermore, New Left theorists tend to assume that people in general want to extend the sphere of control over their lives. What if they do not want to do so? What if they do not really want to participate in the management of social and economic affairs? What if they do not wish to become creatures of democratic reason? Or, what if they wield democratic power 'undemocratically' – to limit or end democracy?

These are complex and difficult questions, not all of which, of course, one could reasonably expect each theorist to address fully. None the less, they are important questions to ask of 'participatory democracy', precisely because it is a version of democratic theory which champions not only a set of procedures, but a form of life as well.

Fundamental issues

The New Left theorists are correct, I believe, to pursue the implications of democratic principles for the organizational structure of society as well as of the state. However, this leaves them vulnerable to criticism. In particular, it leaves them vulnerable to the charge that they have attempted to resolve prematurely the highly complex relations between individual liberty, distributional matters (questions of social justice) and democratic processes. By focusing squarely on the desirability of collective decision-making, and by allowing democracy to prevail over all other considerations, they tend to leave these relations to be specified in the ebb and flow of democratic negotiation.

But it is precisely in criticizing such a standpoint that the New Right thinkers are at their most compelling. Should there be limits on the power of the *demos* to change and alter political circumstance? Should the nature and scope of the liberty of individuals and minorities be left to democratic decision? Should there be clear constitutional guidelines which both enable and limit democratic operations? By answering questions such as these in the affirmative, the New Right recognizes the possibility of severe tensions between individual liberty, collective decision-making and the institutions and processes of democracy. By not systematically addressing these issues, the New Left, in contrast, has too hastily put aside the problems.[4] In making democracy at all levels the primary social objective to be achieved, the New Left thinkers have relied upon 'democratic reason' – a wise and good democratic will – for the determination of just and positive political outcomes. Can an essentially democratic *demos* be relied upon? Can one assume that the 'democratic will' will be wise and good? Can one assume that 'democratic reason' will prevail? Hayek and other New Right thinkers have suggested good grounds for at least pausing on this matter.

It was precisely around these issues that the New Right generated so much political capital by directly acknowledging the uncertain outcomes of democratic politics – the ambiguous results, for instance, of the 'well-intentioned' democratic welfare state. By highlighting that democracy can lead to bureaucracy, red tape, surveillance and excessive infringement of individual options (and not just in East European societies), they have struck a chord with the actual experience of those in routine contact with certain branches of the modern state, experience which by no means necessarily makes people more optimistic about collective decision-making. The New Right has, then, contributed to a discussion about the desirable limits of democratic collective regulation with which others must engage if the model of a more participatory democracy is to be adequately defended. Such an engagement might well have to concede more to the liberal tradition than has hitherto been allowed by left-wing thinkers. The central question then is: how can individuals be 'free and equal', enjoy equal opportunities to participate in the determination of the framework which governs their lives, without surrendering important issues of individual liberty and distributional questions to the uncertain outcomes of the democratic process?

The surrender need not take place, I believe, if enhanced political participation is embedded in a legal framework that protects and nurtures individuals as 'free and equal' citizens. Accordingly, one cannot escape the necessity of recognizing the importance of a number of fundamental liberal tenets: concerning the centrality, in principle, of an 'impersonal' structure of public power, of a constitution to help guarantee and protect rights, of a diversity of power centres within and outside the state, of mechanisms to promote competition and debate between alternative political platforms. What this amounts to, among other things, is confirmation of the fundamental liberal notion that the 'separation' of the state from civil society must be a central feature of any democratic political order. Models of democracy that depend on the assumption that 'state' could ever replace 'civil society' or vice versa must be treated with the utmost caution.

Within the history of liberalism alone the concept of 'civil society' has been interpreted in a variety of different ways (cf. Cohen, 1982; Bobbio, 1985; Pelczynski, 1985; Keane, 1988). There is a profound sense, moreover, in which civil society can never be 'separate' from the state; the latter, by providing the overall legal framework of society, to a significant degree constitutes the former. None the less, it is not unreasonable to claim that civil society retains a distinctive character to the extent that it is made up of areas of social life – the domestic world, the economic sphere, cultural activities and political interaction – which are organized by private or voluntary arrangements between individuals and groups outside the direct control of the state (see Hall, 1983). It is in this sense that the notion is used here. Thus understood, the terms of the argument I wish to make in the remainder of the essay can be stated as follows: centralized state institutions – *pace* the advocates of highly radical models of the market or democratic life – must be viewed as necessary devices for, among other things, enacting legislation, enforcing rights, co-ordinating new policies and containing inevitable conflicts between particular interests. And representative electoral institutions, including parliament and the competitive party system, must be seen as an inescapable element for authorizing and coordinating these activities.

However, to make these points is not to affirm any one liberal-democratic model as it stands. There are profound difficulties with each major model of liberal democracy (see Held, 1987). For advocates of liberal democracy representing positions as diverse as those of Bentham, J. S. Mill and Schumpeter have tended to be concerned, above all else, with the proper principles and procedures of democratic government. By focusing on 'government', they have detracted attention from a thorough examination of the relation between: formal rights and actual rights; commitments to treat citizens as free and equal and practices which do neither sufficiently; conceptions of the state as, in principle, an independent authority and involvements of the state in the reproduction of the inequalities of everyday life; notions of political parties as appropriate structures for bridging the gap between state and society and the array of power centres which such parties and their leaders cannot reach; conceptions of politics as governmental affairs and systems of power which negate this concept. No current conception of liberal democracy is able to specify adequately, as the New Left thinkers have rightly pointed out, the conditions for the possibility of political participation by all citizens, on the one hand, and the set of governing institutions capable of regulating the forces which actually shape everyday life, on the other. The problems, in sum, are twofold. First, the structure of civil society (including private ownership of productive property, vast sexual and racial inequalities) – misunderstood or endorsed by liberal-democratic models – does not create conditions for effective participation, proper political understanding and equal control of the political agenda (see Dahl, 1985). And, second, the structure of the liberal-democratic state (including large, frequently unaccountable bureaucratic apparatuses, institutional dependence on the process of capital accumulation, political representatives preoccupied with their own re-election) does not create an organizational force which can adequately regulate 'civil' power centres.

Democracy: a double-sided process

The implications of these points are profound: for democracy to flourish today it has to be reconceived as a *double-sided* phenomenon: concerned, on the one hand, with the reform of state power and, on the other hand, with the restructuring of civil society (Held and Keane, 1984). This entails recognizing the indispensability of a process of 'double democratization': the interdependent transformation of both state and civil society. Such a process must be premised on the acceptance of the principle that the division between state and civil society must be a central feature of democratic life, and the notion that the power to make decisions must be free of the inequalities and constraints imposed by the private appropriation of capital. But, of course, to recognize the importance of both these positions is to recognize the necessity of recasting substantially their traditional connotations. This requires us to rethink the forms and limits of state action and the forms and limits of civil society.

The questions arise: How, and in what ways, might state policy be made more accountable? How, and in what ways, might 'non-state' activities be democratically reordered? To address these problems with any thoroughness is beyond the scope of this essay (though it is a task begun in Held and Pollitt, 1986, and a central concern of Held, forthcoming). However, it is clearly important to add some institutional detail to the argument presented so far, if the conditions of enactment of a double-sided conception of democracy are to be envisaged at all. What follows, however, is nothing other than the briefest of sketches: some elements of an agenda for further thought and research.

In many countries, West and East, the limits of 'goverment' are explicitly defined in constitutions and bills of rights which are subject to public scrutiny, parliamentary review and judicial process. This idea is fundamental, and fundamental to democracy conceived as a double-sided process. However, such a conception of democracy requires these limits on 'public power' to be reassessed in relation to a far broader range of issues than has been hitherto commonly presupposed. If people are to be free and equal in the determination of the conditions of their own lives, and enjoy equal rights in the specification of the framework which generates and limits the opportunities available to them, they must be in a position to enjoy a range of rights not only in principle, but also in practice. The rights of citizens must be both formal and concrete. This entails the specification of a far broader range of rights, with a far more profound 'cutting-edge', than is allowed typically.

A democracy would be fully worth its name if citizens had the actual power to be active as citizens; that is to say, if citizens were able to enjoy a bundle of rights which allowed them to *command* democratic participation and to treat it as an entitlement (cf. Sen, 1983, ch. 1). Such a bundle of rights, it is important to stress, should not be thought of as merely an extension of the sphere of accumulated private demands for rights and privileges over and against the state, as many liberal thinkers have conceived rights (see Held, 1987, ch. 2). Nor should it be thought of as simply redistributive welfare measures to alleviate inequalities of opportunity, as many of the theorists of the welfare state have interpreted rights (see Marshall, 1973). Rather, it should be seen as entailed by, and integral to, the very notion of democratic rule itself. It is a way of specifying certain socio-economic conditions for the possibility of effective democratic participation. *If one chooses democracy, one must choose to operationalize a radical system of rights.*

What would be included in such a system of rights? A constitution and bill of rights which enshrined the idea of democracy as a double-sided process would specify equal rights with respect to the processes that determine state outcomes. This would involve not only equal rights to cast a vote, but also equal rights to enjoy the conditions for enlightened understanding, involvement in all stages of collective decision-making and the setting of the political agenda. Such broad 'state' rights would, in turn, entail a broad bundle of social rights linked to reproduction, childcare, health and education, as well as economic rights to ensure adequate economic and financial resources for democratic autonomy. Without tough social and economic rights, rights with respect to the state could not be fully enjoyed; and without state rights new forms of inequality of power, wealth and status could systematically disrupt the implementation of social and economic liberties.

A system of rights of this type would specify certain responsibilities of the state to groups of citizens, which particular governments could not (unless permitted by an explicit process of constitutional amendment) override. The authority of the state would thus, in principle, be clearly circumscribed; its capacity for freedom of action bounded. For example, a right to reproductive freedom for women would entail making the state responsible not only for the medical and social facilities necessary to prevent or assist pregnancy, but also for providing the material conditions which would help make the choice to have a child a genuinely free one, and, thereby, ensure a crucial condition for women if they are to be 'free and equal'. A right to economic resources for women and men, in order that they may be in a position to choose among possible courses of action, would oblige the state to be preoccupied with the ways in which wealth and income can be far more equitably distributed. Such resources might be made available through, among other things, a guaranteed income for all adults irrespective of whether they are engaged in wage-labour or household-labour (see Jordan, 1985). Strategies of the latter type should be treated with some caution; their implications for collective or societal wealth creation and distribution are complex, and by no means fully clear. However, without a minimum resource-base of some kind, many people will remain highly vulnerable and dependent on others, unable to exercise fully an independent choice or to pursue different opportunities that are formally before them. The 'rule of law', then, must involve a central concern with distributional questions and matters of social justice: anything less would hinder the realization of democratic rule.

Accordingly, in this scheme of things, a right to equal justice would entail not only the responsibility of the state to ensure formal equality before the law, but also that citizens would have the actual capacity (the health and resources) to take advantage of opportunities before them. Such a constitution and bill of rights would radically enhance the ability of citizens to take action against the state to redress unreasonable encroachment on liberties. It would help tip the balance from state to parliament and from parliament to citizens. It would be an 'empowering' legal system. As such, it would break with any assumption that the state can successfully define citizens' wants and needs and become the 'caretaker of existence' (see essay 6). Of course, 'empowerment' would not thereby be guaranteed; no legal system alone is able to offer such guarantees. But it would specify rights which could be fought for by individuals, groups and movements (wherever pressure could most effectively be mounted), and which could be tested in, among other places, open court.[5]

The implications for civil society are in part clear. To the extent that its structures comprise elements that undermine the possibility of effective collective decision-making, they would have to be progressively transformed. A democratic state and civil society is incompatible with the existence of powerful sets of social relations and organizations which can – by virtue of the very basis of their operations – distort democratic processes and hence outcomes. At issue here is, among other things, the curtailment of the power of corporations to constrain and influence the political agenda, the restriction of the activities of powerful interest groups (whether they be representatives of particular industries or some trade unions with workers in key industrial sectors) to pursue unchecked their own interests, and the erosion of the systematic privileges enjoyed by some social groups (for instance, certain racial groups) at the expense of others. The state and civil society must, then, become the condition for each other's democratic development.

Under such conditions, strategies would have to be adopted to break up old patterns of power in civil society and to create new circumstances which allow citizens to enjoy greater control of their own projects (see Keane, 1988). If individuals are to be free and equal in the determination of the conditions of their own existence, there must be an array of social spheres – for example, cooperatively owned enterprises, independent communications media and health centres – which allow their members control of the resources at their disposal without direct interference from the state, political agencies or other third parties. The models for the organization of such spheres would have much to learn from the conceptions of direct participation mentioned earlier.

But an experimental view of such organizational structures would have to be taken. The state of democratic theory and the knowledge we have of radical democratic experiments does not allow wholly confident predictions about the most suitable strategies for organizational change (see Held and Pollitt, 1986). In this particular sense, the 'music of the future' (Marx) can only be composed in practice through innovation and research.

Outstanding questions

The model of democracy sketched above – which I call 'democratic autonomy' or 'liberal socialism' – seeks to place at its centre the right of all citizens to participate in public affairs. What is at issue is the provision of a *rightful share* in the process of 'government'. However, it is one thing to recognize a right, quite another to say it follows that everyone must, irrespective of choice, actually participate in public life. Participation is not a necessity.

It has been argued that one of the most important negative liberties established since the end of the ancient world is 'freedom from politics', and that such a liberty is an essential part of the contemporary democratic heritage (Arendt, 1963, p. 284). The model of democratic autonomy strives to be compatible with this element of our heritage. Citizens may decide that extensive participation is unnecessary in certain circumstances, and they may decide this for very rational reasons, including a conviction that their interests are already well protected (see Mansbridge, 1983). Clearly, all systems of law – and the legal system of democratic autonomy would be no exception – specify a variety of obligations. Within the model of democratic autonomy obligations would clearly exist. Citizens would be obliged to accept democratic decisions in a variety of circumstances – at sites of politics, work and community life – unless it could be proved that their rights were violated by such decisions. But the obligation to get involved in all aspects of public life would not be a legal obligation. The right to a life of one's own, within a framework of democratic autonomy, is indisputably important.

This position, of course, raises difficult issues. What exact bundle of rights and obligations does the model of democratic autonomy create? What exact obligations would citizens have to accept? Under what circumstances could they legitimately refuse such obligations? If citizens would be entitled to refuse a decision on the grounds that it violated their rights, what means of resistance would they be justified to deploy in these circumstances? These are just a few of the problems which a fully explicated model of democratic autonomy would have to address, and which require further theoretical inquiry.

In any given political system there are clearly constraints on the extent of liberty which citizens can enjoy: liberty is limited. What distinguishes the model of democratic autonomy from other models, especially those in the liberal tradition, such as that of the New Right, is a fundamental commitment to the principle that the liberty of some individuals must not be allowed at the expense of others, where others are often a majority of citizens. In this sense, the concept of liberty presupposed by the model of democratic autonomy allows in some respects a smaller range of actions for certain groups of individuals. If the aims of the model are to be realized, then some people will no longer have the scope to, for instance, accumulate a vast amount of resources, or pursue their own careers at the expense of the careers of their lovers, wives or children. The liberty of persons within the framework of democratic autonomy will have to be one of progressive accommodation to the liberty of others. While, therefore, the scope of action may be more limited for some in certain respects, it will be radically enhanced for others.

It does not follow from this, as is sometimes remarked about related theoretical positions, that such a fundamental transformation of life opportunities entails the end of the division of labour or the end of a role for specialized competencies. As one critic rightly commented: 'a political future which promised to dispense with expertise will be necessarily an idiot's promise or a promise made in the deepest bad faith' (Dunn, 1979, p. 19). The model of democratic autonomy is and must be fully compatible with people choosing to develop particular talents and skills. The conditions of such choices will be different, but this does not mean that there will be no choices (cf. Burnheim, 1985). Moreover, the model of democratic autonomy presupposes explicitly the existence of centralized decision-making in government. Democratic autonomy does not promote the levelling of all authority and of those clusters of institutions which can provide skilled, predictable administration. Weber's argument about the importance of the latter in preventing public affairs becoming a quagmire of in-fighting among factions, . wholly inefficient in settling pressing collective issues, is particularly significant (see Weber, 1978, vol. II, pp. 949, 951-2). But the form and structure of such institutions would have to be changed. It would, again, be quite fallacious to claim one can know exactly how and in what precise ways this should happen. Much further reflection and research is unquestionably necessary on the types and forms of possible political organization and their connecting relations with markets when the latter function within a framework of broad equality of conditions.

If democratic life involves no more than a periodic vote, the locus of people's activities will be the 'private' realm of civil society and the scope of their actions will depend largely on the resources they can command. Few opportunities will exist for citizens to act as citizens, as participants in public life. But if democracy is understood as a double-sided process this state of affairs might be redressed by creating opportunities for people to establish themselves 'in their capacity of being citizens' (Arendt, 1963, p. 256). Of course, this model of democracy faces an array of possible objections which cannot be pursued here. Hopefully, however, the necessity to think beyond the positions of the New Right and New Left has – at the very least – been established.

Notes

1   I have discussed these issues at greater length in *Models of Democracy* (1987) and in *New Forms of Democracy* (Held and Pollitt, 1986). Some of the material in this chapter is adapted from *Models* as well as from chapter 1 of *New Forms*, although I have sought to tighten up some of my earlier formulations here. I am indebted to Adrian Leftwich for many helpful comments on a draft of this essay.
2   See Levitas (1986) for an analysis of different elements in New Right thinking.
3   The New Left, like the New Right, consists of more than one strand of political thought: at the very least, it consists of ideas inspired by Rousseau, anarchists and a variety of Marxist positions. A number of figures have contributed to the reformulation of left conceptions of democracy and freedom; see Pierson (1986) and Held (1987, ch. 8).
4   This is not to say that the problems are unrecognized (see, e.g., Macpherson, 1977, ch. 5).
5   The existing judicial system in most countries is unlikely to provide sufficiently representative personnel to oversee such a judicial process. An alternative would have to be found, comprising perhaps judicial bodies composed of people who were chosen from a 'statistically representative' sample of the population; that is, who were statistically representative of key social categories (gender, race, age) (see Burnheim, 1985). There is no reason to suppose that such bodies would be less capable of independent judgement than the existing judiciary and many reasons for believing that their judgements over the specific matter of how to interpret human rights would be more representative of collective opinion.

References

Arendt, H. 1963: *On Revolution*. New York: Viking Penguin.
Bobbio, N. 1985: *Stato, Governo and Societa: Per Una Teoria Generale della Politica*. Turin: Einaudi.
Burnheim, J. 1985: *Is Democracy Possible?* Cambridge: Polity Press.
Cohen, J. L. 1982: *Class and Civil Society: The Limits of Marxian Critical Theory*. Oxford: Martin Robertson.
Dahl, R. A. 1985: *A Preface to Economic Democracy*. Cambridge: Polity Press.
Dunn, J. 1979: *Western Political Theory in the Face of the Future*. Cambridge: Cambridge University Press.
Friedman, M. R. 1980: *Free to Choose: A Personal Statement*. Harmondsworth: Penguin.

Hall, S. 1983: Themes and questions. In *The State and Society*, 3(7), Milton Keynes: Open University Press.

Hayek, F. A. 1960: *The Constitution of Liberty*. London: Routledge & Kegan Paul.

Hayek, F. A. 1976: *The Road to Serfdom*. London: Routledge & Kegan Paul.

Hayek, F. A. 1982: *Law, Legislation and Liberty*, vol. 3. London: Routledge & Kegan Paul.

Held, D. 1987: *Models of Democracy*. Cambridge: Polity Press.

Held, D. forthcoming: *Foundations of Democracy*. Cambridge: Polity Press.

Held, D. and Keane, J. 1984: Socialism and the limits of state action. In J. Curran (ed.), *The Future of the Left*. Cambridge: Polity Press.

Held, D. and Pollitt, C. (eds) 1986: *New Forms of Democracy*. London: Sage.

Jordan, B. 1985: *The State: Authority and Autonomy*. Oxford: Basil Blackwell.

Keane, J. 1988: *Democracy and Civil Society*. London: Verso.

Levitas, R. (ed.) 1986: *The Ideology of the New Right*. Cambridge: Polity Press.

Lindblom, C. E. 1977: *Politics and Markets*. New York: Basic Books.

McLennan, G. 1984: Capitalist state or democratic polity? Recent developments in Marxist and pluralist theory. In G. McLennan, D. Held and S. Hall (eds), *The Idea of the Modern State*, Milton Keynes: Open University Press.

Macpherson, C. B. 1977: *The Life and Times of Liberal Democracy*. Oxford: Oxford University Press.

Mansbridge, J. J. 1983: *Beyond Adversary Democracy*. Chicago: Chicago University Press.

Marshall, T. H. 1973: Citizenship and social class. In T. H. Marshall (ed.), *Class, Citizenship and Social Development*, Westport, Conn.: Greenwood Press.

Nozick, R. 1974: *Anarchy, State and Utopia*. Oxford: Basil Blackwell.

Offe, C. 1984: *Contradictions of the Welfare State*. London: Hutchinson.

Offe, C. 1985: *Disorganized Capitalism*. Cambridge: Polity Press.

Pateman, C. 1970: *Participation and Democratic Theory*. Cambridge: Cambridge University Press.

Pateman, C. 1985: *The Problem of Political Obligation: A Critique of Liberal Theory*. Cambridge: Polity Press.

Pelczynski, Z. A. (ed.) 1985: *The State and Civil Society*. Cambridge: Cambridge University Press.

Pierson, C. 1986: *Marxism or Politics?* Cambridge: Polity Press.

Polan, A. J. 1984: *Lenin and the End of Politics*. London: Methuen.

Poulantzas, N. 1980: *State, Power, Socialism*. London: Verso/New Left Books.

Rutland, P. 1985: *The Myth of the Plan*. London: Hutchinson.

Sen, A. 1983: *Poverty and Famine*. Oxford: Oxford University Press.

Weber, M. 1978: *Economy and Society*, 2 vols. Berkeley: University of California Press.

7

Citizenship and Autonomy

This essay focuses on the nature of citizenship by examining the work of two people who have sought to explore its meaning in the context of social and economic structures: T. H. Marshall and Anthony Giddens.* Marshall's famous study, 'Citizenship and social class' (1973a), is a, if not the, classic treatment of the relationship between class and citizenship, capitalism and democracy, and any discussion of citizenship must address his work.[1] But the main emphasis below will be on Giddens's thought. Giddens is one of the foremost political and social theorists today and his writings on class, citizenship and related phenomena raise fundamental questions about some of the key features of modern society and about some of the key contributions of the major traditions of political and social theory: above all, those of liberalism and Marxism. It will be my contention that there are ambiguities at the very heart of Giddens's formulations and that, while he unquestionably makes a major contribution to rethinking citizenship and aspects of democratic life, there are a number of difficulties which remain unresolved in his work – difficulties which cast doubt on the coherence of central elements of his views as they are currently presented.

The essay has a number of sections. In the first part, I examine Marshall's 'Citizenship and social class'. In the second part, I assess Giddens's critique of Marshall and show that many of Giddens's specific criticisms of Marshall are misconceived. After elaborating elements of Giddens's attempt to move beyond Marshall's views in the third part, I will contend in the fourth that the entire framework through which Marshall and Giddens examine the relationship between class and citizenship is partial and limited. The terms of reference of their analysis are such that they exclude from view a whole range of substantive problems, conflict areas and struggles. In the fifth and final part, I will

---

* This essay is published here for the first time; it will appear in David Held and John B. Thompson (eds), *Social Theory of Modern Societies: Anthony Giddens and his Critics* (Cambridge: Cambridge University Press, forthcoming).

explore some of the implications of this position. Focusing in particular on Giddens's recent work, I shall show that the failure to examine class and citizenship in broader terms has created ambiguities in his characterization of rights, of the political realm, of social structure, and finally of the political choices that face us today. I shall argue that there are fundamental ambivalences in Giddens's account of central elements of contemporary society.

Citizenship and class

By citizenship, Marshall meant 'full membership of a community', where membership entails *participation* by individuals in the determination of the conditions of their own association (Marshall, 1973a, p. 70). Citizenship is a status which bestows upon individuals *equal* rights and duties, liberties and constraints, powers and responsibilities (p. 84). While there is no universal principle that determines what exactly the citizen's rights and duties shall be, societies in which citizenship is a developing force create, Marshall contended, an image of an 'ideal citizenship' and, thereby, a goal towards which aspirations can be directed. Within all such societies, the urge to attain the ideal is 'an urge towards a fuller measure of equality' – an enrichment of the stuff of which citizenship is made and an increase in the number of those upon whom the status of citizenship is bestowed (p. 84). If citizenship is a principle of equality, class, by contrast, is a system of inequality anchored in property, education and the structure of the national economy (pp. 84–5). According to Marshall, class functions, among other things, to erode and limit the extent to which citizenship creates access to scarce resources and participation in the institutions which determine their use and distribution. Class and citizenship are contrary principles of organization: they are basically opposed influences.

The concept and reality of citizenship are, Marshall argued, among the great driving forces of the modern era. There has been a long, uneven but persistent, trend towards the expansion of the rights of citizenship which for analytical purposes can be broken down into three 'bundles' of rights: civil, political and social.[2] Essentially, he maintained, political reform in each of these domains can modify the worst aspects of economic inequality and can, therefore, make the modern capitalist system and the liberal polity more equal and just, without revolutionary activity. The dynamic of class inequalities stemming from the capitalist market system can be moderated to some degree: the excesses of class inequality can be contained, or in his word 'abated', through the successful development of democratic citizenship rights. Citizenship can remould the class system.

Marshall's discussion is explicitly focused on Britain and, although he sometimes generalizes beyond this context, he does not claim that his argument can be applied with equal cogency to other countries (p. 72). With respect to Britain itself, his argument is that the three elements of citizenship developed at different rates over the past two or three centuries. He sought to show that civil rights were the first to develop, and were established in something like their modern guise before the first great Reform Act in 1832. Political rights developed next, and their extension was one of the main features of the nineteenth century, although it was not until 1928 that the principle of universal political citizenship was fully recognized. Social rights, by contrast, almost vanished in the eighteenth and early nineteenth centuries, but were revived in the latter part of the nineteenth century (p. 83). Their revival and expansion began with development of public elementary education, but it was not until the twentieth century that social rights in their modern form were fully established. Marshall's principal evidence for this is the history of the modern welfare state. The great redistributive measures of the post-war welfare state, including measures introducing the health service, social security, new forms of progressive taxation and so on, created better conditions and greater equality for the vast majority of those who did not flourish in the free market. And they provided a measure of security for all those who are vulnerable in modern society, especially those who fall into the trap of the 'poverty cycle'. Marshall's proposal is that social rights form a vital element in a society which is still hierarchical, but which has mitigated the inequalities – and mellowed the tensions – deriving from the class system.

While Marshall interpreted the development of modern citizenship rights as an uneven process, he conceived each bundle of rights as a kind of step or platform for the others (see pp. 71–83; 95–6; see also Giddens, 1985, pp. 203–5, for a succinct statement of this issue). The eighteenth century was the main formative period for civil or legal rights, when the rights of liberty of the individual, and full and equal justice before the law, became firmly established. Civil rights created new freedoms – although initially, of course, it was the male property-owning individual who was to benefit from them directly. The new freedoms gradually allowed the male citizen liberty from subservience to the place in which he was born and from the occupation to which he was typically tied by custom or statute. While these freedoms (and others relating to them) threatened the traditional forms of power and inequality imposed by feudal society, they did not strain the new forms of inequalities created by the emergence of the competitive market society; on the contrary, Marshall argued, they were 'indispensable to it' (1973a, p. 87). The fundamental reason for this is that the new rights 'gave . . . each man . . . the power to engage as an independent unit in the economic struggle'. They created individuals who were 'free and equal in status' – a status which was the foundation of modern contract. Paradoxically, then, 'the single uniform status of citizenship', in its early form, 'provided the foundation of equality on which the [modern] structure of inequality could be built' (p. 87).

The slow but progressive achievement of civil rights was a prerequisite to the secure establishment of the liberty of the subject. It was also an indispensable first stage in the development of political rights, for, as Giddens usefully explains it, 'only if the individual is recognised as an autonomous agent does it become reasonable to regard that individual as politically responsible' (1985, p. 203). The establishment of political rights belongs, above all, to the nineteenth century and involves a growing interest in equality as a principle to be applied to a range of domains. It involves, moreover, an appreciation of a tension between, on the one hand, the formal recognition of the individual as 'free and equal' in civil matters and, on the other, the actual liberty of the individual to pursue his interests free from political impediment. Political rights were gradually recognized as indispensable to guaranteeing individual freedom. Since there is no good reason for believing that those who govern will act ultimately in anything other than a self-interested way (as will those who are governed), government must, to avoid abuse, be directly accountable to an electorate called upon regularly to decide if their objectives have been met.

The establishment of 'political liberty' involved a process whereby the political rights which had previously been the monopoly of the privileged few were extended to the adult population as a whole. The rise of the trade-union movement and of the labour movement more generally was a critical factor in the development of political citizenship. If citizenship was an entitlement, it had to be an entitlement to full political membership of society. Thus, the search for citizenship became the search for the conditions under which individuals could enjoy a sense of equal worth and equal opportunity. The scene was set for struggle over the enactment of political rights, and of social rights as well.

The ascendance of industrial capitalism created massive disparities in wealth, income and life conditions. Those who were unsuccessful in the market-place experienced profound inequalities in all aspects of their lives. With the establishment of the universal franchise, the organized working class was able to secure, Marshall argued, the political strength to consolidate welfare or social gains *as rights*. While citizenship and class have been 'at war' in the nineteenth and twentieth centuries, the labour movement has succeeded in imposing modifications on the capitalist class system. In the twentieth century, demands for social justice have, in Marshall's words, 'contained contract' (p. 111). The preservation of economic inequalities has been made more difficult by the expansion or enrichment of the notion of citizenship. Class distinctions certainly survive, Marshall recognized, but there is less room for them today, and they are more under pressure and are more likely to be challenged. As he eloquently put it, the expansion of social rights

> is no longer merely an attempt to abate the obvious nuisance of destitution in the lowest ranks of society . . . it is no longer content to raise the floor level in the basement of the social edifice, leaving the superstructure as it was. It has begun

to remodel the whole building, and it might even end by converting the skyscraper into a bungalow. (pp. 96–7)

Contract has been challenged by status, and the rule of market forces has begun to be subordinated to social justice (p. 111). Marshall's view of the likely progress of social democratic reforms (unsurprisingly perhaps, given that many of his ideas were formulated in the late 1940s) is decidedly optimistic.

Giddens versus Marshall

While Anthony Giddens affirms the significance of Marshall's analysis of citizenship for contemporary social and political theory, he has a number of criticisms to make (see 1981, pp. 226–9; 1982, pp. 171–3; 1985, pp. 204–9). In the first place, he is critical of what he sees as the teleological and evolutionary elements in Marshall's analysis (see especially 1982, p. 171). Giddens criticizes Marshall for treating the development of citizenship as if it were something that unfolded in phases according to some inner logic within the modern world. In Giddens's account, Marshall tends to overstate the extent to which citizenship rights can be understood in terms of a threefold staged process. In addition, Giddens sees in Marshall's account an oversimplification of the role of politics and the state. Marshall, according to Giddens, understood the unfolding of citizenship rights from the eighteenth to the twentieth century as a process which is supported and buttressed by 'the beneficent hand of the state'. In Giddens's analysis, Marshall seriously underestimated the way 'citizenship rights have been achieved in substantial degree only through struggle' (1982, p. 171). Furthermore, Giddens argues, Marshall underestimated the degree to which the balance of power was tipped to the underprivileged only during times of war, particularly during the periods of world war.

These criticisms are, in my view, misleading in a number of respects.[3] Far from suggesting a general evolutionary framework for the explanation of the development of citizenship rights, Marshall, in my assessment, takes a more contingent view of historical change.[4] There seems little, if any, evidence to suggest that Marshall's scheme rests on the assumption of an evolutionary logic. Marshall emphasized that institutions and complexes of rights developed at their 'own speed' and under the direction of varying forces and principles (1973a, pp. 73–4). The development of rights by no means followed, he stressed, a linear path in any one time-period; there were often losses as well as gains. Further, the chief factor which Marshall saw underpinning the development of rights was, in fact, struggle – struggle against hierarchy in its traditional feudal form, struggle against inequality in the market-place, and struggle against social injustice perpetuated by state institutions. Rights had to be fought for, and when they were won they had to be protected. At the root of these processes was (and is) the delicate balance between social and political forces. When Marshall discussed citizenship and class, and when he described the relationship between the two as one of 'warfare', he was addressing himself explicitly to some of the major social movements which have shaped the contemporary world. In writings after 'Citizenship and social class', Marshall is even more explicit about the formative role of political and social conflict (see, for example, 1981, particularly pp. 104–36).

A second area of criticism voiced by Giddens concerns Marshall's treatment of the expansion of citizenship rights as a purely 'one-way phenomenon' (1982, p. 173). Marshall is criticized for regarding the development of citizenship as an 'irreversible process'. There are passages in Marshall which certainly justify this criticism. However, it seems in general to be misplaced. For instance, Marshall documented the way in which primitive forms of social rights – rooted in membership of local communities and functional associations (guilds) – existed prior to the eighteenth century and yet practically vanished in the latter half of the eighteenth and the early nineteenth centuries. He argued that their revival began with the development of public elementary education, but that this process of revival itself had by no means a stable history, and depended on the particular strength of the various social movements supporting reform (1973a, pp. 79–83; 95ff.). More fundamentally, Marshall pointed to the emergence of nationalism – 'modern national consciousness', as he put it – as a critical factor in the stimulation of the demand for the recognition of equal social worth (p. 92). Nationalist movements inspired a direct sense of 'community membership' and the aspiration that all nationals become full and equal members of the community. Marshall did not develop this insight, and he did not provide a detailed analysis of the international context within which the demands for citizenship rights developed. None the less, he did not ignore this context and in various writings stressed the significance of nationalism and warfare to the history of rights, particularly social rights (see Marshall, 1975, especially part 1). Moreover, Marshall concluded his reflections on class and citizenship by arguing that the balance achieved between these two great forces in the twentieth century by no means promised a simple stable future. In Marshall's view, how long the current balance lasts cannot easily be determined. And, he concluded, 'it may be that some of the conflicts within our system are becoming too sharp for the compromise to achieve its purpose much longer' (1973a, p. 122). Marshall appears to have been quite sensitive to the potential instabilities which might wreck any period of social equilibrium. Written four decades before the epoch of Reagan and Thatcher, and the new Right's attack on welfare rights, this certainly was an insightful observation.

A third set of criticisms Giddens makes is concerned with Marshall's threefold classification of rights. Giddens objects in particular to Marshall's treatment of civil rights as a homogeneous category. He emphasizes that the civil rights of individual freedom and equality before the law were fought for and achieved in large part by an emergent bourgeoisie. These rights helped consolidate industrial capitalism and the modern representative state. As such, they are to be distinguished from what Giddens calls 'economic civil rights' (or 'industrial citizenship', as Marshall put it). This latter group of rights had to be fought for by working-class and trade-union activists. The right to form trade unions was not gracefully conceded, but was achieved and sustained only through bitter conflicts. The same applies to the extension of the activities of unions in their attempt to secure regularized bargaining and the right to strike. All this implies that there is 'something awry in lumping together such phenomena with civil rights in general' (Giddens, 1982, p. 172). If individual civil rights tended to confirm the dominance of capital, economic civil rights tended to threaten the functioning of the capitalist market.

More fundamentally, Giddens maintains that each category of citizenship right should be understood as an area of contestation or conflict, each linked to a distinctive type of regulatory power or surveillance, where that surveillance is both necessary to the power of superordinate groups and an axis around which subordinate groups can seek to reclaim control over their lives (see 1985, pp. 205ff.). For instance, he writes,

> Civil rights are intrinsically linked to the modes of surveillance involved in the policing activities of the state. Surveillance in this context consists of the apparatus of judicial and punitive organizations in terms of which 'deviant' conduct is controlled . . . [Like the other kinds of rights] civil rights have their own particular locale. That is to say, there is an institutionalized setting in which the claimed universality of rights can be vindicated – the law court. The law court is the prototypical court of appeal in which the range of liberties included under 'civil rights' can be both defended and advanced. (1985, pp. 205–6)

From Giddens's writings, the following classificatory scheme of rights, and the modes of power and institutional sites to which they are related, is suggested:

	Types of right			
	civil	economic civil	political	social
Type of regulatory power or surveillance	policing	control of work-place	political	'management' of population
Institutional centre or locale where rights are championed and fought over	law courts	work-place	parliament or legislative chamber	(state administrative offices?)*

* *Note*: This category is particularly underdeveloped in Giddens's writings.

It is hard to be sure that the above scheme is exactly what Giddens has in mind because he is inconsistent in his use of key terms. In some publications, for example, economic civil rights figure prominently while in others they do not; in some writings social rights are themselves referred to as economic rights although in others they are not. The same can be said about the treatment of the locale of rights (see 1982, ch. 12; 1985, ch. 8). In addition, while Giddens recognizes that the struggle for types of rights is not restricted to one particular setting, the precise connections that are drawn (and the significance of them) remains vague. For instance, the category of civil rights includes a variety of important rights ranging over matters as diverse as marriage, religion and economic affairs. This involves bundles of rights which have quite different origins, conditions of existence and institutional mechanisms of support, from the local community to the courts or parliament.[5] Why, and in what particular ways, types of rights are linked to particular forms of power and locale is not sufficiently elaborated. And while there is much to recommend Giddens's emphasis on the achievement of rights through contestation, it does not separate him as decisively from Marshall as he claims: Marshall does grant conflict a central place in the achievement of rights.

However, underpinning Giddens's concern with conflict, and the domains in which it is located, is a wider concern to develop a new explanatory framework for the development of rights. It is worth dwelling on this for a moment, for it has a number of advantages over Marshall's account, although, as I shall show, it is itself by no means fully satisfactory.

The roots of modern citizenship

In Giddens's view, the development of citizenship and of modern democracy in general has to be linked to the expansion of state sovereignty or the build-up of administrative power from the late sixteenth century (cf. essay 1). The development of the state's 'apparatus of government' was made possible to a significant extent by the extension of the state's capacity for surveillance; that is, the collection and storing of information about members of society, and the related ability to supervise subject populations (Giddens, 1981, pp. 169ff.). As the state's sovereign authority expanded progressively and its administrative centres became more powerful, the state's dependence on force as a direct medium of rule was slowly reduced. For the increase in administrative power via surveillance increased the state's dependence on cooperative forms of social relations; it was no longer possible for the modern state to manage its affairs and sustain its offices and activities by force alone. Accordingly, greater reciprocity was created between the governors and the governed, and the more reciprocity was involved the more opportunities were generated for subordinate groups to influence their rulers. Giddens refers to this 'two-way' expansion of power as 'the dialectic of control' (1985, pp. 201ff.).

The struggle for rights, Giddens argues, can be understood in this context. The expansion of state sovereignty helped foster the identity of subjects as political subjects – as citizens. As Giddens puts it, 'the expansion of state sovereignty means that those subject to it are in some sense – initially vague, but growing more and more definite and precise – aware of their membership in a political community and of the rights and obligations such membership confers' (p. 210). Nationalism is a critical force in the development of this new identity. In fact, Giddens contends, nationalism is 'the cultural sensibility of sovereignty' (p. 219). The conditions involved in the creation of the modern state as a 'surveillance apparatus' are the same as those that help generate nationalism. Nationalism is closely linked to the 'administrative unification of the state'. And citizenship mediates this process. The development of citizenship, as pertaining to membership of an overall political community, is intimately bound up with the novel (administrative) ordering of political power and the 'politicization' of social relations and day-to-day activities which follows in its wake (see Giddens, 1985, ch. 8).

The pursuit of equal membership in the new political communities reconstituted the shape of the modern state itself. Although the struggle for citizenship took a variety of forms, the most enduring and important was, Giddens claims, class conflict: first, the class conflict of the bourgeoisie against the remnants of feudal privilege; and, second, the class conflict of the working classes against the bourgeoisie's hold on the chief levers of power. These conflicts shaped two massive institutional changes, respectively. The first of these was the progressive separation of the state from the economy. It was the establishment of civil and political rights by the bourgeoisie which first and foremost helped free the economy, and more generally civil society, from the direct political interference of the state. The 'separation' of the state from the economy remoulded both sets of institutions. As Giddens explains it, the new rights and prerogatives

> should not be seen as being created 'outside' the sphere of the state, but as part and parcel of the emergence of the 'public domain', separated from 'privately' organised economic activity. Civil rights thus have been, from the early phases of capitalist development, bound up with the very definition of what counts as 'political'. Civil and political citizenship rights developed together and remain, thereafter, open to a range of divergent interpretations which may directly affect the distribution of power. (1985, p. 207)

The development of polyarchy (rule by the many, or liberal democracy as it became in the West) can be understood against this background. The new 'public' domain became concerned in principle with protecting the space for citizens to pursue their activities unimpeded by illegitimate state action and with ensuring the responsiveness of government to the preferences of its citizens considered as political equals (Giddens, 1985, pp. 198–201).[6] The 'public' and the 'private' spheres were formed through interrelated processes.

The second massive institutional change was linked, after the general achievement of the franchise, to the success of the working classes in the late nineteenth and twentieth centuries struggling for 'social rights', or for what Giddens sometimes prefers to call 'economic rights'. This second set of struggles produced the welfare order – the modern welfare interventionist state. Social or economic rights cannot be regarded as a mere extension of civil and political rights, for they are in part the creation of an attempt to ameliorate the worst consequences of the worker-citizen's lack of formal control of his or her activities in, above all, the work-place.

In sum, in Giddens's assessment, class conflict has been and remains the medium of the extension of citizenship rights and the basis of the creation of an insulated economy, polyarchy and the welfare state. The forging of state sovereignty was a critical impetus to the struggle for rights and to the remould-ing of citizenship. The increase in state administrative power led to the creation of new aspirations and demands, and to the development of insti-tutions which were responsive to them. These were major historical changes. But there is nothing inherent about them, Giddens notes, which would prevent their erosion in different political or economic circumstances. They remain fragile achievements.

There is much that is compelling about this position. In particular, Giddens's emphasis on the way in which an increase in state power led to the progressive reliance of the state on new relationships with its subjects – relationships based on consent, rather than force – has much to recommend it as a basis for explaining why new forms of political relations were called into being in the modern era. Likewise, his emphasis on the contingent nature of these develop-ments has much to be said for it, especially if one is seeking to explain the different forms citizenship has taken, and the complex articulation of these forms with industrial capitalism (see Therborn, 1977; Mann, 1987). None the less, it is my view that the value of Giddens's analysis is weakened consider-ably by a number of difficulties. It will be my contention that problems in Giddens's position derive from accepting too much of Marshall's initial terms of reference, and from lack of precision in central formulations. The upshot of these problems is a fundamental underestimation of the complexity of citizen-ship: its multidimensional roots and the way the struggle for different types of rights is 'inscribed' into, or embedded in, changing conceptions of citizenship. A few reflections on the nature of citizenship provide a useful starting-point from which to highlight these shortcomings.

Citizenship, rights and obligations

From the ancient world to the present day, all forms of citizenship have had certain common attributes. Citizenship has meant a certain reciprocity of rights against, and duties towards, the community (see Brinkmann, 1968). Citizenship has entailed membership, membership of the community in which one lives one's life. And membership has invariably involved degrees of participation in the community. The question of who should participate and at what level is a question as old as the ancient world itself. There is much significant history in the attempt to restrict the extension of citizenry to certain groups: among others, owners of property, white men, educated men, men, those with particular skills and occupations, adults. There is also a telling story in the various conceptions and debates about what is to count as citizenship and in particular what is to count as participation in the community. (For an account see Held, 1987.)

If citizenship entails membership in the community and membership implies forms of social participation, then it is misleading to think of citizenship primarily in relationship to class or the capitalist relations of production. Citizenship is about involvement of people in the community in which they live; and people have been barred from citizenship on grounds of gender, race and age among many other factors. To analyse citizenship as if it were a matter of the inclusion or exclusion of social classes is to eclipse from view a variety of dimensions of social life which have been central to the struggle over citizenship. In light of this fact, the debate about citizenship initiated by Marshall requires elaboration and modification.[7]

The argument against Marshall and Giddens can, thus, be put as follows. Class conflict may well be an important medium for the development of citizenship rights but it is by no means the only one which requires detailed examination. If citizenship involves the struggle for membership and participation in the community, then its analysis involves examining the way in which different groups, classes and movements struggle to gain degrees of autonomy and control over their lives in the face of various forms of stratification, hierarchy and political oppression. The post-Marshall debate needs to extend the analysis of citizenship to take account of issues posed by, for instance, feminism, the black movement, ecology (concerned with the moral status of animals and nature) and those who have advocated the rights of children (see Turner, 1986, pp. 85–92). Different social movements have raised different questions about the nature and dimensions of citizenship. As one commentator aptly put it, 'citizenship rights are the outcome of social movements which aim either to expand or to defend the definition of social membership . . . The boundaries which define citizenship . . . ultimately define membership of a social group or collectivity' (Turner, 1986, pp. 92, 85). The struggle over the nature and extent of citizenship has *itself* been a, if not the, central medium of social conflict – the medium through which various classes, groups and movements strive to enhance and protect their rights and opportunities. The very meaning of particular rights cannot be adequately understood if the range of concerns and pressures which have given rise to them is not properly grasped.

Now, it is the case that Giddens does acknowledge a range of movements which have been significant in shaping the struggle for citizenship rights. But this acknowledgement has come 'late' in the sense that it leaves the impression of being tacked on to his existing explanatory framework. This is the case for at least two reasons. First, whenever Giddens offers substantive explanations of the development of citizenship, class conflict is the major determining factor (1981, pp. 227–9; 1982, pp. 171–2; 1985, ch. 8). Second, little attention is devoted to understanding the nature and activities of social movements, and particular movements' advocacy of certain rights is not properly explained.[8] Giddens's attempt in his most recent work to provide a 'conceptual map' that links together diverse sources of social protest with particular sets of institutions and particular forms of rights does not solve the problems (1985, pp. 310–25). Significant movements are missed out altogether (such as the anti-racist movements),[9] and the connections between those that are there and particular struggles for rights seem tenuous. For example, many would argue with the view taken within Giddens's scheme that social rights[10] are the prime objective of the labour movement, that political rights are the prime concern of the 'free speech movement' (a dubious catch-all category itself), that civil rights are the main focus of the peace movement and that 'moral imperatives' are the preoccupation of the ecological movement. Moreover, different movements changing orientations over time (from civil concerns to perhaps wider political and social issues), their different institutional locations at any given moment (economy, polity, local community, etc.) and their different views of the meaning of rights cannot be accommodated on a map which essentially plots static relations between phenomena. In short, although Giddens acknowledges different clusters of movements and rights in the struggle for citizenship, this is not elaborated into a coherent framework. If Giddens is serious about the necessity to encompass a diverse range of groups and movements in his account of citizenship, then he will have to depart decisively from the terms of reference of his debate with Marshall, which affirm class as the key variable affecting, and the determining influence on, citizenship rights.

It is important to be clear about the meaning of rights if a more adequate account of citizenship is to be developed. The type of rights which are central to the Marshall–Giddens discussion can be defined as *legitimate spheres of independent action (or inaction)*.[11] Accordingly, the study of rights can be thought of as the study of the domains in which citizens have sought to pursue their own activities within the constraints of community. If the early attempts to achieve rights involved struggles for autonomy or independence from the locale in which one was born and from prescribed occupations, later struggles involved such things as freedom of speech, expression, belief and association, and freedom for women in marriage. The autonomy of the citizen can be represented by that bundle of rights which individuals can enjoy as a result of their status as 'free and equal' members of society. And to unpack the domain of rights is to unpack both the rights citizens formally enjoy and the conditions under which citizens' rights are actually realized or enacted. Only this 'double focus' makes it possible to grasp the degrees of autonomy, interdependence and constraint that citizens face in the societies in which they live.[12]

There is insufficient space in this essay to elaborate fully a new classificatory scheme of rights which would do justice to the range of rights which have been established or advocated in the struggle for citizenship. But it is important at least to indicate that the set of rights compatible with citizenship in modern societies has to be conceived more broadly than either Marshall or Giddens has allowed. The broad cluster of rights Marshall refers to under the headings 'civil', 'political' and 'social', and Giddens refers to as 'civil', 'economic civil', 'political' and 'social', can usefully be thought of as pertaining to four distinct spheres which I prefer to call civil, economic, political and social. Giddens's reasons for not lumping together civil and economic civil rights are sound, but little is gained by retaining the label 'civil' in this category. Accordingly, economic rights means all those rights which have been won by the labour movement over time and which create the possibility of greater control for employees over the work-place. Removing this category from civil rights distinguishes usefully those rights which are concerned with the liberty of the individual in general from those sub-categories of rights which seek to recover elements of control over the work-place, and which have been at the centre of conflicts between labour and capital since the earliest phases of the industrial revolution.[13] The category of political and social (or welfare) rights can, following Marshall and Giddens, be treated as fairly unproblematic for the purposes of this essay.

But apart from these broad sets of rights, there are other categories which neither Marshall nor Giddens develops, linked to a variety of domains where, broadly speaking, (non-class-specific) social movements have sought to re-form power centres according to their own goals and objectives. Among these is the area of struggle for reproductive rights – at the very heart of the women's movement (cf. Petchesky, 1986). Reproductive rights are the very basis of the possibility of effective participation of women in both civil society

and the polity. A right to reproductive freedom for women entails making the
state or other relevant political agencies responsible not only for the medical
and social facilities necessary to prevent or assist pregnancy, but also for
providing the material conditions which would help make the choice to have a
child a genuinely free one and, thereby, ensure a crucial condition for women
if they are to be 'free and equal'. Giddens's lack of attention to reproductive
rights is symbolic of his disregard of the whole question of the social organization of reproduction, and of women and gender relations more generally
(see Murgatroyd, forthcoming). He has not made the latter an integral
component of his work and the inevitable result, I believe, is major lacunae in
his conception of the conditions of involvement of women (and men) in public
life.

Marshall's and Giddens's accounts of rights suffer, in addition, from a
further limitation: a strict focus on the citizen's relation to the nation-state.
While this is unquestionably important, the whole relation of rights to the
nation-state has itself become progressively more problematic in the twentieth
century. For a gap has opened up, linked to processes of globalization, between
the idea of membership of a national political community, that is, citizenship,
and the development of international law which subjects individuals, non-
governmental organizations and governments to new systems of regulation
(see Vincent, 1986). Rights and duties are recognized in international law
which transcend the claims of nation-states and which, whilst they may lack
coercive powers of enforcement, have far-reaching consequences. For
example, the International Tribunal at Nuremberg (1945) laid down, for the
first time in history, that when *international rules* that protect basic humanitarian
values are in conflict with *state laws*, every individual must transgress the state
laws (except where there is no room for 'moral choice'). The legal framework
of the Nuremberg Tribunal marked a highly significant change in the legal
direction of the modern state; for the new rules challenged the principle of
military discipline and subverted national sovereignty at one of its most
sensitive points: the hierarchical relations within the military.[14] In addition,
two internationally recognized legal mainstays of national sovereignty –
'immunity from jurisdiction' and 'immunity of state agencies' – have been
progressively questioned by Western courts. While it is the case that national
sovereignty has most often been the victor when put to the test, the tension
between citizenship, national sovereignty and international law is marked,
and it is by no means clear how it will be resolved.

A satisfactory account of the meaning and nature of citizenship today must
transcend the terms of reference which Marshall and Giddens have set down.
The study of citizenship has to concern itself with all those dimensions which
allow or exclude the participation of people in the communities in which they
live and the complex pattern of national and international relations and

processes which cut across these. Neither Marshall nor Giddens has provided an adequate basis for such a study.

Rights, states and societies

The restricted conception of citizenship in Marshall's and Giddens's work has serious sociological and political implications for central areas of inquiry. The section below will explore these implications in relation to Giddens's treatment of the ideological nature of rights, the critical dimensions of the state, the social structure of post-war society and contemporary political directions.

Rights: sham or real?

When setting out the meaning of citizenship rights, Giddens criticizes Marshall from a Marxist perspective and then uses Marshall against Marxism, pursuing the question: are rights an ideological sham or of real significance? In recent writings, Giddens has affirmed that capitalism is, as Marx argued, a class society. Pivotal to Giddens's analysis is the capitalist labour contract, the basic concept, he suggests, for analysing the class structure of capitalism from the eighteenth century to the present time.

The creation of a market-place for both labour power and capital involved two fundamental developments. The first of these was the progressive separation of the economic from the political, referred to earlier. The creation of a distinctive sphere of the political was effected by the overthrowing of feudal, courtly power, and by its progressive replacement by parliamentary representative government (Giddens, 1982, p. 173). The struggle for civil and political rights consolidated this development, giving distinctive form to the public domain. While the separation of the economic from the political was in many respects a progressive development in political terms, it served also to undercut the new-won freedoms. For although the new freedoms were universal in principle, they favoured the dominant class in practice. The rights of the citizens to elect or stand as representatives were not extended to work and, accordingly, the sphere of politics was not extended to industry. Once citizens entered the factory gates, their lives were fully determined by the dictates of capital. To quote Giddens: 'the capitalist labour contract . . . excludes the worker from formal rights over the control of the workplace. This exclusion is not incidental to the capitalist state, but vital to it since the sphere of industry is specifically defined as being "outside politics"' (1985, p. 207). 'In substantial degree', Giddens argues, 'Marx was surely right' (1982, p. 173; 1985, p. 207). Many of the new freedoms were 'bourgeois freedoms' (1981, p. 228; 1982, pp. 173-4).

In prior types of society it was taken for granted that the worker or peasant had a significant degree of control over the process of labour. But with the birth of industrial capitalism this substantial degree of control was lost and had to be won all over again. The formation of the labour movement, and of trade unions in particular, created a minimum basis of power for workers in the industrial sphere. Labour and socialist parties were able to build on this despite often bitter opposition. Together, unions and socialist parties took advantage of and fought for the development of political and social rights. It is very important, Giddens concludes from this, to see the different kinds of citizenship rights distinguished by Marshall as – contra Marx and Marxism – 'double-edged'. Citizenship rights do serve to extend the range of human freedoms possible within industrial capitalist societies; they serve as levers of struggle which are the very basis on which freedoms can be won and protected. But at the same time they continue to be the sparking-points of conflicts. In the final analysis, therefore, citizenship rights have not simply been bourgeois freedoms. To use Marshall against Marx is, according to Giddens, to recognize that Marxism has failed to understand, and anticipate, the very way in which certain types of citizenship rights have been actualized within the framework of liberal industrial capitalist society. As he puts it:

> Among the industrialized societies at least, capitalism is by now a very different phenomenon from what it was in the nineteenth century and labour movements have played a prime role in changing it. In most of the capitalist countries, we now have to speak of the existence of 'welfare capitalism', a system in which the labour movement has achieved a considerable stake and in which economic [social] citizenship rights brook large. (1985, p. 325)

Citizenship rights helped cement the industrial capitalist order while at one and the same time creating new forms of politics linked to new rights for all its citizens.

There is a fundamental ambiguity in Giddens's analysis. This ambiguity derives from his attempt to reconcile three different positions. First, he wants to argue that Marx was right: citizenship rights have been so much ideology – a sham (1981, p. 228). Giddens affirms the view that citizenship rights have for long periods largely been the province of the bourgeoisie and can legitimately be referred to as 'bourgeois freedoms' (1981, pp. 227–8). Second, he argues that Marx was only partially right. Marx was right about the extent to which citizenship rights served to legitimate and cement the industrial capitalist order. But Marx was wrong as well because citizenship rights have proven to be 'double-edged'. Third, Giddens argues that Marx was simply wrong about the nature of rights. The fact that rights are double-edged – the fact that citizenship rights can be actualized within the framework of liberal democracy – seems to him to imply that the revolutionary socialist project is quite unjustified. To support this view Giddens singles out the fact that citizenship rights have been actually developed and extended within the sphere of industrial capitalism modifying and altering industrial capitalism itself. Giddens's overall equivocation on this issue, and the consequences this equivocation has, can be highlighted by considering his appraisal of the political significance of the separation of the 'political' and 'economic'.

For Giddens, the separation of the political and economic is linked fundamentally to the nature of modern domination – the rule of capital. While Giddens is surely right to stress the way the institutionalized separation of the economic from the political creates the very basis for the development and expansion of capital – and secures the interests of the capitalist class – his analysis fails to explore systematically the ways in which this separation also creates a significant space for the realization of political rights and freedoms. The relative separation of the political and economic means that there is a realm in which the citizen can enjoy rights unavailable to those in societies where this separation has not been established. What this amounts to, among other things, is the necessity to recognize the fundamental liberal notion that the 'separation' of the state from civil society is (and must be) a central feature of any democratic political order; without it, a number of critical modern political innovations – concerning the centrality, in principle, of an 'impersonal' structure of public power, of a constitution to help guarantee and protect rights, of a diversity of power centres within and outside of the state, of mechanisms to promote competition and debate between alternative political platforms – cannot be enjoyed.[15] While one consequence of the differentiation of the economic and political is to give the economy relative freedom and, thereby, to produce and reproduce massive asymmetries in income, wealth and power, as Giddens rightly maintains, another is to create a space for the enjoyment of civil and political rights (see Turner, 1986, pp. 37–44). The significance of this requires detailed comparative investigation (between countries West and East, North and South) which is missing in Giddens's work.

An additional problem of analysing and assessing citizenship rights primarily in terms of their ideological significance for class relations and capitalist society is that the very diverse origins of rights and the distinctively modern conception of citizenship gets put aside. The modern conception of citizenship is inseparable from a series of multiple and complexly overlapping conflicts. Struggles between monarchs and barons over the domain of rightful authority; peasant rebellions against the weight of excess taxation and social obligation; the spread of trade, commerce and market relations; the flourishing of Renaissance culture with its renewed interest in classical political ideas (including the Greek city-state and Roman law); the consolidation of national monarchies in Europe (England, France and Spain); religious strife and the challenge to the universal claims of Catholicism; the struggle between church and state – all these played a part in the emergence of the modern idea of the state, the citizen and citizenship.[16] The idea of the individual as a citizen is, moreover, an idea deeply connected with the doctrine of freedom of choice, a doctrine which raises questions about choice in matters as diverse as marriage, economic and political affairs (cf. Macpherson, 1966, ch. 1). If the modern idea of citizenship crystallized at the intersection of a variety of struggles, it did so in the context of struggles concerned with rights which are fundamental to most aspects of choice in everyday life. The significance of these rights goes far beyond that which can be embraced in an analysis which simply places class first.

Giddens's emphasis on separating out the formal rights that people enjoy from the actual capacities they have to enact rights is important. But this insight is not original, and his use of it is marred by terms of reference which are too narrow and do not permit the adequate specification of the diverse range of rights that emerge with the development of modern citizenship. The right to freedom of choice in marriage, the right to choice about one's religion – these and many other rights cannot simply be understood or their meaning explicated within the framework of concerns 'rights: sham or real?' They suggest a diversity of issues, and a diversity of conditions, which need much more careful analyses than Giddens has hitherto provided. They also require a much more sophisticated classificatory scheme of rights if many of them are to be given adequate treatment at all. A satisfactory theory of rights, which attends to the diverse range of rights which have been essential to the shaping of the modern world, will require an analysis which goes far beyond that provided by Marx, Marshall or Giddens.

State: capitalist or modern?

In modern Western political thought, the idea of the state is often linked to the notion of an impersonal and privileged legal or constitutional order with the capability of administering and controlling a given territory (see essays 1 and 8 in this volume; Skinner, 1978). While this notion found its earliest expression in the ancient world, it did not become a major object of concern until the late sixteenth century (see Skinner, 1978, vol. 2, pp. 349–58). The idea of an impersonal and sovereign political order, that is, a legally circumscribed structure of power separate from ruler and ruled with supreme jurisdiction over a territory, could not predominate while political rights and duties were closely tied to religious institutions and the feudal system of property rights. Similarly, the idea that human beings were 'individuals' or 'a people', with a right to be citizens of their state, could not develop under the constraining influences of the 'closed circle' of medieval intellectual life.

These notions are sometimes argued to be constitutive of the very concept of the modern state. There are passages in which Giddens seems to share this view, and as a corollary an emphasis on the extraordinary innovatory power of these notions, recognizing that they provided a critical impetus to the form (constitutional, representative) and limits ('separation' of state and civil society, division of powers) of the modern 'apparatus of government' (see Giddens, 1984, ch. 6). From this perspective it follows that an understanding of the state requires a detailed appreciation of its institutional and legal bases – a 'state-centred' perspective (see Evans et al., 1985). While Giddens sometimes seems to recognize this, there are other passages in his work where the very idea of the modern state is eclipsed by the idea of the 'capitalist state'.

By the 'capitalist state' Giddens means, following Claus Offe, a state 'enmeshed' in class relations (see especially Giddens, 1981, pp. 210-14, 219-26; cf. Offe, 1984). The following points are central to the position:

1 The state in capitalism 'is a state in a class society' – a society in which class relations (via control over allocative resources) enter into the very constitution of the productive process; class struggle is a chronic feature of everyday life, and class conflict is a 'major medium' of the internal transformation of society (Giddens, 1981, pp. 214, 220-1).

2 Unlike other ruling classes in history, 'the ruling class does not rule' in capitalism; that is, the 'capitalist class does not generally compose . . . the personnel of the state' (Giddens, 1981, p. 211). None the less, 'the state, as a mode of "government", is strongly influenced by its institutional alignments with private property and with the insulated "economy"' (Giddens, 1985, p. 136).

3 The state is dependent upon the activities of capitalist employers for its revenues and, hence, operates in the context of various capitalist 'imperatives' (Giddens, 1981, p. 211). It has, accordingly, to sustain the process of accumulation and the incentives for the private appropriation of resources while not undermining belief in itself as an impartial arbiter of all class interests, thereby eroding its power-base.

4 The state is 'directly enmeshed in the contradictions of capitalism'. In so being, it is 'not merely a defender of the status quo' (Giddens, 1981, p. 220). For if it is enmeshed in the contradictions of capitalism, it can in some part be seen as a force able to shape the very nature of interests and policies.

In this analysis, the explanatory and political axis 'class–state' is once again granted the central role. Class and state power are directly linked, and class power is held to be the basis of political power. Such a position clearly grants primacy to the capitalist nature of modern societies *and* states.

While there is some scope within this framework for understanding the political or strategic intelligence which government and state agencies often display, the general emphasis is one which denies what is central to the idea of the modern state, that is, that the state apparatus itself has sufficient primacy over social classes and collectivities that the nature and meaning of political outcomes – constitutional forms, particular institutional structures and the like – cannot be inferred directly from the configuration of class relations. Giddens's account of the capitalist state sits uneasily with his recognition of the *sui generis* powers of the modern state, and of the necessity to see the state as 'a set of collectivities concerned with the institutionalized organization of political power' (Giddens, 1981, p. 220). Further, it sits in some tension with his own argument that Marx's treatment of the capitalist state is deficient because it generally ignores the non-capitalist features of the state and fails to separate out the institutional elements of modern politics from the broad pattern of social relations (see Giddens, 1985, pp. 141, 160).

Giddens's equivocation on the critical dimensions of the modern state is related to his equivocation about rights. It is one thing to argue that the modern state has (as do civil and political rights) central 'functions' for the reproduction of capital – an argument, however, that would need very careful elaboration. But it is quite another thing to stress the capitalist character of the state to the point at which the significance of the institutional, constitutional and legal innovations of the modern state tends to be eclipsed from view altogether. A systematic treatment of the idea of rights, and of the new freedoms they formally allow, and a systematic understanding of the relationship between formal rights and the actual possibilities of their realization, requires a much more substantial account of the modern state than can be found in Giddens's work. Only such a treatment could do justice to the fact that the modern state developed partly in response to the demand to articulate and protect a range of rights and interests which cannot be reduced to issues of property and property relations.

Society: pluralist or class-ridden?

In *A Contemporary Critique of Historical Materialism* and other texts, Giddens argues at length that capitalism is a class society. In fact, it is his view that capitalism is the only social formation to which the concept of 'mode of production' is applicable. As he puts it, 'I do . . . want to claim that capitalism is the first and only form of society in history of which it might be said with some plausibility that it both "has" and "is" a mode of production' (1985, p. 134).

However, there are many other places in Giddens's work where he rejects (even in the case of capitalism) the direct connection Marx drew between the history of classes, exploitation, conflicts of interest and political power or the state. Here he argues that there are multiple routes of domination and different types of exploitation within and between classes, states, the sexes and ethnic groups. He suggests that it is a mere delusion to imagine that the end of capitalism means the end of oppression in all its forms. In a typical passage he writes:

> The validity of much of what Marx has to say in analysing the nature of capitalist production need not be placed in doubt . . . However, Marx accords undue centrality to capitalism and to class struggle as the keys to explaining inequality or exploitation, and to providing the means of their transcendence. (1985, p. 336)

The difficulty here is that ultimately Giddens has not resolved the issues posed by the debate between Marxism and pluralism – and no amount of elaborate syntheses seems to have settled the questions (see McLennan, forthcoming). Giddens wishes to affirm the centrality of class in the determination of the character of contemporary society while at the same time recognizing that this very perspective itself marginalizes or excludes certain types of issue from consideration. This is true of all those issues which cannot be reduced, as Giddens himself recognizes, to class-related matters. Classic examples of this are the domination of women by men and of certain racial and ethnic groups by others. Other central concerns include the power of public administrators or bureaucrats over their 'clients' and the role of 'authoritative resources' (the capacity to coordinate and control the activities of human beings) which build up in most social organizations.

Giddens's affirmation of class analysis is certainly not unqualified; he argues strenuously on behalf of class analysis in social theory but does not grant class relations primacy over many critical areas: from ecology to the military. Further, he recognizes, of course, the social and political significance of a number of social movements (1985, ch. 11). But how exactly these movements are to be linked into the overall emphasis on class is not clarified. As one critic has remarked: 'Giddens wants to affirm the centrality of class while not giving up pluralist insights' (McLennan, forthcoming). Earlier equivocations and ambiguities are reflected in the decisive issue of how he characterizes the very nature of contemporary society. There are fundamental unresolved tensions in Giddens's account of the core relations and conflicts of modern life.

Political choices: liberalism or socialism or . . . ?

These problems are carried over into the political dimension of Giddens's work. Giddens does not see himself as a champion of liberalism, but neither does he stray far from some of liberalism's central prescriptions. He does not straightforwardly advocate socialist positions, but nor does he wish to jettison central socialist ideals. He is critical, in addition, of a variety of intermediate positions, for example pluralism, and of 'reformist' political views like those of Marshall. Yet he shares some of the terms of reference of the 'middle ground'. In *The Nation-State and Violence*, Giddens appears to advocate the necessity to go beyond liberalism, pluralism and Marxism. The contemporary world, he argues, is far more complex than any of these doctrines anticipated and it has left none of them with their 'hands clean' (1985, ch. 11). He maintains, moreover, that there are trends at work in the late twentieth century – particularly global trends – which render incoherent most contemporary conceptions of the political good (1985, pp. 325ff.).

Traditionally, concepts of the political good have been elaborated at the level of state institutions; the state has been at the centre of bold interpretations of political life (see Dunn, 1985). The problems facing these traditional concepts are immense today, as Giddens stresses. The developments of a world economy which threaten to erode the sovereignty of states; the expansion of transnational links which creates new forms of collective decision-making; the emergence of 'power blocs' which divide and frequently rule the political world – all these phenomena raise, I believe, fundamental questions about the terms of reference of liberalism, pluralism and Marxism (see essay 8). It is, of course, important to recognize the new questions on the political agenda. But it remains a, if not the, central task of political and social theory to think them through. One cannot be wholly optimistic about Giddens's future contribution in this area while there is such ambiguity at the heart of his critique and reconstruction of social and political theory. On the other hand, if Giddens fails here we will all almost certainly be the losers; for there are very few with his scope and range of insight.

Notes

1 Marshall's later work alters some of the emphases of his earlier essay; see, for instance, Marshall (1973b).
2 By 'civil rights' Marshall means 'rights necessary for individual freedom', including liberty of the person, freedom of speech, thought and faith, the right to own property and enter into contracts, and the right to be treated equally with others before the law. 'Political rights' refers to those elements of rights which create the possibility of participation in the exercise of political power 'as a member of a body invested with political authority or as an elector of the members of such a body'. 'Social rights' are defined as involving a whole range of rights 'from the right to a modicum of economic welfare and security to the right . . . to live the life of a civilized being according to the standards prevailing in . . . society' (pp. 71–2). The adequacy of Marshall's categories will be discussed in

several places in this essay and additional rights categories – the economic, reproductive and those deriving from international law – will be examined. The meaning of these latter categories will be set out as they are introduced.

3 I am by no means the first to make this observation; see Turner (1986, pp. 45–6) for a particularly helpful discussion.

4 This is not the emphasis, it should be acknowledged, which has generally been put on Marshall's work in recent times. The chief reason for the discrepancy lies in the way Marshall's ideas were incorporated and popularized by writers who dominated sociological thought in the 1950s and 1960s, such as Seymour Martin Lipset, Reinhard Bendix and David Bell. Some of the latters' concerns and perspectives, in my view, distorted the reception of Marshall's key notions. While Marshall's writings are not without some ambiguity on these matters, they cannot, for reasons set out below, simply be interpreted as offering an 'evolutionary' account of citizenship rights.

5 I shall return to this point at some length below.

6 Giddens's conception of polyarchy is directly informed by Dahl's and Lindblom's views; see Dahl (1971) and Lindblom (1977).

7 This argument is stated very usefully in Turner (1986, especially chs 1, 2 and 4).

8 The women's movement, for example, typically gets half a paragraph in Giddens (1985, p. 321). In addition, the contemporary women's movement is connected, without explanation, to concerns with civil and political rights. Some of the difficulties involved in such a view – above all, the neglect of the struggle for reproductive rights – are discussed below.

9 Giddens would counter this criticism by arguing that all social movements can in principle be located on his 'map' (see 1985, p. 318). It is quite unclear, however, how movements concerned with matters such as racial prejudice or sexual freedom can be fitted into his categories. The same kind of consideration is raised in the note above about the prime orientation of the women's movement.

10 Giddens actually uses the term 'economic rights' here instead of 'social rights'. I have stayed with Marshall's term in order to help keep clear the key concepts under discussion.

11 Not all types of rights can, of course, be reduced to this conception. But it is, I believe, the pivotal notion underpinning the issues raised by Marshall and Giddens. I discuss this and related conceptions of rights further in my *Foundations of Democracy* (forthcoming).

12 For an elaboration of the issues underpinning the necessity of a 'double focus' in the analysis of citizenship rights see Held (1987, ch. 9).

13 Separating these categories in this way also helps illuminate why certain types of rights may not always be complementary (as illustrated, for instance, in recent controversy over whether 'the closed shop' undermines the individual's freedom of choice).

14 For an excellent discussion of these issues see Cassese (1988).

15 I trace the importance of these issues at some length in Held (1987, chs 2, 3, 8 and 9).

16 See, e.g., Benn and Peters (1959); Tilly (1975); Poggi (1978); Skocpol (1979); Bendix (1980); Keane (1984); Held (1987).

References

Bendix, R. 1980: *Kings or People*. Berkeley: University of California Press.

Benn, S. I. and Peters, R. S. 1959: *Social Principles and the Democratic State*. London: Allen & Unwin.

Brinkmann, C. 1968: Citizenship. In *International Encyclopedia of Social Sciences*, New York: Macmillan.

Cassese, A. 1988: *Violence and Law in the Modern Age*. Cambridge: Polity Press.

Dahl, R. A. 1971: *Polyarchy: Participation and Opposition*. New Haven: Yale University Press.

Dunn, J. 1985: Responsibility without power: states and the incoherence of the modern conception of the political good. Lecture delivered to the IPSA, Paris, July. Forthcoming in M. Banks (ed.), *The State in International Relations*, Hassocks, Sussex: Wheatsheaf.

Evans, P. B., Rueschemeyer, D. and Skocpol, T. (eds) 1985: *Bringing the State Back In*. Cambridge: Cambridge University Press.

Giddens, A. 1981: *A Contemporary Critique of Historical Materialism*. London: Macmillan.

Giddens, A. 1982: *Profiles and Critiques in Social Theory*. London: Macmillan.

Giddens, A. 1984: *The Constitution of Society*. Cambridge: Polity Press.

Giddens, A. 1985: *The Nation-State and Violence*. Vol. II of *A Contemporary Critique of Historical Materialism*. London: Macmillan.

Held, D. 1987: *Models of Democracy*. Cambridge: Polity Press.

Held, D. forthcoming: *Foundations of Democracy*. Cambridge: Polity Press.

Keane, J. 1984: *Public Life and Late Capitalism*, essay 6. Cambridge: Cambridge University Press.

Lindblom, C. E. 1977: *Politics and Markets*. New York: Basic Books.

McLennan, G. forthcoming: *Pluralism, Marxism and Beyond*. Cambridge: Polity Press.

Macpherson, C. B. 1966: *The Real World of Democracy*. Oxford: Oxford University Press.

Mann, M. 1987: Ruling strategies and citizenship. *Sociology*, 21(3).

Marshall, T. H. 1973a: Citizenship and social class. In T. H. Marshall (ed.), *Class, Citizenship and Social Development*, Westport, Conn.: Greenwood Press.

Marshall, T. H. 1973b: The welfare state – a comparative study. In T. H. Marshall (ed.), *Class, Citizenship and Social Development*, Westport, Conn.: Greenwood Press.

Marshall, T. H. 1975: *Social Policy in the Twentieth Century*. London: Hutchinson.

Marshall, T. H. 1981: *The Right to Welfare and Other Essays*. London: Heinemann.

Murgatroyd, L. forthcoming: In D. Held and J. Thompson (eds), *Social Theory of Modern Societies*, Cambridge: Cambridge University Press.

Offe, C. 1984: *Contradictions of the Welfare State*. London: Hutchinson.

Petchesky, R. P. 1986: *Abortion and Women's Choice*. London: Verso.

Poggi, G. 1978: *The Development of the Modern State*. London: Hutchinson.

Skinner, Q. 1978: *The Foundation of Modern Political Thought*, 2 vols. Cambridge: Cambridge University Press.

Skocpol, T. 1979: *States and Social Revolutions: A Comparative Analysis of France, Russia and China*. Cambridge: Cambridge University Press.

Therborn, G. 1977: The rule of capital and the rise of democracy. *New Left Review*, 103.

Tilly, C. 1975: Reflections on the history of European state-making. In C. Tilly (ed.), *The Formation of National States in Western Europe*. Princeton, NJ: Princeton University Press.

Turner, B. S. 1986: *Citizenship and Capitalism: The Debate over Reformism*. London: Allen & Unwin.

Vincent, R. J. 1986: *Human Rights and International Relations*. Cambridge: Cambridge University Press.

8

Sovereignty, National Politics and the Global System

The concept of the nation-state – the idea of a people determining its own fate within the framework of a national political apparatus – has been at the heart of both the normative political theory of the modern world and of political analysis in the social sciences generally.* On the one hand, concepts of the political good have been elaborated at the level of state institutions, practices and operations; the state has been at the intersection of intellectually and morally ambitious conceptions of political life (Dunn, 1985). On the other hand, the state has been seen as the key unit of political analysis in the social sciences and this has been allied to an emphasis on *endogenous* models of social and political change. That is to say, the leading perspectives on societal change have assumed the origins of social transformation are to be found in processes internal to society. Change is presumed to occur via mechanisms 'built in', as it were, to the very structure of a given society, and governing its development (Giddens, 1985).

The challenge facing political theory today is daunting. For the fundamental terms of reference of political theory – including the assumption that one can understand the proper nature of the polity by reference to the nation-state – appear to be under strain in the face of major twentieth-century developments. Among the latter are the dynamics of a world economy which seem to produce instabilities and difficulties within states and between states that outreach the control of any single 'centre'; the rapid growth of transnational links which have stimulated new forms of collective decision-making involving states, intergovernmental organizations and an array of international pressure-groups; the build-up of military arms and the means of warfare as a 'stable feature' of the contemporary world. Such phenomena raise fundamental

* This essay is published here for the first time; it will appear in the revised Open University course, *State and Society* (Milton Keynes: Open University Press, 1989). © The Open University, 1988, D209: *State and Society*.

questions about the nature of political theory, the fate of the modern state and the fate of one of the defining ideas of the state – sovereignty.

The idea of sovereignty will be explored in this essay through a number of sections which discuss in turn: the historical background of the idea; classic conceptions of sovereignty; the notion of the sovereign equality of states; 'disjunctures' between the concept of sovereignty and the economic and political structures of the global system; and the relevance of the idea of national sovereignty to contemporary political analysis. The ultimate purpose of the essay is to assess whether the idea of the sovereign state can be sustained in the face of current economic and political circumstances. The argument will be that the classic concept of sovereignty – as set out in Anglo-American and continental traditions of political theory – is problematic. A number of 'gaps' will be identified between the idea of 'a national community of fate' and the pattern of global interconnections – above all, those set by international econ-omic processes, international regimes and organizations, international law and power blocs.[1] While it will be concluded that the concepts of political theory today are inadequate to describe the foundations of national states, it will also be shown how the idea of sovereignty remains cogent in a number of respects – above all, in underlying the determination of 'friend' and 'foe' and marshalling the 'means of violence' in the relations within and between states.

Sovereignty and national politics

The idea of sovereignty is intimately linked to the idea of the state; for its origin and history is closely connected to the origin and development of the state. Despite the fact that what is meant by sovereignty is difficult to dis-entangle fully, it is possible at the outset to provide a fairly straightforward definition. By 'sovereignty' I mean, following Hinsley's classic discussion, 'the idea that there is a final and absolute authority in the political community' (1986, p. 1). The meaning of sovereignty becomes a little clearer if we add to this definition, as Hinsley does, the following: 'and no final and absolute authority exists elsewhere' (1986, p. 26). For what the idea of sovereignty entails is that there is a political authority in a community which has undis-puted right to determine the framework of rules and regulations in a given territory and to govern accordingly.

The doctrine of sovereignty has two distinct dimensions: the first concerned with the 'internal' aspect of sovereignty; the second concerned with the 'external'. The former involves the belief that a political body established as sovereign rightly exercises the 'supreme command' over a particular society. Government – however defined – must enjoy the 'final and absolute authority' within that terrain. The latter, external, dimension involves the claim that no final and absolute authority above and beyond the sovereign state. ...ie international context, the theory of sovereignty has implied that states ,nould be regarded as independent in all matters of internal politics, and should in principle be free to determine their own fate within this framework. External sovereignty is an attribute which political societies possess in relationship to one another; it is associated with the aspiration of a community to determine its own direction and policies, without undue interference from other powers.

Sovereignty has been an important and useful concept for legal analysis, but it can be a misleading notion if applied uncritically as a political idea. One needs to bear in mind a crucial distinction between *de jure* and *de facto* supreme power, between '(a) supreme legal *authority*, *competence* or entitlement (i.e. a *de jure* use of "power"), or (b) a supreme ability to induce . . . [people] to take a desired course of action, by bringing some sort of pressure to bear upon them (a *de facto* use)' (Benn and Peters, 1959, p. 257). To attribute sovereignty in the first sense to anyone or any office would be to give an account of the provisions of a legal order, for example a constitution – an account which would specify what form sovereignty should take as specified in law. To attribute sovereignty in the second sense would be to give an account of the actual (political, economic or social) determinants of the exercise of supreme power. For analytical purposes, these different levels of analysis need to be kept separate, although one must always bear in mind that the legal aspect of sovereignty is never politically neutral – a set of rules and regulations which simply determine the framework within which politics unfolds (King, 1987, p. 494). Law is always shaped by politics, by the struggles and conflicts of individuals, groups and collectivities to determine the nature of the rules which govern their lives.

The historical backdrop of sovereignty

If the basic idea of sovereignty seems a fairly straightforward one, it must be noted that it was by no means always so. It is worth saying something briefly about the history of the idea of sovereignty, because it tells us something about how fundamentally innovative this notion was when developed systematically in the early modern era. The idea of sovereignty was not part of the ancient classical Greek world. The city-state, or *polis*, did not differentiate between state and society – ruled as it was by citizen-governors. In ancient Athens citizens were at one and the same time subjects of state authority and the creators of public rules and regulations. The people, the *demos*, engaged in legislative and judicial functions; for the Athenian concept of 'citizenship' entailed taking a share in these functions, participating *directly* in the affairs of the state. Athenian democracy required a general commitment to the principle of civic virtue: dedication to the republican city-state and the subordination of private life to public affairs and the common good. 'The public' and 'the private' were intertwined. Humans could only properly fulfil themselves and live honourably as citizens in and through the *polis* (see Finley, 1983).

It was not until the rise of the Roman Empire that a new type of rule, *rule by a single central authority*, crystallized. A clear record of this notion can be found in the *lex regia* doctrine noted by Justinian, the sixth-century Byzantine emperor, in his *Corpus iuris* (compilation of Roman law). According to this doctrine, what pleases an emperor has the force of law but only in so far as 'the people' transfers to him and into his hands 'all its own right and power' (see Hinsley, 1986, pp. 43–4). Rulership entails ultimate power, but it is a power that has to be understood in relation to its proper origins: the will of the people. With the *lex regia* doctrine the idea of sovereignty as a distinct form of law-making power was firmly established, but its influence, in the first instance, did not outlive the Roman Empire.

With the fall of the Roman Empire the idea of sovereignty became progressively submerged by the rise of the Christian faith. While it would be quite misleading to suggest that Christianity effectively banished secular considerations from the life of rulers and ruled, it unquestionably shifted the source of authority and wisdom from this-worldly to other-worldly representatives. The Christian world-view transformed the rationale of political action from that of the *polis* or empire to a theological framework. The Hellenic view of humanity, for example, as formed to live in a city was replaced by a preoccupation with how humans could live in communion with God (Pocock, 1975, p. 84). The Christian world-view insisted that the good lay in submission to God's will.

The integration of Christian Europe gradually came to depend above all on two theocratic authorities, the Papacy and the Holy Roman Emperor. During the Middle Ages there was no theoretical alternative to the theocratic positions of pope and emperor. One of the most striking manifestations of this was the absence of clear distinctions between ideal and positive law, between public and private rights, between legality and religious morality. The medieval view of society as 'a whole' – a divinely ordained hierarchy of rank and order in a 'Great Chain of Being' – is well articulated in the following commentary:

> in the feudal world the primary concept was not the state but law – a law not made by politicians but part of a universal and eternal order, to be discovered by a study of custom and precedent. Kings, councils and judges found and formulated it but could not make it; for to create new law would be to impose a new obligation by an act of will, and only God could do that. Political authorities – i.e. those exercising legal authority backed by coercive power – were regarded as being as much under law as any other corporate institution; the law was not thought of as the creation of the political order, nor as linked to it any more

intimately than to any other. Law was thought of as the eternal and objectively valid normative system within which all associations were contained, and from which all roles drew appropriate rights and duties. (Benn and Peters, 1959, p. 256)

The whole fabric of medieval thought had to be shattered before the idea of a sovereign political order could once again be conceived independently of religious authority, as something different in kind from religious, kindred or economic groupings. Until about the end of the twelfth century when, among other things, the principles and precepts of Roman law were rediscovered and began to stimulate Western legal interest, the 'closed circle' of medieval intellectual life went unchallenged.

It was not until the end of the sixteenth century, however, that the nature and limits of political authority, law, rights and obedience emerged as a preoccupation of European political thought. Of all the developments that helped trigger new ways of thinking about political authority, it was perhaps the Protestant Reformation that was the most significant. The Reformation did more than just challenge papal jurisdiction and authority across Europe; it raised questions about political obligation and obedience in a most stark manner. Whether allegiance was owed to the Catholic Church, a Protestant ruler, or particular religious sects, was an issue that did not easily resolve itself. The bitter struggles between religious factions which spread across Europe during the last half of the sixteenth century, and reached their most intense expression during the Thirty Years War in Germany, made it clear that religion was becoming a highly divisive force (see Sigler, 1983). Very gradually it became apparent that the powers of the state would have to be separated from the duty of rulers to uphold any particular faith (Skinner, 1978, p. 352). This conclusion alone offered a way forward through the dilemmas of rule created by competing religions, all seeking to secure for themselves the kind of privileges claimed by the medieval church.

The impetus to re-examine the nature of the relationship between society and state was given added force by a growing awareness in Europe of the variety of possible social and political arrangements which followed in the wake of the discovery of the non-European world (see Sigler, 1983, pp. 53–62). The relationship between Europe and the 'New World', and the nature of the rights (if any) of non-Europeans, became a major focus of discussion. It sharpened the sense of a plurality of possible interpretations of the nature of political life. The direction these interpretations actually took was, of course, directly related to the context and traditions of particular European countries: the changing nature of politics was experienced differently throughout Europe. But it is hard to underestimate the general significance of the events and processes which ushered in a new era of political reflection.

In this context sovereignty became a way of thinking about an old problem

– the nature of power and rule. When established forms of authority could no longer be taken for granted it was the idea of sovereignty which provided a fresh link between political power and rulership. In the struggle between church, state and community, sovereignty offered an alternative way of conceiving the legitimacy of claims to power. In the debate about sovereignty which ensued, there was, unsurprisingly perhaps, little initial agreement about its meaning; differing account were offered of the proper locus of 'supreme power' in society, the source of authority for that power, limitations upon that power, if any, and the ends to which that power might or should be directed. The section below examines the notions of a number of the key figures who provided significant contributions to the debate on sovereignty. Their contrasting views set out much of the basic framework in the debate about the nature and role of ultimate political power.

Conceptions of sovereignty

Reflecting on the religious and civil conflicts of the sixteenth century, Jean Bodin (1529/30–90), a French philosopher and political writer, contended that these conflicts could only be solved if it was possible to establish the existence of an unrestricted ruling power competent to overrule all religious and customary authorities. He argued strenuously that an 'ordered commonwealth' depended upon the creation of a central authority which could wield unlimited power within a community. Bodin was not the first to make this case; for example, Machiavelli (1469–1527), a significant influence on Bodin, had done so earlier. But unlike Machiavelli, Bodin developed this notion into what is commonly regarded as the first statement of the modern theory of sovereignty: that there must be within every political community or state a determinate sovereign authority whose powers are decisive and whose powers are recognized by the community as the rightful (or legitimate) basis of authority.

Bodin developed one of the most celebrated definitions of sovereignty in his major text, *Six Books of a Commonwealth* (1576). Sovereignty, in this account, is the untrammelled and undivided power to make laws. It is the supreme power over subjects unrestrained by law; 'the right to impose laws generally on all subjects regardless of their consent' (*Six Books*, 1, 8, p. 32). Law is, accordingly, 'nothing else than the command of the sovereign in the exercise of his sovereign power' (*Six Books*, 1, 8, p. 35). The sovereign has the capacity to make and alter the law for all his subjects. 'There are none on earth, after God, greater than sovereign princes, whom God establishes as His lieutenants to command the rest of mankind' (*Six Books*, 1, 10, p. 40). The sovereign power 'cannot be subject to the commands of another', for it is the sovereign that 'makes law for the subject' (*Six Books*, 1, 8, p. 28). Sovereign power is rightfully exercised if it is exercised 'simply and unconditionally' (*Six Books*, 1, 8, p. 26).

Bodin was a critic, however, of Machiavelli's defence of centralized power – a defence which, Bodin held, firmly placed the ends of the state or community above those of the individual subject and uncritically affirmed that 'reasons of state' held priority over the 'rights of individuals' (cf. Skinner, 1981, pp. 51–77). In contrast to Machiavelli, Bodin sought to show that a sovereign authority could only be properly established if, as it has been aptly put, 'the body politic was regarded as being composed of both ruler and ruled, integrated as previous beliefs and politics had failed to integrate them, and if the governing power respected legal and moral rules' (Hinsley, 1986, p. 121). In Bodin's work, good government, or sovereignty properly exercised, is subject to the laws of God and of nature as well as to the fundamental or customary rights and laws of the political community (including the property rights of citizens) (*Six Books*, 1, 8, pp. 29, 33).

Sovereignty, in Bodin's innovative account, is the defining characteristic or constitutive power of the state. Different types of state can, he further argued, be differentiated according to the locus of this supreme power – monarchy, aristocracy or democracy. Bodin's clear preference was for a monarchical polity with a just form of government: an all-powerful monarch who would temper power with justice by following the laws of God and of nature, and by upholding customary rules. In maintaining this position – in championing, on the one hand, a supreme power unrestrained by law and, on the other, necessary limits upon this power – Bodin has often been charged with inconsistency. However, this particular criticism misses the mark; for Bodin's primary concern is with *lawful* government (see, for example, *Six Books*, 1, 8, p. 36). Sovereignty may be unlimited, but the sovereign is bound in morals and religion to respect the laws of God, nature and custom (see Benn, 1967, p. 502). An additional suggestion made by Bodin that sovereignty can and ought to be limited by constitutional laws, raises further difficulties for the coherence of his position, but even these, it can be shown, do not necessarily raise decisive problems (Bodin, *Six Books*, 1, 8, p. 31; cf. Benn, 1967; King, 1974; Parker, 1981).

Bodin's preoccupation with establishing the necessity of monarchical sovereignty meant that he did not pursue many of the tensions inherent in the idea of a sovereign power comprising both rulers and ruled – an integrated body politic of 'law-makers' and 'law-takers', of governors and subjects. It was tensions, in particular, between the principle of rulership and the principle of self-government, between power and community, which were to lead to fundamentally discrepant conceptions of the nature of sovereign power and of the criteria of legitimacy of government and state. At the extremes were, on the one hand, Hobbes's classic statement about *state* sovereignty (*Leviathan*,

1651) and, on the other hand, Rousseau's powerful account of the doctrine of *popular* sovereignty (*The Social Contract*, 1762).

In his great work, *Leviathan*, Hobbes provided one of the most elegant rationales for the primacy of the state, for the necessary unity of the state as the representative of the body politic, and for the necessity of the state as the creator and maintainer of positive law. Like Bodin, he wrote against the background of social disorder and political instability; in this case, the English Civil War. Like Bodin, he sought to establish the necessity of an all-powerful sovereign capable of securing the conditions of 'peaceful and commodious living'. But Hobbes took these concerns in a radically new direction by arguing that it was only when individuals 'lay down their right to all things' that their long-term interest in security and peace can be upheld. His position was that individuals ought willingly to surrender their rights to a powerful single authority – thereafter authorized to act on their behalf – because, if all individuals were to do this simultaneously, the condition would be created for effective political rule. A unique relation of authority would be created – the relation of sovereign to subject – and a unique political power would be established: sovereign power or sovereignty – the authorized, hence, rightful, use of power by the person (or assembly) established as sovereign (see Benn, 1955; Peters, 1956).

The sovereign has to have sufficient power to ensure that the laws governing political and economic life are upheld. Since, in Hobbes's view, 'men's ambitions, avarice, anger and other passions' are strong, the 'bonds of words are too weak to bridle them . . . without some fear of coercive power': 'covenants, without the sword, are but words, and of no strength to secure a man at all' (*Leviathan*, p. 223). Beyond the sovereign state's sphere of influence there will always be the chaos of constant warfare; but within the territory controlled by the state, with 'fear of some coercive power', social order can be sustained.

It is important to stress that, in Hobbes's opinion, sovereignty must be self-perpetuating, undivided and ultimately absolute (*Leviathan*, pp. 227–8). The justification for this is '*the safety of the people*'. By 'safety' is meant not merely minimum physical preservation. The sovereign must ensure the protection of all things held in property: 'Those that are dearest to a man are his own life, and limbs; and in the next degree, (in most men) those that concern conjugall affection; and after them riches and means of living' (*Leviathan*, pp. 376, 382–3). Although Hobbes acknowledges certain limits to the legitimate range of the sovereign's actions (see *Leviathan*, ch. 21), the state is regarded by him as pre-eminent in all spheres. For the state is authorized to represent all individuals and, accordingly, absorbs all popular or public right. State sovereignty embraces all elements of the body politic.

With Hobbes, the justification of state power received its fullest expression and became a central theme in European political thought. But his position was controversial and challenged on at least two grounds (see Hinsley, 1986, pp. 144ff.). The first objection raised the fundamental question of where sovereign authority properly lay, with the ruler, the monarch, the state or (as was increasingly to be argued) with the people; the second objection was concerned with the proper form and limits, the legitimate scope, of state action.

Rousseau did not reject the concept of sovereignty, but insisted on retaining for the people the sovereignty which Hobbes had transferred to the state and its rulers. In Rousseau's view, sovereignty originates in the people and ought to stay there (*The Social Contract*, p. 141). For the very essence of sovereignty is the creation, authorization and enactment of law according to the standards and requirements of the common good. And the nature of the common good can only be known through public discourse and public agreement. Only citizens themselves can articulate 'the supreme direction of the general will' – it is the sum of their publicly generated judgements of the common good (*The Social Contract*, pp. 60–1). Moreover, Rousseau argued, citizens can only be obligated to a system of laws and regulations they have prescribed for themselves with the general good in mind (*The Social Contract*, p. 65, cf. p. 82).

Taking arguments about sovereignty in a new direction, Rousseau held that, ideally, individuals should be involved directly in the creation of the laws by which their lives are regulated. The sovereign authority is the people making the rules by which they live. All citizens should meet together to decide what is best for the community and enact the appropriate laws. The ruled should be the rulers: the affairs of the state should be integrated into the affairs of ordinary citizens (see *The Social Contract*, pp. 82 and 114, and for a general account, book 3, chs 1–5). Rousseau was critical of the classical Athenian conception of direct democracy because it failed to incorporate a division between legislative and executive functions and, consequently, became prone to instability, internecine strife and indecision in crisis (*The Social Contract*, pp. 112–14, pp. 136ff.). But while he wished to defend the importance of dividing and limiting 'governmental power', the executive or government in his scheme was legitimate only to the extent to which it fulfilled 'the instructions of the general will'. In so arguing, Rousseau undermined the distinction between the state and the community, the government and 'the people' but in the opposite direction to Hobbes. Government was reduced to a 'commission'; public right absorbed the state.

Hobbes and Rousseau may be portrayed as representing opposing ends of the debate about the locus of sovereignty. However, both cast their arguments in such a way as to face a common objection: that they projected models of political power with potentially tyrannical implications. For if Hobbes placed the state in an all-powerful position with respect to the community, Rousseau placed the community (or a majority thereof) in a position to wholly dominate individual citizens – the community is all-powerful and, therefore, the sovereignty of the people could easily destroy the liberty of individuals (Berlin, 1969, p. 163). The problem is that just as Hobbes failed to articulate either the principles or institutions necessary to delimit state action, Rousseau assumed that minorities ought to consent to the decisions of majorities, and posited no limits to the reach of the decisions of a democratic majority, and therefore to political intervention. Conceptions of sovereignty which fail to demarcate the limits or legitimate scope of political action need to be treated with the utmost caution.

An alternative to the theses of the sovereignty of the state and the sovereignty of the people is to reaffirm the location of sovereignty in the body politic as a whole and regard the community as the source of sovereignty and the state as the proper instrument for its exercise (Hinsley, 1986, pp. 222–3). The motivation for such a position lies precisely in doubts both about unaccountable state power and about the necessity to provide limits to the legitimate scope of political action. Doubts such as these were given lasting expression in the constitutional arguments of John Locke (1672–1704) and in the subsequent tradition of political thinking inspired by his work.

Locke held that the institution of 'government' can and should be conceived as an instrument for the defence of the 'life, liberty and estate' of its citizens; that is, government's *raison d'être* is the protection of individuals' rights as laid down by God's will and as enshrined in law (see Dunn, 1969, part 3). In Locke's view, the formation of the state does not signal the transfer of all subjects' rights to the state (*Two Treatises of Government*, pp. 402–3, para. 135 and pp. 412–13, para. 149). The rights of law-making and enforcement (legislative and executive rights) are transferred, but the whole process is conditional upon the state adhering to its essential purpose: the preservation of 'life, liberty and estate'. Supreme power remains ultimately with the people. Locke believed that the integrity and ultimate ends of society require a constitutional state in which 'public power' is legally circumscribed and divided. He argued on behalf of a constitutional monarchy holding executive power and a parliamentary assembly holding the rights of legislation, although he did not think this was the only form government might take.

It is important to emphasize that, in Locke's account, political authority is bestowed by individuals on government for the purpose of pursuing the ends of the governed; and should these ends fail to be represented adequately, the final judges are the people – the citizens of the state – who can dispense both with their deputies and, if need be, with the existing form of government itself. Faced with a series of tyrannical political acts, rebellion to form a new government, Locke contended, might not only be unavoidable but justified. One commentator has summarized Locke's position thus:

Rulers . . . hold their authority under law; and entitlement to the obedience of their subjects derives from the impartial administration of this law. Where they act against or outside this law to the harm of their subjects, they become tyrants. Wherever law ends, tyranny begins [*Two Treatises*, p. 448, para. 202]. For a ruler in authority to use force against the interests of his subjects and outside the law is to destroy his own authority. He puts himself into a state of war with his injured subjects, and each of these has the same right to resist him as they would have to resist any other unjust aggressor [*Two Treatises*, p. 448, para 202 and p. 467, para 232]. (Dunn, 1984, p. 54)

In relation to Bodin's or Hobbes's ideas, this was a most radical doctrine which has had an enduring impact on Western political thought. For it affirmed that supreme power was the inalienable right of the people; that governmental supremacy was a *delegated* supremacy held on trust; that government enjoyed full political authority so long as this trust was sustained; and that a government's legitimacy or right to rule could be withdrawn if the people judged this necessary and appropriate, that is, if the rights of individuals and 'ends of society' were systematically flouted.

Although Locke maintained that political power was held 'on trust', he did not develop a detailed account of who were to count as 'the people' and under what conditions 'trust' should be bestowed (cf. Dunn, 1984, pp. 22–59; Held, 1987, pp. 51–5). He certainly did not explore systematically how possible tensions between the sovereignty of the people – the idea of the people as an active sovereign body with the capacity to make or break governments – and government – as the trustee of the people with the right to make and enforce the law – might be resolved in principle. He did not anticipate, that is to say, many of the arguments and institutional innovations of democratic theory (see Held, 1987). However, his attempt to transcend the old dualism between ruler and people, state and community, became highly influential in the West, as did his attempt to enshrine this new political understanding in the notion of constitutional government: a legal and institutional mechanism to protect both the 'sovereign people' and 'the sovereign state' – the right of the people to hold political power accountable and the right of the state to govern. For it was Locke's case that neither public nor state right alone could be left unmediated, unchecked and unbalanced.

While the history of the concept of sovereignty in modern times has been marked by further dispute and complexity, it can be argued that it has generally affirmed the location of sovereignty in the political community or body politic as a whole; the necessary embodiment of sovereignty in a constitution (written or unwritten); and the necessary articulation of sovereignty by a set of rules and relations which marks and delimits both state and society (see Jouvenal, 1957; James, 1986). In keeping with these emphases, 'sovereignty' has come to be defined, as it was, for example, in one recent encyclopaedia of political thought, as 'the power or authority which comprises the attributes of an ultimate arbitral agent – whether a person or a body of persons – entitled to make decisions and settle disputes within a political hierarchy with some degree of finality' but 'bound by some rules from which it cannot free itself' (King, 1987, p. 492, p. 495). Further, sovereignty by its very nature implies a degree of independence from external powers and dominance or ultimate authority over internal groups. In modern democratic states, it has come to be recognized that sovereignty is the supreme law-making and decision-taking power of a community, that the ultimate source of sovereignty is the people, that sovereignty is necessarily delegated by the people to the state and exercised on their behalf through government, and that constitutional arrangements or well-established precedents are necessary to safeguard these political goods.

The sovereign equality of states

In the international context, sovereignty has involved the assertion by the state – whether it be democratic or not – of independence; that is, of its possession of sole rights to jurisdiction over a particular people and territory. This 'external' dimension of sovereignty has, in addition, been associated with the claim that, by virtue of the very argument which establishes the sovereignty of a particular state, that state must accept that it will be one among many states with, in principle, equal rights to self-determination. In the world of relations among states, the principle of the sovereign equality of all states has, since the early years of the nineteenth century, become paramount in the formal conduct of states toward one another (see Hinsley, 1963). And in this world, it is Hobbes's way of thinking about power and power relations which has often been regarded as the most insightful account of the meaning of sovereignty at the global level (see, for example, Aron, 1966).

Hobbes drew a direct comparison between international relations and the state of nature. He described the international system of states as being in a continuous 'posture of war' since;

> in all times, Kings, and Persons of Soveraigne authority, because of their Independency, are in continuall jealousies, and in the state and posture of Gladiators; having their weapons pointing, and their eyes fixed on one another; that is, their Forts, Garrisons, and Guns upon the Frontiers of their Kingdomes; and continuall Spyes upon their neighbours. (*Leviathan*, pp. 187–8)

In these circumstances, a war of 'all against all' is a constant threat; and each state is at liberty to act to secure its own interests unimpeded by any higher religious or moral strictures.

[I]n States, and Common-wealths not dependent on one another, every Common-wealth (not every man) has an absolute Libertie, to doe what it shall judge (that is to say, what that Man, or Assemblie that representeth it, shall judge) most conducing to their benefit. (*Leviathan*, p. 266)

The upshot of this view is, as one commentator has written, that 'states are not subject to international moral requirements because they represent separate and discrete political orders with no common authority among them' (Beitz, 1979, p. 25). The world consists of separate national powers, pursuing their own interests, backed ultimately by their organization of coercive power.

In the study of international affairs, Hobbes's account has become associated with the 'realist' theory of international politics (cf. Morgenthau, 1948; Wight, 1986; S. Smith, 1987). Realism posits, in the spirit of Hobbes's work, that the system of sovereign states is inescapably anarchic in character; and that this anarchy forces all states, in the inevitable absence of any supreme arbiter to enforce moral behaviour and agreed international codes, to pursue power politics in order to attain their vital interests. This *Realpolitik* view of states has had a significant influence on both the analysis and practice of international relations in recent times; for it offers a convincing *prima facie* explanation of the chaos and disorder of twentieth-century world affairs (McGrew, 1986, pp. 53–5). On this account, the modern system of nation-states is a 'limiting factor' which will always thwart any attempt to conduct international relations in a manner which transcends the politics of the sovereign state.

There are alternative views (see, for example, McKinley and Little, 1986). Among the most significant was that laid down by the Dutch jurist and philosopher Hugo Grotius (1583–1645). Grotius was one of the first to insist on the necessity of a body of international positive law, distinct from divine and natural law, to enshrine and articulate the principle of sovereignty. While Grotius's understanding of the relations among states shared some emphases with Bodin, Grotius was unique in his systematic pursuit of questions about the nature and status of international law, the rights and obligations of states, and the relation between international law and justice (Grotius, *The Law of War and Peace*).

Grotius asserted, against the sceptics of his age, that there could be universal moral standards which might be used to adjudicate disputes in international conflicts, standards which could be derived from two fundamental principles. 'The first was that self-preservation must always be legitimate, and the second was that *wanton* injury of another (i.e. not for reasons of self-preservation) must always be illegitimate' (Tuck, 1987, p. 187). Grotius argued that these principles were constitutive of social and moral life and, accordingly, obligated human beings independently of all other considerations even if, he wrote in a famous phrase, 'there is no God' (see Tuck, 1987, pp. 186–7 and, for a fuller account, 1983). He contended, moreover, that rules cᵣ ·'·' be derived from this foundation for resolving conflict or, if need be, justifying its necessary pursuit.

Elaborating these arguments, Grotius advanced a most significant analysis of the idea of the 'just war', maintaining that no war could be just if it were based purely on the aggressive pursuit of self-interest. In his view, the only wars that were justified were those based on defence and retaliation, and then only when all other means had been thoroughly exhausted and armed conflict was the last resort. Although there are significant ambiguities in Grotius's work which have led to quite different interpretations of its meaning (cf. Bull, 1977; Beitz, 1979; Tuck, 1983; Hinsley, 1986), he consistently pursued the distinction between the legality of an act when judged by the standards of a sovereign state and the justice of that act when assessed by the standards of a system of international jurisprudence. Pursuing this distinction he argued that a subject's obligation was above all to justice and that it was not a duty to serve a state in the pursuit of an unjust cause. This notable argument, along with other elements of Grotius's thinking, was taken up and applied on a number of occasions in international politics, including, significantly, in the years following the Second World War in the International Tribunal at Nuremberg (1945) and in the original deliberations and declarations of the United Nations, both of which I shall return to later.

Grotius belongs to a line of thinkers who have contributed to the creation of a counterpoint to the 'realist' view of international relations. This alternative tradition of analysis, often referred to as 'idealism' but more appropriately referred to as the 'liberal' conception of international politics, has at its centre a belief in a potential 'harmony of interests' among states (McGrew, 1986, pp. 544ff.). While this belief has been defended in different ways over time, it has generally involved two claims: first, that humankind has a common interest in peaceful co-existence which alone would allow individuals to develop their objectives unimpeded by naked aggression and the pursuit of sectoral interests; and, second, that humanity's interest in peace can never be fully realized while undemocratic state forms exist. The whole idea of international relations as a war of all against all is, according to this liberal view, a doctrine contrived 'to preserve the power and the employment of princes, statesmen, soldiers, diplomats and armaments manufacturers, and to bind their tyranny ever more firmly upon the necks of people' (Howard, 1981, p. 31).

This position received its most elaborate development during the nineteenth century, although it was often asserted in the wake of the wreckage of the First World War in support of hopes to establish 'a community of like minded nations', cooperating fully with one another and 'settling their differences like reasonable men, enjoying peace under a law . . . which if need be they would pool their resources to enforce' (Howard, 1981, p. 91). These aspirations were dashed with the failure of the League of Nations; and their fate was sealed, in the view of many commentators, by the outbreak of the Second World War (see, for example, Hinsley, 1963; Carr, 1981). There certainly seemed an abundance of evidence to suggest that few states, particularly among the most powerful nations, were willing to surrender one of the most integral elements of the idea of sovereignty: the freedom to define friend or enemy and to adopt the most suitable strategies toward them. 'Realist' scepticism about the plausibility of any programme to transform the principles and operational basis of the sovereign state gained support in the face of the difficulties of sustaining liberal convictions.

The issues which divide 'realist' and 'liberal' conceptions of international politics cannot be traced further here. But at least it can and should be noted that the two poles represented by Hobbes's and Grotius's accounts of the nature of the international order represent two recognizable poles of modern international relations today: the one articulating the nature of state power, the pursuit of national interests, and the way states have sought to retain control over issues of war and peace; the other articulating some of the central issues that necessarily are raised by states which seek to find ways of cooperating with others in order to bring about a more stable and regulated framework within which the complex interconnections and dealings of the international environment can be managed. But whichever account is more plausible in general terms, the contrasts between them raise starkly the question of whether in the international context sovereignty means that states participate in international relations as wholly independent members of a system of states, free to pursue their own interests unimpeded by any higher authority or any transsocietal political arrangements; or whether, by virtue of the way in which states are inescapably embedded in a complex system of international relations, the very idea of states as autonomous, self-governing and essentially self-referring political units is fundamentally unsustainable.

Sovereignty in the face of the global system

It is commonplace today to hear politicians say they do not control many of the factors which determine the fate of a nation-state. It is international forces, it is often said, which limit the choices facing a state or make it impossible for a particular national policy to be pursued. Leaving aside for a moment the accuracy of such claims, it is useful to keep in mind a distinction introduced earlier between *de jure* and *de facto* sovereignty or, as I shall put it below, between sovereignty and autonomy. This distinction is sometimes made in order to separate out problems facing a state due to loss of aspects of legal sovereignty from problems which stem from a loss of political and economic autonomy. For example, it may be that what underpins politicians' anxiety about a 'loss of control' is not a diminution of legal and actual control over the *process* of determining policy directions, but rather a diminution of their capacity to *achieve* these policies once they have been set (Keohane and Nye, 1972, p. 393). As one economist expressed the point: '[i]n fact, nations retain actual as well as legal control over their instruments of policy (sovereignty); the problem arises because these instruments of policy lose their effectiveness, so that countries find themselves able to pursue their objectives but unable to achieve them' (Cooper, 1986, p. 21). In what follows, I shall explore whether sovereignty has remained largely intact while the autonomy of the state has diminished, or whether the modern state actually faces a loss of sovereignty.

There are many issues that are important to disentangle here – issues which centre on the challenges to political authority deriving, on the one hand, from the system of nation-states and the world political economy and, on the other, from the divergence that sometimes exists between those affected by a decision and those who participated in making it, however indirectly, within a sovereign state. I shall take each set of issues in turn, although it must be recognized that what follows is only the briefest of sketches of arguments which would benefit from extensive development.

A number of fundamental 'gaps', I believe, are apparent in the relation between the political theory of the sovereign state and the nature of the twentieth-century world, gaps which highlight a discrepancy between the terms of reference and explanatory reach of the theory and the actual practices and structures of the state and economic system at the global level (Morse, 1976; Pettman, 1979; Beetham, 1984; Dunn, 1985; Giddens, 1985). There are at least five gaps worth noting.

Gap 1: the world economy

There is a gap between the formal domain of political authority and the actual economic system of production, distribution and exchange which in many ways serves to limit or undermine the actual power or scope of national political authorities (Keohane and Nye, 1977; Gourevitch, 1978; Katzenstein, 1978).[2] No adequate account, for example, of the pressures on the welfare state and the evolution of government policy in Europe in the 1970s and 1980s can be given independently of the international mechanisms which transmitted inflation and recession, the deterioration of the terms of trade experienced by many European countries, and the steady expansion of industrial capitalism at the so-called 'periphery' of the international economy – South Korea, Taiwan, Singapore and the other newly industrializing countries (Warren, 1980; Keohane, 1984).

Economic processes have become progressively internationalized in a number of key spheres: communications, production, trade, finance and in many matters of economic coordination. New technology, in addition, has radically increased the mobility of economic units and the sensitivity of markets, and societies, to one another. There is considerable evidence to support the claim that technological advances in transportation and communication are eroding the boundaries between hitherto separate markets – boundaries which were a necessary condition for autonomous national policies (see Keohane and Nye, 1972, pp. 392–5). The very possibility of a national economic policy is, accordingly, reduced. The monetary and fiscal policies of individual national governments, one survey of the international political economy recently concluded, 'are dominated by the movements in international financial product markets' (R. Smith, 1987, section 11, p. 21). Likewise, the levels of employment investment and revenue within a country are often 'subordinated to the production location decisions of MNCs [multinational corporations]' (R. Smith, 1987, section 11, p. 21). Even when MNCs have a clear national base, their interest is above all in global profitability, and their country of origin may contribute relatively little to their overall financial position.

The loss of control of national economic programmes is, of course, not uniform across economic sectors or societies more generally: some markets and some countries can isolate themselves from transnational economic networks by, among other things, attempts to restore the boundaries or 'separateness' of markets and/or extend national laws to cover internationally mobile factors and/or adopt cooperative policies with other countries for the coordination of policy (see Cooper, 1986, pp. 1–22). The particular tensions between political and economic structures are likely to be different in different spheres, and between them: West–West, North–South, East–West (see R. Smith, 1987). And while there is still insufficient evidence to conclude that the very idea of a national economy is superseded, the internationalization of production, finance and other economic resources is unquestionably eroding the capacity of the state to control its own economic future. At the very least, there appears to be a diminution of state autonomy, and a disjuncture between the premises of the theory of the sovereign state and the conditions of modern economies.

Gap 2: hegemonic powers and power blocs

Connected with the above, there is a gap between the idea of the state as an autonomous strategic, military actor and the development of the global system of states, characterized by the existence of hegemonic powers and power blocs, which sometimes operate to undercut a state's authority and integrity. The dominance of the USA and USSR as world powers, and the operation of alliances like the North Atlantic Treaty Organization (NATO) and the Warsaw Pact, clearly constrains decision-making for many nations. A state's capacity to initiate particular foreign policies, pursue certain strategic concerns, choose between alternative military technologies and control certain weapon systems located on its own territory may be restricted by its place in the international system of power relations (see Kaldor and Falk, 1987).

Within NATO, for example, clear evidence of what might be called the 'internationalization of security' can be found in its joint and integrated military command structure. When NATO was originally established in the late 1940s, the US sought to limit (if not erode) the political sovereignty of the European states by the introduction of a clause in the founding treaty which would have allowed NATO forces to intervene in a NATO country in cases of 'indirect aggression'; that is, 'an internal *coup d'état* or political change favourable to an aggressor' (quoted in Wiebes and Zeeman, 1983; see Smith, 1984, pp. 124–5). The clause was successfully resisted by European states, but ever since then NATO's concern with collective security has trodden a fine line between, on the one hand, maintaining an organization of sovereign states (which permits, in principle, an individual member state *not* to act if it judges this appropriate) and, on the other, developing an international organization which *de facto*, if not *de jure*, operates according to its own logic and decision-making procedures. The existence of an integrated supranational command structure – headed by the Supreme Allied Commander in Europe, who has always been an American General appointed by the US president – ensures that, in a situation of war, NATO's 'national armies' would operate within the context of NATO strategies and NATO decisions (Smith, 1984, p. 131). The sovereignty of a national state is necessarily and decisively qualified once its armed forces are committed to a NATO conflict.

But even without such a commitment state autonomy as well as sovereignty can be limited and checked; for the routine conduct of NATO affairs involves the integration of national defence bureaucracies into international defence organizations; these, in turn, create transgovernmental decision-making systems which can escape the control of any single member state. Such systems can lead, moreover, to the establishment of informal, but none the less powerful, transgovernmental personnel networks or coalitions which are difficult to monitor by national mechanisms of accountability and control (Kaiser, 1972; Richelson and Ball, 1985). Having said this, no brief account of NATO would be complete without emphasizing also that its members are rivals competing for scarce resources, arms contracts, international prestige and other means of national enhancement. Membership of NATO does not eliminate sovereignty; rather, 'for each state, in different ways, membership . . . qualifies sovereignty' (Smith, 1984, p. 133). Aspects of sovereignty are negotiated and renegotiated in the NATO alliance.

Gap 3: international organizations

A third major area of disjuncture between the political theory of the sovereign state and the contemporary global system lies in the vast array of international regimes and organizations (of which NATO is only one type) which have been established to manage whole areas of transnational activity (trade, the oceans, space and so on) (Luard, 1977; Krasner, 1983). The growth in the number of these new forms of political association (see table 8.1 below) reflects the general expansion of transnational links. The development of international and transnational organizations has led to important changes in the decision-making structure of world politics. New forms of multinational politics have been established and with them new forms of collective decision-making involving states, intergovernmental organizations and a whole variety of transnational pressure groups. The International Monetary Fund (IMF), for example, pursuing a particular line of economic policy, may insist, as a condition of its loan to a government, that the latter cut public expenditure, devalue its currency and cut back on subsidized welfare programmes (see Harris, 1984).

Table 8.1

	Intergovernmental organizations	International non-governmental organizations
1909	37	176
1951	123	832
1972	280	2173
1984	365	4615

In a Third World country, for example, this may create hunger among large sections of the local population, trigger bread riots and perhaps the fall of a government or it might contribute directly to the imposition of martial law (Girvan, 1980). It has to be borne in mind that IMF intervention is routinely at the request of governmental authorities or particular political factions within a state and, therefore, cannot straightforwardly be interpreted as a threat to sovereignty. None the less, a striking tension has emerged between the idea of the sovereign state – centred on national politics and political institutions – and the nature of decision-making at the international level. The latter raises serious questions about the conditions under which a community is able to determine its own policies and directions.

The European Community is a significant illustration of these issues. Its significance, however, perhaps reaches further than any other kind of international organization due to its right to make laws which can be imposed on member states. Within Community institutions, the Council of Ministers has a unique position; for it has at its disposal powerful legal instruments (above all, 'Regulations', 'Directives' and 'Decisions') which allow it to make and enact policy. Of all these instruments 'Regulations' are the most notable because they have the status of law independently of any further negotiation or action on the part of member states (see Wickham, 1984). Moreover, the Community's extensive range of activities and control over resources makes it a form of 'public power' at the intersection of relatively new types of politics. As one observer noted:

> The Community commands resources, distributes benefits, allocates markets and market shares, and adjudicates between conflicting interests – all on a modest scale, within limited sectors, but all taking it into the central issues of politics. Unlike conventional international organizations, it is also a highly visible forum for politics, in which national politicians perform for both domestic and international audiences. National governments make valiant efforts to impose coherence and coordination on their activities at the European level, but the operation of transgovernmental coalitions among both ministers and officials is a long accepted aspect of Community politics. Transnational groups have mushroomed, representing the interests of European steel producers and pig farmers, trade unionists and environmentalists. (Wallace et al., 1982, p. 166)

The member states of the European Community are no longer 'the sole centres of power within their own territorial boundaries' (Wickham, 1984, p. 166). On the other hand, it is important to bear in mind that the Community's powers are limited when considered in relation to those of a typical European state; for the Community does not possess, for instance, coercive powers of its own – an army, a police force and other institutions of direct law-enforcement. The Community's powers were gained by the 'willing surrender' of aspects of sovereignty by member states – a 'surrender' which, arguably, has actually helped the survival of the European nation-state faced, on the one hand, with the dominance of the USA in the first three decades following the Second World War and, on the other, with the rise of the Japanese economic challenge. As one well-informed commentator put it:

> the nation-state today survives even though some of its powers have to be pooled with others, and even though many apparently sovereign decisions are seriously constrained, or made ineffective by, the decisions of others as well as by economic trends uncontrolled by anyone. [The European Community helps] . . . the state survive, by providing a modicum of predictability and a variety of rewards . . . [it has] strengthened the nation-state's capacity to act at home and abroad. (Hoffman, 1982, pp. 34–5)

In short, the European Community provides opportunities and restraints. The states of the Community retain the final and most general power in most areas of their domestic and foreign affairs – and the Community itself seems to have strengthened their options in these domains. However, within the Community sovereignty is now also clearly divided: any conception of sovereignty which assumes that it is an indivisible, illimitable, exclusive and perpetual form of public power is defunct.

Gap 4: international law

There is a fourth significant gap to note – a gap between the idea of membership of a national political community, that is, citizenship, which bestows upon individuals both rights and duties, and the development of international law, which subjects individuals, governments and non-governmental organizations to new systems of regulation (Vincent, 1986). Rights and duties are recognized in international law which transcend the claims of nation-states and which, whilst they may not be backed by institutions with coercive powers of enforcement, have far-reaching consequences. For example, the International Tribunal at Nuremberg – in the spirit of thinkers like Grotius – laid down, for the first time in history, that when *international rules* that protect basic humanitarian values are in conflict with *state laws*, every individual must transgress the state laws (except where there is no room for 'moral choice') (Cassese, 1988, p. 132). The legal framework of the Nuremburg Tribunal marked a highly significant change in the legal direction of the modern state; for the new rules challenged the principle of military discipline and subverted national sovereignty at one of its most sensitive points: the hierarchical relations within the military (Cassese, 1988, p. 141).

Of all the international declarations of rights which were made in the postwar years, the European Convention for the Protection of Human Rights and Fundamental Freedoms (1950) is especially noteworthy (see Negro, 1986). In marked contrast to the United Nations' Universal Declaration of Human Rights (1947) and subsequent UN charters of rights, the European Convention was concerned, as its preamble indicates, 'to take the first steps for the *collective enforcement* of certain of the Rights of the UN Declaration' (my emphasis). The European initiative was committed to a most remarkable and radical legal innovation: an innovation which in principle would allow individual citizens to initiate proceedings against their own governments. Nearly all European countries have now accepted an (optional) clause of the Convention which permits citizens to petition directly the European Commission on Human Rights, which can take cases to the Committee of Ministers of the Council of Europe and then (given a two-thirds majority on the Council) to the European Court of Human Rights. While the system is far from straightforward and is problematic in many respects, it has been claimed that, alongside legal changes introduced by the European Community, it no longer leaves the state 'free to treat its own citizens as it thinks fit' (Capotorti, 1983). In Britain alone, for example, telephone-tapping laws have been altered after intervention by the European Commission and findings of the European Court of Justice have led to changes in British law on issues as far-reaching as sexual discrimination and equal pay.

Within international law more generally, there are two legal rules which, since the very beginnings of the international community, have been taken to uphold national sovereignty: 'immunity from jurisdiction' and 'immunity of state agencies'. The former prescribes that 'no state can be sued in courts of another state for acts performed in its sovereign capacity'; and the latter stipulates that 'should an individual break the law of another state while acting as an agent for his country of origin and be brought before that state's courts, he is not held "guilty" because he did not act as a private individual but as the representative of the state' (Cassese, 1988, pp. 150ff.). The underlying purpose of these rules is to protect a government's autonomy in all matters of foreign policy and to prevent domestic courts from ruling on the behaviour of foreign states (on the understanding that all domestic courts everywhere will be so prevented). And the upshot has traditionally been that governments have been left free to pursue their interests subject only to the constraints of the 'art of politics'. It is notable, however, that these internationally recognized legal mainstays of sovereignty have been progressively questioned by Western courts. And while it is the case that national sovereignty has most often been the victor when put to the test, the tension between national sovereignty and international law is now marked, and it is by no means clear how it will be resolved.

Gap 5: the end of domestic policy

Finally, there is a gap between states as in principle representative of their citizens in the determination of public policy at home and in the protection of their interests overseas, and the global political system which makes the distinction between domestic and foreign policy harder and harder to sustain. One of the clearest manifestations of this is in the whole area of state security. The Cold War elevated communism and politics on the left generally to a political threat which knew no territorial limits: the enemy within was to be feared as much as the enemy without (Whitaker, 1984). Within NATO, accordingly, the domestic stability of each member state became a routine concern; for it was regarded as a vital condition of the political and military cohesion of the alliance (McGrew, 1986, p. 66). Matters of military security and international prestige readily spilt over into questions about appropriate industrial infrastructure, investment priorities, health care and educational policy (Kaiser, 1971; Morse, 1976; among others).

In the name of 'national security interests', moreover, controversial public matters can be placed beyond public debate; for instance, in the initial extension of surveillance in Britain to industrial disputes and to a wide range of civilian activities (including those of some journalists and politicians) (see essay 4, pp. 141–3). When 'national security interests' are invoked, public policy can readily become a matter for state personnel alone locked into, among other things, the networks of power blocs. The questions this poses for the idea of the sovereign democratic state are considerable.

Against this background of 'gaps' or 'disjunctures', the limits of a political theory that derives its terms of reference exclusively from the nation-state become apparent. This point is reinforced by a further consideration of the efficacy of the principle of majority rule. The application of this principle is, of course, at the centre of Western democracy: it is at the root of the claim of political decisions to be regarded as 'worthy' or legitimate (Spitz, 1984). Majority rule presupposes that 'equal' and 'secret' voting rights when combined with 'universal' and 'direct' voting rights create a congruent relation between the participants in the decision and those affected by it (see Offe, 1985, pp. 263ff.). Problems arise, however, not only because decisions made by *other* states, or by quasi-supranational organizations such as the EEC, NATO or the World Bank, diminish the range of decisions open to a given 'majority', but also because decisions of a nation do not only affect (or potentially affect) its citizens. For example, a decision made against the siting of an international airport near a capital city for fear of upsetting the local rural vote may have disadvantageous consequences for airline passengers throughout the world who are without direct means of representation. Or a decision to build a nuclear plant near the borders of a neighbouring country is likely to be a decision taken without considering whether those in the nearby country (or countries) ought to be among those who are consulted. Or a decision to suspend food aid to a country may stimulate the sudden escalation of food prices in that country and contribute directly to the outbreak of famine amongst the urban and rural poor (McHenry and Bird, 1977; Sobhan, 1979). Or the decision by a government in West or East to suspend or step up military aid to one side or another in a political struggle in a distant country may decisively influence the outcome of that conflict, or fan it into a further vortex of violence (Leftwich, 1983).

The modern theory of the sovereign state presupposes the idea of a 'national community of fate' – a community which rightly governs itself and determines its own future. The idea is certainly challenged by the nature of the pattern of global interconnections and the issues that have to be confronted by a modern state. National communities do not exclusively 'programme the action and decisions of governmental and parliamentary bodies' and the latter by no means simply determine what is right or appropriate for their own citizens (Offe, 1985, pp. 286ff.).

The issue of sovereignty today

While a complex pattern of global interconnections was already evident in the early phases of the development of the modern state, there is little doubt that there has been in recent times a further 'multinationalization of previously domestic activities' and an intensification of the 'intermeshing of decision making in multinational frameworks' (Kaiser, 1972, p. 370). The evidence that transnational relations have eroded the powers of the modern sovereign state is certainly strong. From considerations such as these some observers have concluded that sovereignty is fundamentally weakened and that the democratic system of Western states is progressively unviable: a national system of accountability and control risks obsolescence in the face of international forces and relations (see, for example, Burnheim, 1985). The conclusion, however, requires qualification.

While I have mapped some of the common challenges to the sovereign state – above all, to the European sovereign state – in the modern post-war world (gaps 1–5), it is important to stress that the effect of these challenges is likely to vary under different international and national conditions – for instance, a nation's location in the international division of labour, its place in particular power blocs, its position with respect to the international legal system, its relation to major international organizations. At issue, in part, is the meaning of what is sometimes called 'globalization'. Although globalization is a useful concept as a means of referring to the rapid growth of complex interconnections and interrelations between states and societies, it fails to recognize the discontinuities in world politics. Not all states, for example, are equally integrated into the world economy and, thus, while national political outcomes will be heavily influenced by global processes in some countries, in others regional or national forces might well remain supreme (Barry-Jones, 1983; Dicken, 1986).

Further, it would be wrong to conclude that because a particular state has experienced a decline in its international freedom of action, sovereignty is thereby wholly undermined. To argue in this way is, as has been so aptly remarked, 'to associate the attribute of sovereignty with the possession by the state of freedom to act as it chooses instead of with the absence over and above the state of a superior authority' (Hinsley, 1986, p. 226). Politicians may often have aspired to a world marked by total freedom of action, but they have always been forced to recognize, in the end, that states do not exist in isolation and that the international system of states is a power system *sui generis*. The critical question, therefore, is: do states face a loss of sovereignty because new types of 'superior authority' have in fact crystallized in the international world and/or because their freedom of action (autonomy) has declined to a point at which it is no longer meaningful to say that supreme authority rests in their hands?

The discussion of the five disjunctures between the political theory of the sovereign state and the late twentieth-century political world reveals a set of forces which combine to restrict the freedom of action of governments and states by blurring the boundaries of domestic politics; transforming the conditions of political decision-making; changing the institutional and organizational context of national polities; altering the legal framework and administrative practices of governments; and obscuring the lines of responsibility and accountability of national states themselves. On the other hand, one thing is also unquestionably the case: states on the whole remain unready to submit their disputes with other states to arbitration by a 'superior authority', be it the United Nations, an international court or any other international body. At the heart of this 'great refusal' is the protection of the right of states to go to war (cf. Hinsley, 1986, pp. 229–35). Despite the fact that states today operate in a world of international political economy, military alliances, international and transnational organizations, international law and so on, it remains the case that the modern state is still able to determine the most fundamental aspect of people's life-chances – the question of life and death. In a complex interdependent world, sovereignty remains a powerful force.

Moreover, one way in which states continue to exercise their sovereignty is – as indicated in the discussion of the EEC in particular – by participating in the creation of organizations which might better monitor and regulate transnational forces and relations beyond their control. While such organizations frequently create new restraints upon national states, they also create new forms of political participation and intervention. At issue here is the active renewal of the rights and obligations of states in and through the international system.

In short, the idea of *de jure* sovereignty remains compelling, especially with regard to the state's capacity to wield coercive power. However, the operation of states in an ever more complex international system, which limits their autonomy and infringes their sovereignty, undermines the cogency of those traditions of sovereignty – stemming from Hobbes, on the one side, and Rousseau, on the other – which interpret sovereignty as an illimitable and indivisible form of political power. Instead, if sovereignty as a concept is to retain its analytical and normative force – as the rightful capacity to take final decisions and make and enact the law within a given community – it has to be conceived as divided among a number of agencies and limited by the very nature of this plurality and the rules and procedures which protect it. Such an idea is implicit in the Lockean conception of political community, and is central to the traditions of political analysis which do not locate and reduce sovereignty to either state or society. However, it requires further extension to the new international circumstances in which the state is located today, a task which modern political theory has barely begun.

Notes

1   I do not mean to imply that these gaps are new, that, for example, global inter-connections are recent phenomena. Rather it seems to be the case that a dense pattern of global interconnections began to emerge with the initial expansion of the world economy and the rise of the modern state (see Wallerstein, 1974). None the less, there are new dimensions to these patterns, e.g. the growth of international organizations, and some of these will be highlighted below.

2   This point is, of course, at the centre of the Marxist analysis of the state. It is not the state, Marx emphasized, that underlies the socio-economic order, but the socio-economic order that underlies the state. For Marx and the subsequent Marxist tradition, the very idea of the sovereign state is to a large extent illusory; it is socio-economic relations at the national and international level that are the key to the analysis of political power. Although Marxism has a great deal to contribute to, among other things, the analysis of gap 1, it too readily displaces the terms of reference of *political* analysis and offers too narrow a set of explanatory terms to encompass sufficiently all the dimensions of the challenges to the idea of the sovereign state (see gaps 1–5). For reasons of space I shall not pursue these issues here (see Held, 1987, ch. 4; cf. Sweezy, 1942; Mandel, 1972; Harris, 1984).

References

Aron, R. 1966: *Peace and War: A Theory of International Relations*. New York: Doubleday.

Barry-Jones, R. J. 1983: *Interdependence On Trial*. London: Francis Pinter.

Beetham, D. 1984: The future of the nation state. In G. McLennan, D. Held and S. Hall (eds), *The Idea of the Modern State*, Milton Keynes: Open University Press.

Beitz, C. 1979: *Political Theory and International Relations*. Princeton, NJ: Princeton University Press.

Benn, S. I. 1955: The uses of sovereignty. *Political Studies*, 3(2).

Benn, S. I. 1967: Sovereignty. In *The Encyclopaedia of Philosophy*, vol. 7. New York: Macmillan.

Benn, S. I. and Peters, R. S. 1959: *Social Principles and the Democratic State*. London: Allen & Unwin.

Berlin, I. 1969: *Four Essays on Liberty*. Oxford: Oxford University Press.

Bodin, J.: *Six Books of a Commonwealth*, trs. and ed. M. J. Tooley. Oxford: Basil Blackwell, 1967.

Bull, H. 1977: *The Anarchical Society: A Study of Order in World Politics*. London: Mac-millan.

Burnheim, J. 1985: *Is Democracy Possible?* Cambridge: Polity Press.

Capotorti, F. 1983: Human rights: the hard road towards universality. In R. St. J. Macdonald and D. M. Johnson (eds), *The Structure and Process of International Law*, The Hague: Martinus Nijhoff.

Carr, E. H. 1981: *The Twenty Year Crisis 1919–1939*. London: Macmillan.

Cassese, A. 1988: *Violence and Law in the Modern Age*. Cambridge: Polity Press.

Cooper, R. N. 1986: *Economic Policy in an Interdependent World*. Cambridge, Mass.: MIT Press.

Dicken, P. 1986: *Global Shift*. London: Harper & Row.

Dunn, J. 1969: *The Political Thought of John Locke*. Cambridge: Cambridge University Press.

Dunn, J. 1984: *Locke*. Oxford: Oxford University Press.

Dunn, J. 1985: Responsibility without power: states and the incoherence of the modern conception of the political good. Lecture delivered to the IPSA, Paris, July. Forthcoming in M. Banks (ed.), *The State in International Relations*, Hassocks, Sussex: Wheatsheaf.

Finley, M. I. 1983: *Politics in the Ancient World*. Cambridge: Cambridge University Press.

Giddens, A. 1985: *The Nation-State and Violence*. Cambridge: Polity Press.

Girvan, N. 1980: Swallowing the IMF medicine in the seventies. *Development Dialogue*, 2.

Gourevitch, P. A. 1978: The second image reversed: the international sources of domestic politics. *International Organization*, 32.

Grotius, H. 1925: *The Law of War and Peace*, trs. F. W. Kelsey. Oxford: Clarendon Press.

Harris, L. 1984: Governing the world economy: Bretton Woods and the IMF. In *The State and Society*, 6(26). Milton Keynes: Open University Press.

Held, D. 1987: *Models of Democracy*. Cambridge: Polity Press.

Hinsley, F. H. 1963: *Power and the Pursuit of Peace*. Cambridge: Cambridge University Press.

Hinsley, F. H. 1986: *Sovereignty*, 2nd edn. Cambridge: Cambridge University Press.

Hobbes, T.: *Leviathan*, ed. C. B. Macpherson. Harmondsworth: Penguin, 1968.

Hoffman, S. 1982: Reflections on the nation-state in Western Europe today. *Journal of Common Market Studies*, XXI (1 and 2).

Howard, M. 1981: *War and the Liberal Conscience*. Oxford: Oxford University Press.

James, A. 1986: *Sovereign Statehood*. London: Allen & Unwin.

Jouvenal, B. de 1957: *Sovereignty*. Cambridge: Cambridge University Press.

Kaiser, K. 1971: Transnational politics: toward a theory of multinational politics. *International Organization*, 25(4).

Kaiser, K. 1972: Transnational relations as a threat to the democratic process. In R. O. Keohane and J. S. Nye (eds), *Transnational Relations and World Politics*, Cambridge, Mass.: Harvard University Press.

Kaldor, M. and Falk, R. 1987: *Dealignment*. Oxford: Basil Blackwell.

Katzenstein, P. J. (ed.) 1978: *Between Power and Plenty: Foreign Economic Policies of Advanced Industrial States*. Madison: University of Wisconsin Press.

Keohane, R. O. 1984: The world political economy and the crisis of embedded liberalism. In J. H. Goldthorpe (ed.), *Order and Conflict in Contemporary Capitalism*, Oxford: Oxford University Press.

Keohane, R. O. and Nye, J. S. (eds) 1972: *Transnational Relations and World Politics*. Cambridge, Mass.: Harvard University Press.

Keohane, R. O. and Nye, J. S. 1977: *Power and Interdependence: World Politics in Transition*. Boston: Little, Brown.

King, P. 1974: *The Ideology of Order: A Comparative Analysis of Jean Bodin and Thomas Hobbes*. London: Allen & Unwin.

King, P. 1982: *Federalism and Federation*. London: Croom Helm.

King, P. 1987: Sovereignty. In D. Miller, J. Coleman, W. Connolly and A. Ryan (eds), *The Blackwell Encyclopaedia of Political Thought*, Oxford: Basil Blackwell.

Krasner, S. 1983: *International Regimes*. Ithaca, NY: Cornell University Press.

Leftwich, A. 1983: *Redefining Politics*. London: Methuen.

Locke, J. 1963: *Two Treatises of Government*. Cambridge and New York: Cambridge University Press.

Luard, E. 1977: *International Agencies: The Emerging Framework of Interdependence*. London: Macmillan.

McGrew, A. 1986: Global challenges to democratic government. In *Democratic Government and Politics*, 4(14). Milton Keynes: Open University Press.

McHenry, D. F. and Bird, K. 1977: Food bungle in Bangladesh. *Foreign Policy*, 27(Summer).

McKinley, R. D. and Little, R. 1986: *Global Problems and World Order*. London: Francis Pinter.

Mandel, E. 1972: *Marxist Economic Theory*, 2 vols. New York: Monthly Review Press.

Morgenthau, H. J. 1948: *Politics Among Nations*. New York: Knopf.

Morse, E. L. 1976: *Modernization and the Transformation of International Relations*. New York: Free Press.

Negro, J. 1986: International institutions. In *Democratic Government and Politics*, 4(13). Milton Keynes: Open University Press.

Offe, C. 1985: *Disorganized Capitalism*. Cambridge: Polity Press.

Parker, D. 1981: Law, society, and the state in the thought of Jean Bodin. *History of Political Thought*, 2.

Peters, R. S. 1956: *Hobbes*. Harmondsworth: Penguin.

Pettman, R. 1979: *State and Class: A Sociology of International Affairs*. London: Croom Helm.

Pocock, J. G. A. 1975: *The Machiavellian Moment: Florentine Political Thought and the Atlantic Republican Tradition*. Princeton, NJ: Princeton University Press.

Richelson, J. and Ball, D. 1986: *The Ties that Bind*. London: Allen & Unwin.

Rousseau, J.-J. *The Social Contract*. Harmondsworth, Penguin, 1968.

Sigler, J. 1983: *Minority Rights*. Westport, Conn.: Greenwood Press.

Skinner, Q. 1978: *The Foundations of Modern Political Thought*, 2 vols. Cambridge: Cambridge University Press.

Skinner, Q. 1981: *Machiavelli*. Oxford: Oxford University Press.

Smith, D. 1984: States and military blocs: NATO. In *The State and Society*, 6(27). Milton Keynes: Open University Press.

Smith, R. 1987: Political economy and Britain's external position. In *Britain in the World*, a compilation of papers presented for an ESRC conference, 12–13 November, King's College, London.

Smith, S. 1987: Reasons of state. In D. Held and C. Pollitt (eds), *New Forms of Democracy*. London: Sage.

Sobhan, R. 1979: Politics of food and famine in Bangladesh. *Economic and Political Weekly*, 1 December.

Spitz, E. 1984: *Majority Rule*. Chatham, NJ: Chatham House.

Sweezy, P. 1942: *The Theory of Capitalist Development*. New York: Monthly Review Press.

Tuck, R. 1979: *Natural Rights Theories*. Cambridge: Cambridge University Press.

Tuck, R. 1983: Grotius, Carneades and Hobbes. *Grotiana*, new ser., 4.

Tuck, R. 1987: Hugo Grotius. In D. Miller, J. Coleman, W. Connolly and A. Ryan (eds), *The Blackwell Encyclopaedia of Political Thought*, Oxford: Basil Blackwell.

Vincent, R. J. 1986: *Human Rights and International Relations*. Cambridge: Cambridge University Press.

Wallace, H. et al. 1982: *Policy Making in the European Communities*. London: John Wiley.

Wallerstein, I. 1974: *The Modern World-System*. New York: Academic Press.

Warren, B. 1980: *Imperialism: Pioneer of Capitalism*. London: Verso.

Whitaker, R. 1984: Fighting the cold war on the home front. In R. Miliband (ed.), *The Uses of Anti-Communism*. London: Merlin Press.

Wickham, A. 1984: States and political blocs: the EEC. In *The State and Society*, 6(28). Milton Keynes: Open University Press.

Wiebes, C. and Zeeman, B. 1983: The Pentagon Negotiations March 1948: the launching of the North Atlantic Treaty. *International Affairs*, 59(3).

Wight, M. 1986: *Power Politics*. Harmondsworth: Penguin.

9

A Discipline of Politics?

I

Politics denotes an activity about which many people today feel a combination of cynicism, scepticism and mistrust.* It is experienced as something distant and remote from everyday life. The affairs of government and national politics are not things many people claim to understand, nor are they often a source of sustained interest. Not surprisingly perhaps, those closest to both power and privilege are the ones who have most interest in and are most favourable to political life. For the rest, the fact that something is a recognizably 'political' statement is almost enough to bring it instantly into disrepute – it marks the statement as in all probability a strategic utterance and an evasion of the truth. Politics is, thus, a 'dirty' word, associated frequently with self-seeking behaviour, hypocrisy and 'public relations' activity geared to selling policy packages to those who might otherwise purchase elsewhere. Accordingly, people often mistrust and dislike politicians, who are thought to be concerned first and foremost with their own careers and hence all too likely to sidestep pressing questions and to downplay or ignore problems (see essay 4).

The discipline of politics (or political science or government) does little, if anything, to dispel this image of politics and politicians. Focusing as it often does on the nature and structure of government as a decision-making process and on those who press their claims upon it, it tends to portray politics as a distinct and separate sphere in society, a sphere set apart from, for instance, personal, family and business life (cf. essay 1, pp. 14–28). By focusing on governmental institutions, the discipline of politics marginalizes and provides little basis for understanding the very stuff of politics, that is, those deep-rooted problems that actually face us all daily as citizens, for example, issues of

* This essay, written jointly with Adrian Leftwich, first appeared in Adrian Leftwich (ed.), *What is Politics?* (Oxford: Basil Blackwell, 1984), pp. 139–59. I have edited and revised it for this volume.

war and violence, unemployment and poverty, health and welfare. It is one of the claims of this essay that a discipline of politics which fails to address systematically these problems reinforces the widely held notion of politics as a more or less unworthy activity for the self-interested. It is also a claim of this essay that the discipline of politics does generally fail to address central problems and to develop the necessary originality and skills for their resolution. It is not therefore a surprise that the initial commitment, enthusiasm and keenness which many students bring to the study of politics in colleges and universities is gradually but steadily eroded, giving way to a preoccupation with learning (memorizing) a set curriculum and with individual examination performance.

II

We live in a world which is increasingly punctuated by crises which daily affect the welfare and life-chances of countless millions of human beings. For instance, one can point to evidence of major and often increasing inequalities within societies between, say, classes, cultures, sexes and regions, in respect of the ownership or control of crucial resources, or access to them (whether these be land, capital, income or jobs). The rising tide of unemployment in many societies is one concrete manifestation of this, with all the enormous personal and social costs this brings about, and the waste of human resources it represents. Stark contrasts are often associated with it. In the United Kingdom, for instance, where unemployment has been very high and remains a crucial matter – especially in areas like Merseyside and the North-East, and particularly amongst the young and the ethnic minorities – it may seem paradoxical that in recent years the number of new private cars sold has been ever greater and that house prices have generally soared (see essay 4). In many parts of the Third World – notably Asia and Latin America – the number of landless poor and urban unemployed increases each year, while small and extremely wealthy elites live in conditions of more or less sumptuous luxury, often in houses and estates guarded by dogs, high fences and electronic security devices.

One can point, too, at the increasing militarization of the globe in terms of escalating national expenditures on arms, the swelling number of military personnel, the booming trade in arms exports and the steady build-up of nuclear warheads, despite recent international arms reduction agreements between the superpowers. In addition, the evidence shows that increasingly, civilians are the main casualties of war, that between 1960 and the early 1980s there have been some sixty-five major wars and that, at a conservative estimate, nearly eleven million lives have been lost in them (Sivard, 1982). Famines often erupt in the wake of such conflicts. But they also occur where there have been no such conflicts and where, as often as not, national and global food availability has been no worse and sometimes better than in previous non-famine years. They even occur where food is being exported from the country concerned (Lappé and Collins, 1979; Sen, 1982).

A glance at the annual reports of organizations such as Amnesty International will show, moreover, a dismal global record on human rights, as more or less repressive regimes emerge to try to stamp out opposition to political, social and economic inequalities and the attempts by the dispossessed, deprived or powerless to alter them.

Furthermore, it is simply not the case that these problems occur in isolation from each other in particular societies. As often as not they are related, sometimes directly and sometimes in long, looping chains of cause and effect. It is also clear that the people who are usually most directly affected by these events have little control over the forces which may cause them, since major decisions which influence their lives are often taken thousands of miles away. For example, a decision, or threatened decision, to suspend US food aid to Bangladesh, taken in the White House in Washington, may stimulate the sudden escalation of food prices in Dacca and contribute directly to the outbreak of famine amongst the urban and rural poor (see McHenry and Bird, 1977; Sobhan, 1979). Or the board of directors of a transnational corporation, assessing its global operations from their headquarters in New York, London, Paris or Tokyo, may decide to shift production of one of its lines from one country to another, thus creating unemployment in a town at a stroke. Or the decision by a government in West or East to suspend or step up military aid to one side or another in a political struggle in a distant country may decisively influence the outcome of that conflict. Or the International Monetary Fund (IMF), pursuing a particular line of economic policy, may insist as a condition of its loan to a government that the latter cut public expenditure, devalue its currency and pull back on subsidized welfare programmes. This may provoke hunger and anger amongst the urban poor, bring about bread riots and perhaps the fall of a government, or it might contribute directly to the imposition of martial law (see Girvan, 1980). In each and every one of these and many other instances, the effect on human lives and conditions is inevitably far-reaching and sometimes devastating.

III

Now, it is central to the argument of this essay that politics, as we shall shortly define the activity, is at the heart of all such problems. Any discipline advertising itself as 'politics' must therefore engage with such issues, and it must seek to train those who study it to analyse, understand and hence know how, potentially, to act upon them, though there may certainly be more than one course of action which flows from such understanding. It is our contention that the discipline of politics as conventionally taught has in general failed to do this. We shall explain, first, why we think this has happened and we shall go on, second, to suggest what can and should be done to try to remedy the situation.

We recognize that it is both a difficult and a delicate time to raise some of these questions, for the social sciences in general, and politics in particular, do not currently enjoy rave notices nor wholehearted support from the state or private funding agencies. Indeed, the social sciences (with sociology as the main target) are often thought of as irrelevant or subversive (see Held, 1987). They are said not to engage with the 'real problems' of society, but to involve themselves in highly abstract and largely internecine theoretical debates on abstruse questions of analytic method or substance. There is some truth in this view, as any teacher or student in a social-science department will readily acknowledge. But there is something fundamentally specious in the criticism about 'irrelevance' when it comes from those – usually in the media or the official agencies of government responsible for higher education – who *do not want* social scientists to engage in 'relevant' work, except at the 'technical' margins, lest they be critical of the fundamental principles of policy and practice of state and society, whether in the West or East, North or South. When social scientists do engage with controversial matters they are more than likely to find their research funds, jobs and – in certain parts of the globe – their citizenship or even their lives under direct attack. (For example, research funds and jobs have been lost in Britain; the citizenship of some social scientists has been effectively withdrawn in some Eastern European societies; and social scientists have been murdered in Chile, Argentina and South Africa in recent years.)

Moreover, it is unnecessary for social scientists always to apologize for theoretical interests: scientific work does progress, and can only progress, through work of this kind. But underlying the argument of this essay is the claim that the kinds of problems indicated above are not only real and urgent, they are relevant and profoundly *political*. If the discipline of politics is to live up to its name, then it must engage directly and theoretically with such problems, by confronting the analytical and pedagogic issues necessary for their understanding and potential resolution, in theory and in practice.

The difficulty, of course, is that problems of this kind are inherently inter-disciplinary, involving complex relations between aspects of social life which are all too often regarded and studied (incorrectly in our judgement) as distinct: such as economy, polity, social structure and international relations. It is the interplay of *all* these phenomena which we think of as 'politics': what we would call the 'lived interdisciplinarity' of all collective social life. Hence, if politics as a discipline is to be developed systematically it must, in large part, be interdisciplinary, so that it can generate the explanatory frameworks and teaching methods which enable its students to come to grips with such problems and their possible solutions. It cannot treat politics as a separate institutional sphere, as only the officially 'public' realm of government.

Before proceeding to examine some of these issues further, we offer, first, a broad working definition of politics.

In our view, politics is a phenomenon found in and between all groups, institutions and societies, involving all spheres of human endeavour, public and private. It is manifested in the activities of cooperation, negotiation and struggle over the use, production and distribution of resources. It is an element of all human life: an inescapable dimension of the production and reproduction of society. Accordingly, politics is about power; about the forces which influence and reflect its distribution and use; and about the effect of this on resource use and distribution. Politics is about the 'transformative capacity' of social agents, agencies and institutions: it is not about Government or governments alone (see pp. 1–2, 166–7; and see Giddens, 1979). Where politics is regarded more narrowly as a sphere apart from economy or culture, that is, as governmental activity and institutions, a vast domain of what we would consider politics is excluded from view. There is, in fact, nothing *more political* than the constant attempts to exclude certain types of issues from politics. These attempts represent strategies of depoliticization; that is, strategies to have certain issues treated as if they were not a proper subject for politics. Classic examples of this are the constant attempts to make the organization of the economy in the West, or violence against women in marriage (assault or rape), thought of as non-political – a mere outcome of 'free' private contracts (see Pateman, 1983). Furthermore, administrators and politicians often ask us to 'keep politics out' of things like sport (or vice versa), or not to 'mix' politics with religion or industrial relations or 'race' relations. What they are *actually* asking is that we *refrain* from participating in politics, that is, in decisions about the use and distribution of resources in relation to affairs that are very important to our lives. As such, they are not seeking to promote, defend or even isolate politics, they are seeking to *suppress* it (Leftwich, 1983, p. 26). To study politics, therefore, is to study critically the history of possibilities and the possibilities of history.

IV

We stated in the previous section that the discipline of politics as conventionally taught fails to engage with the central problems of politics in both modern and historical societies. Why is this the case? In addressing this question we make a number of points. Some have to do with higher education more broadly, some with the social and historical sciences generally, and some with politics in particular.

1 The first critical matter is the remarkable degree of specialization that has occurred between disciplines (and within them), especially since the Second World War. While specialization need not always lead to fragmentation, this has in fact happened within both the natural and social sciences and – most dramatically – in the sharp divisions between them. Specialist research proliferates in every field, and it gets more specialized. The almost tidal flow of learned articles, journals and books is overwhelming. New kinds of information-processing systems (such as bibliographies of bibliographies) have emerged in an effort to help students and academic staff to keep up with what has been written. Other than full-time researchers (and seldom amongst them), most of us find it increasingly difficult to keep up, even within our often tight specialisms.

The general problem with specialization in science is that while it may yield highly detailed research and understanding of *particular* parts of problems, it is almost always the case that these accounts are partial and one-sided. And while there have been important advances made in the specialist study of *parts* of the social world and its problems, this has not been matched by comparable advances in attempts to examine their interconnections. To put it bluntly, we seem to know more about the parts and less about the whole; and the trouble is that we risk knowing very little even about the parts because their context and conditions of existence in the whole are eclipsed from view. Moreover, in the course of this specialization and fragmentation, as different disciplines (and special interests within them) have fastened on to *bits* of problems for analytical attention, the explanation of relations *between* the bits has become the concern of none. Specific disciplines, that is to say, have identified their corners of the problem, and departed with them. This is the consequence of specialization. But the complex character of the whole problem has remained unexplained (and certainly unresolved) because – as we pointed out earlier – such problems are simply not amenable to narrow disciplinary analysis or technical treatment.

'The economy', 'the social system' and 'the political system' (though not always referred to by these terms) have been treated by the social sciences as if they were more or less independent arenas of human activity. This is reflected in the conventionally rigorous separation of the disciplines of economics, sociology and politics, and their main concerns. Within each discipline, soaring levels of sometimes breathtakingly abstract theories have emerged, and the more abstract the levels, the further the disciplines have moved away from the complex relations of problems in societies, in all their murky and involved real-world character; and the further they have diverged from each other.

In the natural sciences, the closer one approaches the explanation of a *particular* phenomenon or problem – the structure or malfunctioning of the human body; or pollution; or the weather; or an epizootic – the less and less possible it is to maintain sharp distinctions between disciplines. The same is true for more obviously social and political problems – inflation, unemployment, inequality, poverty and famines, debt in the Third World and so on. Yet their study tends to be confined to particular disciplinary corners with persistently disappointing results, such as the failure to produce an adequate theory of inflation and unemployment.

In politics, the focus on narrow institutional spheres of government and associated political matters, as conventionally understood, has led to wholly inadequate accounts, for instance, of the sources and forms of power in societies. Much standard democratic theory as taught at undergraduate level, for example, has not turned its attention to the enormous concentrations of power in the private and corporate sector of 'the economy', because they are usually considered to be beyond the borders of 'the political system' or simply not political (cf. essays 2 and 6). The daily and lived interdependence of 'polity' and 'economy', of state and society, and of nations with one another have rarely been at the centre of the discipline's pedagogic concerns.

2   It is not too difficult to see why this state of affairs has come about and how it has been reproduced in the politics of the discipline of politics. The twin pillars of studies in politics in Britain, for example, have been political institutions and political philosophy (see Moodie, 1984). The latter provides the clue to the main lineages of the discipline, in constitutional history, law and philosophy. In the post-war years this has been influenced by the behavioural approaches of American political science, and by a variety of streams of Marxism. None the less, it remains fair to say that the pillars stand more or less intact, if somewhat weatherbeaten, though around them have grown up more or less strong areas, such as political sociology, international relations (sometimes in separate departments) and Third World studies. There has also been a proliferation of diverse special interests, including political anthropology, public administration and electoral studies.

Hence traditionalism (the twin pillars) and a multiplicity of specialisms have characterized the academic discipline of politics. With more or less consistency, succeeding generations of graduate students have been socialized into these main streams and have hence sustained the continuity of approach, with interesting but not decisive shifts in orientation of the discipline as a whole.

It is important to recognize that in its theoretical and institutional concerns, the discipline of politics has continued to be subject-centred, not problem-oriented, in respect of both content and methods of teaching. By this we mean that it proceeds on the assumption that there is a body of knowledge to communicate to students – for instance, the distinction between congressional and parliamentary modes of government; or what Mill, Marx or Dahl said. In general, the discipline has not been concerned to develop and deploy particular kinds of analytical skills for the purposes of engaging with, and trying to resolve (at least at the level of explanation), the kinds of problems which continue to occur in and between societies and which – as argued earlier – form the core of politics.

3   Institutions of higher education have many objectives and a variety of functions; these include research, teaching, the transmission of a culture and other services to the community. Whatever may be the proper balance between these, it is generally the case that, as far as teaching is concerned, a claim is made to provide a training which promotes such capacities as, *inter alia*, 'the general powers of the mind', 'critical ability', 'thinking for oneself', 'insight', 'self-education', 'judgement' and so forth. All major reports and books on the question over the last two decades have rightly emphasized the importance of these capacities (although the particular conceptions of them are by no means always ones with which we would agree; see, for instance, the Robbins Report, 1963; and the Hale Report, 1964). Do institutions of higher education actually promote these capacities?

We all know that the vast majority of undergraduates do not go on to *use* what they have 'learned' in their courses (and this is as true for biology and chemistry as it is for the social sciences). We also know from memory-retention studies that, if not used, such 'knowledge' disappears down the memory curve within not too many months. So it is important that the different disciplines (subjects, that is) should be more the media through which general capacities and skills are developed, and less the substance of 'learning'. Yet, in practice, teaching of 'subjects' rather than skills is the norm. In the social and historical sciences, especially, the lecture, the seminar, the tutorial, the essay or dissertation and the unseen examination still prevail as the main modes of teaching, learning and assessment. These methods, linked to the content of the 'subject' (in the books), have the effect of inducing a kind of passive *consumption* of knowledge, rather than stimulating active participation and the *production* of analyses, explanations and resolutions of problems through the development of skills. Passivity and consumer orientations are reinforced by the sheer volume of books and articles students have to digest – a quantity of material which no superperson could ever cope with in the time allotted and which leaves most ordinary mortals frequently bewildered. Anyone who has written essays and exams knows that these exercises are by and large concerned with the re-presentation of standard material in the field; they know additionally what is expected from them in particular cases and will adjust their presentations accordingly. On the other side, anyone who is involved in marking essays, dissertations and examination papers will concede, quite readily in fact, that the overwhelming bulk of them do not show 'independent thought' or 'critical ability'. Those involved in marking regularly find a superficiality of thought, the recycling of certain sets of standard ideas or fashionable orthodoxies of one kind or another, a lack of originality, a fragmentation of understanding through disciplinary monism, and – above all – an incapacity to cope analytically with the *de facto* interdisciplinarity of a difficult world and its complex problems.

A common response to all this from weary and perhaps cynical academics is to blame the 'poor quality' of students these days, the depressed and groggy state of mind in which some students come to higher education after the grim grind of A-level (or the equivalent final high-school examinations in the USA and Europe), or more generally the 'lack of student interest'. But how often, in politics particularly, do we look to ourselves as the bearers of the discipline, to our pedagogy and the institutional arrangements (for instance departmental and course structures) as possible sources of the academic malaise we may diagnose?

It can certainly be said that many students come up to higher education as enthusiasts. The political problems of the world are a source of major interest to them. And then, to put it crudely, we anaesthetize their interests and enthusiasms by dragging them more or less unwillingly through 'the subject', and by feeding them or telling them to find out and learn a body of theoretical ideas and empirical information which (with notable exceptions) – in economics as well as politics and sociology – seldom seems to engage with the 'relevant' issues and *problems* of one's own society (or those abroad).

4   It is important to qualify some of the arguments above. There *are* areas where interdisciplinary work seeks to establish links between the concerns and insight of different disciplines. There *are* areas where courses start with problems. In the developing work in ecology, for instance, important links are being made and taught in the analysis of problems that flow from the relations between human communities and their actions upon the environment, and vice versa. And in the work done in political sociology, development studies and the approach of political economists, there are important contributions being made.

But in general it remains true to say that, as a discipline, politics has remained largely bound to its lineage. It has encouraged the more or less idiosyncratic research of graduate students and staff within its traditional institutional and theoretical concerns; it has continued to stress the teaching of traditional philosophical and empirical bodies of information in standard ways; it has not expanded its concerns to engage with relevant *problems* in historical and contemporary societies; and it has been more or less haphazard about identifying and training the analytical skills and capacities which are needed for tackling such problems.

What, then, can or should be done?

V

It is not possible in a short piece such as this to spell out in every detail the central components of a discipline of politics with respect to syllabus and method, at least as far as undergraduate courses and research priorities are concerned. Nor is it desirable, for there is enormous scope for variety in terms of structure, approach and use of distinctive kinds of illustrative theoretical and empirical materials. But what we can do is to outline the central principles and preoccupations which, in our view, should form the organizing framework and pedagogic priorities of a discipline of politics.[1] It should be clear from what follows that these flow from the definition of politics given above; they are concerned with providing the historical, comparative and analytical understandings and skills which will enable students to handle the problems of our societies and their futures more adequately.

Starting first with the kinds of skills and understandings which students of politics should acquire, we would stress four main (and to a significant degree overlapping) areas. First, there are conceptual–analytical skills. By this we mean the ability to analyse, use, defend and criticize concepts and terms found in political debate, historical and modern (concepts like 'sovereignty', 'freedom', 'democracy' and 'domination'). This involves appreciation of the historical origins, meanings and usages of such concepts, and the development of the capacity to engage in political argument about them. Clarity of understanding is a necessary condition of effective political analysis. But it is not a sufficient condition. For it is essential, if one is to appreciate how political life generally is and can be shaped by ideas, to learn the way in which concepts actually function in particular political arguments and contexts. As an initial illustration one could take a much-publicized debate on many British campuses some ten years ago as to whether certain speakers should be allowed to visit the colleges and give lectures. Using that issue of 'free speech' and the arguments which were developed for and against it at the time, students could be introduced with intensity to wider theoretical concerns about 'freedom' and the rights and obligations of citizens. Through such instances, not only does the pertinence of difficult questions become apparent, but the implications and consequences of various judgements as well. Many other issues could be used in similar ways. For instance, in both the West and East (and also in the

South) many societies advertise their political arrangements as 'democratic'. Are these arrangements the same? If not, how do they differ? And why? How do the distinctive meanings and practices relate to classical and modern theories of democracy? Do the theories help us to grasp and justify particular arrangements? If so, which ones? Can the arrangements be developed and improved? If so, how, and according to what principles and under what conditions? The same kind of approach can be adopted with other central concepts of political discourse. When ministers of state and policy-makers of one kind or another refer, for instance, in the West or East, to the defence of 'freedom', what do they mean? Do the !Kung San of the Kalahari have a notion of 'freedom' which is different to that of transnational corporations in their wish to defend their 'freedom' from state 'interference'? Can we diagnose the distinctive meanings used, and the social and historical contexts of their evolution? In what ways can the various conceptions of 'freedom' in political theory illuminate the problem? Can they help us disentangle rhetoric and self-interest from clarity, consistency and sound judgement? Through the pursuit of such an approach one becomes better equipped not only to recognize good and bad arguments and the nature of different types of reasoning, but also to be clearer about what we can reasonably say about issues that concern us.

Secondly, there are theoretical–analytical skills. By this we mean the ability to understand, compare, criticize, defend and, above all, *use* rival theories about the nature and relations of politics, economics and social structure in the analysis of historical and modern societies. In building on and connecting with the previous set of conceptual skills (and of course they overlap) it is necessary again to stress the importance we attach to starting with problems. The problems should be used as a means of leading students to explore different kinds of theory with a view to assessing their value for explanatory purposes. Take unemployment as an example: given a set of facts and figures (themselves subject to methodological and logistical problems of definition and collection – an issue to be considered shortly), how can it be explained? Is it a problem found in all societies, past and present, or would one simply never have encountered it in traditional Maasai, Eskimo or ancient Greek society? If not, why not? When does it first emerge as a problem in human societies? With what set of conditions is it associated? If, as some theorists argue, it is intrinsic to free enterprise and capitalist societies, why then is it found also in so-called communist societies, in Eastern Europe and China? The same approach can be adopted with respect to other problems of the kind mentioned at the start of this essay: the patterns of escalating violence and conflict in the Third World, or famines, or inequalities between nations, classes, regions and the sexes.

Thirdly, as should be clear from the above, there are essential skills required in the methods and modes of political enquiry and analysis. Few of the above objectives could be met if students were not able to develop a number of skills to do with thinking, counting and researching in politics; of how to gather, use and interpret information; of ways of putting arguments to various tests, or of how to assess both quantitative and qualitative judgements. A course – or a set of courses – concerned with developing such skills would be closely related to the previous two, and the next one, to be discussed shortly. We would want to argue for the centrality of such a course (or set of courses) running throughout an undergraduate degree, involving periods of intensive project work each year. Of course, the kind of work done would depend on other aspects of the degree and would need to be closely related to them, with a careful eye to local issues, problems, resources and sources. But, once again, the starting-point can most effectively be problems or issues. For instance, someone claims that the USA is more 'free' than the Soviet Union; or that Blacks in South Africa are 'better off' than anywhere else in Africa: what can be meant by such claims? Are there criteria which might be elaborated and evidence sought to enable comparisons to be made? Or what do official government statistics offer on a particular topic, for example poverty? How are such statistics generated? What concepts underpin them and how are the data interpreted? Project work, often best undertaken by groups and assessed as a collective endeavour, is an invaluable way of introducing problems and skills, and of enabling those who undertake it to participate actively in shaping their own learning.

Finally, before looking at some of the requirements and implications of this, it is necessary to stress the importance of comparative and historical skills and knowledge. The real laboratory for the social sciences is the history and structure of the enormous range of politics of past and present societies and the relations between them in time and space. It is essential that students of politics have more than a passing familiarity with the ways in which historical and modern societies have organized, explained and justified their affairs – in productive, distributive, decision-making, social, cultural and ideological terms. For these represent the contexts within which the kinds of problems discussed earlier have arisen and do arise. There are a variety of ways in which such historical and comparative understanding can be achieved. But, in broad outline, it would at least seem essential to include elements of the following, with examples depending on other areas of the degree: politics in non-state societies; the emergence of states; the emergence of the modern state (Europe) and the development of world systems; comparative government and institutions of modern states; comparative politics in modern states, for example, with respect to issues of class, race, sex, etc. Again, it is important to emphasize the need to integrate this component of a degree with the other skills discussed before. That is to say, while there may be virtue in historical knowledge for its own sake, a much more important case for such understanding in politics is that it provides the *medium* through which the other skills can be developed and deployed, and the *context* within which the genesis of various theories, concepts and analyses can be appreciated and hence their implications for other contexts assessed.

VI

It should be clear from the above that, in terms of emphasis, we see the development of a set of related analytical skills – and *not* simply the learning of certain bodies of theory and empirical (institutional) information – as being the core of a discipline of politics. The skills, of course, will require understanding of conceptual, theoretical and philosophical approaches from a variety of traditions. The development of such skills will also require historical understanding and knowledge of institutional detail. Such skills can of course be developed in a great variety of different courses, whose structure, relations, sequence, intensity and spread will differ from department to department, as they should. But given the conception of politics we use here, it makes a lot of sense, in our view, for departments of politics to look beyond their institutional boundaries to the availability of staff in other departments, within and beyond the social sciences. This is not simply an argument for more interdepartmental work. The kind, content and shape of interdepartmental collaboration we envisage (though we have no illusions as to how difficult in practice it would be to organize and sustain under present circumstances) would not flow from some abstract commitment to interdisciplinarity, but from the specific requirements of the concrete problems being used for pedagogic purposes. If one thinks of some of the substantive problems we have mentioned above, it is apparent how valuable the contributions of, for instance, economists, economic and social historians, geographers, sociologists, ecologists and biologists would be to their understanding and resolution. And students of politics need, crucially, to be able to know how to *use* and integrate these diverse specialisms and skills in the analysis of the problems before them.

If students are to develop the kinds of skills we have been stressing, it is necessary to have a very serious look at the full range of possibilities of teaching and learning methods (see Leftwich 1981 and 1982; Elton, 1981). There is a case for some of the traditional methods of lecture, seminar, tutorial and essay, but they must be used and integrated intelligently in meeting wider pedagogic purposes. Given that we emphasize problem-analysis, the case for projects of many kinds is overwhelming. We do not mean projects only in the conventional sense of dissertations and individual research essays. There is a variety of possibilities, each of which will enable students and staff to explore topics in depth, either on their own or in groups. For instance, to avoid the usual pattern of individual student isolation (or intellectual agoraphobia), certain courses (or parts of courses) may be best organized through and around reading groups and collectively arranged endeavours.

But group work involves much more than things like reading groups. In a department with particular interests and specialist skills in, for instance, analysing and resolving problems of democratic participation (in organizations, communities or government – local and national), there would be enormous advantage in having groups of students actually go out into the community to look at the structure, processes and problems of local government, industrial organization and community participation, with a view to producing individual or collective projects (cf. Held and Pollitt, 1986). In so doing, they will be able to develop some of the research and enquiry skills (collection of information, interviewing, participant observation, assessment of data and so on) so necessary for political analysis and for the development of the kind of political imagination necessary to resolve problems.

What this type of work requires, from teaching staff, is the commitment of time and imaginative energy to help specify the problems and to ensure that sources and resources are available for students to tap. The problem may be of the more conventional kind (why has revolutionary change not occurred in the most advanced capitalist societies, as some versions of Marxist theory imply it should have?); or the problem may be one less usually tackled in politics departments. For instance, has the collectivization of agricultural production been an effective means of overcoming the food problems of developing societies? What do the experiences of, say, Russia, China, Israel and Tanzania tell us about the forms, details and contexts of successful and unsuccessful collectivization?

In our experience, group work by students, focusing on a concrete problem, is one of the most effective means of liberating their energies and of realizing unfulfilled potential. It enables them to learn, through project and other work, about the intense complexity of politics and the causes, conditions and consequences of problems, past or present. In confronting problems of the kind offered here as examples one cannot avoid getting to grips with issues of an institutional, historical, theoretical and comparative kind. Students (and staff!) learn: how to track down and use relevant sources and resources (staff, library, field-work where appropriate); how to collect, interpret and argue about evidence; how to assess competing concepts and theories, especially with regard to their explanatory or practical usefulness; and how to organize their time and energy (in groups or singly) with project-writing deadlines in mind. It seems to us that lectures, essays, tutorials and formal seminars should *serve* and *complement* these kinds of active and participatory learning methods, rather than being merely substitutes for them as they currently tend to be.

VII

Given the conception of politics which we have outlined, and given the political nature of the problems which face modern societies, it should be clear why we argue for a radical rethink and restructuring of the discipline of politics. At the heart of the approach we suggest are three major points: first, the discipline should shift its primary focus away from its long preoccupation with the teaching of subjects to a more self-conscious concern with the analysis of problems. For politics is, just as the discipline of politics should be, fundamentally concerned with understanding and acting upon problems, with the modes of their analysis and collective resolution. Second, it follows that the appropriate pedagogic priorities of the discipline should be the training and learning of appropriate analytical skills, not the 'learning' of bodies of theoretical and empirical information for their own sake. This is not to say that understanding of theory and evidence is unimportant: on the contrary, it is vital. But what it does mean, thirdly, is that a discipline of politics should be concerned to train its students to be able to *use* theory and evidence for the purposes of analysis and practical action.

Politics (in both senses) is the discourse and struggle over the organization of human possibilities: it is academic and practical. It is concerned with both theoretical and practical questions, with far-reaching organizational and institutional issues. This preoccupation with the theoretical and practical distinguishes it as a discipline from, say, political philosophy, as it is most often taught. The latter frequently considers and espouses political principles, arguments and even arrangements, independently of considering the conditions of their enactment or realization. In so doing, it encourages at a certain level the arbitrary choice of principles, and seemingly endless abstract debates about them. Anthropology and sociology, on the other hand, have generally tended to focus on certain kinds of societies or on certain limited spheres of social behaviour and relations within them. And much economics, in developing sophisticated ways of measuring the costs and benefits of different courses of action, provides no real account of *why* some are chosen and some are not.

The political nature of the problems of the world in practice involves questions of *all* these kinds: the conflicts of interest between diverse social groups in the constitution and reproduction of distinctive societies; the clash of competing principles and philosophical preferences; the consideration of the costs and benefits to different social groups of different courses of action; and the conditions for, or constraints on, the realization of policies, programmes and options. It is precisely for this reason that it is no contradiction (except in semantic terms) to say that the discipline of politics must be interdisciplinary in its focus and its frameworks.

In our view it is this complexity which makes politics so intriguing to students and also of the greatest importance in practice. At a time when the social sciences are under some threat, when contraction seems likely and when it is tempting to play safe, it is necessary to assert this importance again and again. The problems of the modern world will never be solved by technical innovations alone, but only by the development and transformation of our politics in ways that can more effectively shape the kind, and better organize the distribution, of such innovations. Only by defining its purposes in terms of the urgency of the times, and hence its research and teaching priorities in terms of the *kind* of approach suggested here, will the discipline of politics be able to make a serious contribution to the definition and furtherance of human welfare, and to the eradication of the tarnished image of politics.

Note

1   I should like to acknowledge here the contribution to those proposals by friends and colleagues Alex Callinicos, Bill Fuller, David Skidmore and Albert Weale.

References

Elton, L. 1981: Can universities change? *Studies in Higher Education*, 6(1).

Giddens, A. 1979: *Central Problems in Social Theory*. London: Macmillan.

Girvan, N. 1980: Swallowing the IMF medicine in the seventies. *Development Dialogue*, 2.

Hale Report 1964: *Report of the Committee on University Teaching*. London: HMSO.

Held, D. 1987: The future prospects of sociology. *Network*, 39.

Held, D. and Pollitt, C. (eds) 1986: *New Forms of Democracy*. London: Sage.

Lappé, F. M. and Collins, J. 1979: *Food First: Beyond the Myth of Scarcity*. New York: Ballantine.

Leftwich, A. 1981: The politics of case study: problems of innovation in university education. *Higher Education Review*, 13(2).

Leftwich, A. 1982: Social science, social relevance and the politics of educational development. *International Journal of Educational Development*, 1(3).

Leftwich, A. 1983: *Redefining Politics*. London: Methuen.

McHenry, D. F. and Bird, K. 1977: Food bungle in Bangladesh. *Foreign Policy*, 27 (Summer).

Moodie, G. C. 1984: Politics is about government. In A. Leftwich (ed.), *What is Politics?* Oxford: Basil Blackwell.

Pateman, C. 1983: Feminism and democracy. In G. Duncan (ed.), *Democratic Theory and Practice*, Cambridge: Cambridge University Press.

Robbins Report 1963: *Report of the Committee in Higher Education*. London: HMSO.

Sen, A. 1982: *Poverty and Famines*. Oxford: Oxford University Press.

Sivard, R. L. 1982: *World Military and Social Expenditures*. Leesburg, Va: World Priorities.

Sobhan, R. 1979: Politics of food and famine in Bangladesh. *Economic and Political Weekly*, 1 December.

Index

Pages which contain tables and diagrams are in *italics*.

Index by Geraldine Beare